DRUNKS, WHORES
AND
IDLE APPRENTICES

DRUNKS, WHORES AND IDLE APPRENTICES

Criminal biographies of the eighteenth century

Philip Rawlings

London and New York

First published 1992
by Routledge
2 Park Square, Milton Park, Abingdon, Oxon, OX14 4RN

Simultaneously published in the USA and Canada
by Routledge
a division of Routledge, Chapman and Hall Inc.
29 West 35th Street, New York, NY 10001

Printed and bound by Antony Rowe Ltd, Eastbourne

Transferred to Digital Printing 2005

Typeset in 10 on 12 point Garamond Linotron 101 by
J&L Composition Ltd, Filey, North Yorkshire

British Library Cataloguing in Publication Data
Rawlings, Philip
Drunks, Whores and Idle Apprentices:
Criminal Biographies of the 18th Century
I. Title
364.10922

Library of Congress Cataloging in Publication Data
Rawlings, Philip
Drunks, whores and idle apprentices: criminal biographies of the
eighteenth century / Philip Rawlings.
p.   cm.
Includes bibliographical references and index.
1. Criminals—England—History—18th century—Biography.
2. Criminals—England—History—18th century—Biography—History and
criticism. I. Title.
HV6945.R38   1992
364.1′092′242–dc20
[B]   91–46370

ISBN 0–415–05056–1

'Tis in vain to hope for a *Reprieve*,
The Sheriff's come down with his *Warrant*;
An *Account* I behind me must leave
Of my *Birth*, *Education* and Parents.

('Epistle on Jack Sheppard',
Daily Journal, 16 November, 1724)

There is not perhaps in the world a more agreeable study than that of
Biography; nor any thing sought after and read with greater avidity,
than the lives of unfortunate men, and those who suffer under the
hands of the executioner more than any.

(*The Life and Wonderful Transactions of Mr. Charles Speckman,
alias Browne*, 1763)

CONTENTS

CONTENTS

**V The Life, Travels, Exploits, Frauds and
Robberies of Charles Speckman (1763)**

PREFACE

We can understand much about a society from looking at the way in which it treats its criminals. It is not just the punishments which are revealing, but also the literature. In this book I have brought together a small selection of eighteenth-century accounts written about the lives of contemporary criminals. My primary aim is to bring to a wider reading public a flavour of a body of literature which, while it was extremely popular when published, has been all but forgotten for two hundred years. Although the biographies can stand by themselves, in the General Introduction some of the problems surrounding their use are discussed.

In the putting together of this book many people have given me assistance, willingly and unwillingly, knowingly and unknowingly. I will refrain both from praising their virtues and from heaping blame upon myself for the faults which the book has; after all, should not those with whom I discussed it and who failed either to point out these faults or to persuade me to change the book, bear some of the blame? However, I did work in various places around the country on this book and I would like to thank the staff of the many libraries and record offices I used including: the British Library, including the Newspaper Library at Colindale; the Guildhall Library; the Public Records Offices at Kew and Chancery Lane; County Records Offices in Surrey, Essex and Somerset; the Greater London Record Office; the John Rylands Library in Manchester; Brunel University Library. The University Library at Aberystwyth was particularly important in the formation of ideas, through the books there, but, just as importantly, through its provision of a place in which to hold discussions with colleagues: my apologies and thanks both to them and to the students who constantly asked us to be quiet. More specifically, I would like to thank Richard Ireland and Ian Bell; the loan of his computer by Peter Wallington was, viewed objectively, somewhat foolhardy, but I prefer to see it as the act of a farsighted individual who has the benefit of good insurance cover. I would also like to thank my father, who read the whole book several times, my mother and Debbie, three people whose boredom thresholds have been seriously tested.

PREFACE

This book opens with a General Introduction. Its purpose is to provide the novice with not only a discussion of the criminal biographies and their writers and readers, but also an examination of the ways in which scholars have used, or dismissed, these works. The remainder of the book is taken up with reprints of the biographies prefaced by brief introductions. These introductions outline some of the themes which appear in the biographies and provide background and bibliographical information. Each biography is also supplemented by notes intended to clarify the text.

ABBREVIATIONS

GLRO: Greater London Record Office

OBSP: the published reports of the trials held at the Old Bailey

Ordinary of Newgate's *Account*: see the General Introduction and the introduction to the Ordinary of Newgate's *Account*: Mary Young (1741) in this volume

PRO: Public Record Office (Kew and Chancery Lane)

In the citation of books, pamphlets and essays, square brackets have been used as follows:

> where placed around a writer's name, such as [H. Walpole], this indicates that the named writer almost certainly wrote the piece even though his or her name does not appear on the title page. If the name is followed by a question mark, such as [H. Walpole?], then the writer was more likely than not H. Walpole;

> where the brackets are placed around a date, such as [1751], or around a place name and date, such as [London, 1751], this indicates that the date of publication was almost certainly 1751, or the place and date of publication were almost certainly London and 1751. The addition of a question mark has the same effect in reducing certainty as above.

In the chapters where the criminal biographies are reprinted, square brackets around a number, such as [p. 2], indicate the original page breaks.

The peculiarities of spelling, punctuation and grammar in the original texts have been retained.

GENERAL INTRODUCTION

THE BIOGRAPHICAL LITERATURE OF CRIME AND ITS POPULARITY

During the late seventeenth century and throughout the eighteenth century crime provided one of the principal subjects for popular literature. All aspects were covered: the crime itself, the investigation, the trial, the punishment and the life of the offender. The works ranged from newspaper articles through broadsheets and pamphlets to large books, sometimes in several volumes. This book focuses on biographical pamphlets, that is, pamphlets which took as their subjects real people, who had been accused of, usually, a capital crime. Some of these pamphlets proclaim themselves to be autobiographies, although, as is argued later in this General Introduction, it is not easy to decide whether such claims were true or even partly true. These criminal biographies have been the subject of much controversy amongst modern scholars. There is, for example, an argument about the role they played in the development of the novel, and certainly some of the techniques which appear in them were also used by novelists, such as Defoe in *Moll Flanders*. The problem is further complicated by the claim, which is hard to substantiate, that novelists like Defoe also wrote criminal biographies, and by the difficulty in separating 'fact' from 'fiction' in the biographies. One thing is certain: the criminal biography, which became firmly established in the eighteenth century, continues to flourish up to the present day.

Although reliable sales figures are not available, there are plenty of reasons for supposing that criminal biographies sold well in the eighteenth century. First, there is the anecdotal evidence. John Dunton, a well-known publisher of the late seventeenth century, financed the more expensive, and less lucrative, side of his business from the profits of his criminal biographies.[1] The York printer Thomas Gent wrote that in 1722 when he was printing the dying speech of Christopher Layer, who had been hanged for treason, he was so besieged by hawkers anxious for the publication that he was unable to step outside his office until he had finished the work, which

1

took several days.[2] In 1732 Rev. Piddington was said to have sold the confession of Sarah Malcom, who had been convicted of murder, for £20 – the average labourer's weekly wage was, at that time, somewhere between ten and twenty shillings.[3] In 1754 the publishers Goadby and Owen issued an apology for their failure to keep pace with the demand for *The Discoveries of John Poulter*:

> The Press has been kept almost continually going, on the above Work for several Weeks past, yet Orders for great Numbers of them from different Parts of the Country could not be supplied, but as a very large Number is now printed off, and the Press kept still going on it, the Publick may depend on a proper supply for the future.[4]

This may, of course, have been merely a publisher puffing his wares, yet evidence of the literature's popularity comes also from those who saw nothing to applaud in it. In 1750 Horace Walpole complained to a friend of 'the ridiculous rage' of buying biographies of criminals,[5] and in 1786 the commercial success of a lengthy biography of Charles Price, who had been accused of fraud, led to adverse comment in the Press: the *Whitehall Evening Post* remarked, with disgust, that,

> Since the first appearance of THE MEMOIRS OF CHARLES PRICE, little else has been read or talked of. There have been several thousands already sold, and as many more are now printing! This fact is stated as a proof, that the contemplation of the baseness of human nature is become a more pleasing subject than its virtues. If the life of that excellent man, Dr. Jebb, which would form an admirable contrast to that of Price, was published, in all probability the sale would not amount to the expence of advertising it!!![6]

Second, the sheer number of different criminal biographies gives some indication of their popularity. Aside from newspaper articles, somewhere between two and three thousand biographies have survived from the eighteenth century.[7] Notorious cases attracted more than one publication: the trial of Mary Blandy in 1752 for the murder of her father led to more than thirty pamphlets, books and broadsheets, as did the controversy in 1753–4 surrounding the alleged kidnapping of Elizabeth Canning. Biographies often went through many editions: *A Warning to Youth: The Life and Death of Thomas Savage* appeared in at least twenty-two editions in the early eighteenth century; *The Discoveries of John Poulter* went through seventeen editions between 1753 and 1779; and *A Narrative of all the Robberies, Escapes, &c. of John Sheppard* ran to eight editions in the space of two months at the end of 1724.[8]

2

READERS

It is sometimes argued that the expansion of the book trade which began in the seventeenth century was the result of an increase in literacy. But the connection between the trade and readership is more complex: was it advances in literacy which led to more publications, or was it more publications which led to more readers? Looking just at literacy rates ignores other issues which had an effect on the book trade, such as changes in the organization of the publishing business and the enactment of copyright laws. In any case, the various methods of measuring literacy rates are fraught with difficulties.[9] For instance, the ability to sign one's name cannot be assumed to imply the ability to read, or even to write. On the other hand, since reading is learnt before writing, those who could read may not have been able to write, although the likelihood is that the two rates would have been fairly close to one another. Moreover, even if it were possible to calculate the number of people who were able to read, it could not be assumed that they actually used that skill. As might be imagined, measuring reading habits is even more hazardous than estimating literacy: for example, using the sales of a book, such as the Bible, provides an uncertain guide, since it is unclear whether those who bought bibles did so in order to read them, or simply to possess them as religious artefacts.[10]

Turning to the question of who read criminal biographies, it is typically assumed that the bulk of the readers of popular literature came from the labouring classes, but the evidence for this is problematic. The anecdotal evidence rests on sparse and rather exceptional sources. For instance, in her valuable study of late seventeenth-century chapbooks, Spufford refers to the reading habits of John Bunyan and the poet John Clare.[11] Aside from the problem of using Clare as evidence for the habits of those who lived a hundred years before he was born, neither he nor Bunyan could be said to have been typical of labouring people, so their reading habits cannot be assumed to have reflected those of the generality of their social class. It is true that Clare wrote of his father that he 'could read a little in a bible or testament and was very fond of the supersti[ti]ous tales that are hawked about a sheet for a penny', but he also wrote that his mother 'knew not a single letter' and that his neighbours denounced reading as 'a sure indication of laziness'.[12]

Of course, these criticisms do not prove that the poor were not able to read or that they did not read crime literature. On the other hand, reading many of the criminal biographies would have needed more than the simple literacy skills required for the chapbooks in Spufford's study since the texts are sometimes fairly sophisticated. Perhaps stronger evidence on this issue is the price. The labouring people might have been able to afford halfpenny and penny broadsheets and chapbooks and have had the skills to be able to read them,[13] but many of the biographies cost sixpence and some as much as several shillings and so would surely have seemed expensive to all but the better-paid workers. However, there is evidence that people clubbed together to buy newspapers which were then read to the group by literate members,[14] and there may have been similar arrangements for other literature, including criminal biographies. But, on the whole, it seems likely that, while some members of the labouring classes may well have read, or listened to the reading of, criminal biographies, the publishers looked elsewhere for their main market.

Little consideration has been given to the readership of criminal biographies by the eighteenth-century ruling elite: Richetti makes the curious remark that such reading matter 'must have appeared to the educated literate elite of the eighteenth century precisely what comic books and television seem to the contemporary guardians of cultural standards'.[15] Yet, there is plenty of evidence of the gentry's fascination with crime and its literature: James Boswell wrote that having read criminal biographies in his youth gave him 'a sort of horrid eagerness' to attend hangings; and Horace Walpole, in spite of his expressions of contempt for criminal biographies, had many examples in his library at Strawberry Hill.[16]

However, it is likely that the core of the readership for crime literature came from the same broad social group as those who published it: the tradespeople, lawyers, clergy, doctors and so forth who composed the middling classes. The price of the publications was more readily within their range, indeed there was often no need for the urban middling classes to buy them since many could be read free of charge, or for a small fee, in bookshops and coffee-houses.[17] The biographies themselves typically suggest this readership. It was common for them to include advice on crime prevention aimed at, in particular, tradespeople. Furthermore, as will be argued later, much of the literature portrays crime as originating in the lack of self-discipline and idleness of the labouring people, and implicitly asserts that the resolution of these problems lies not in the loose control operated by the landed gentry, which, while possibly suitable for rural areas, is regarded as incompatible with the problems of large cities like London, but in the imposition by middling-class employers of a rigorous discipline at the workplace.

WRITERS AND THE PROBLEMS OF AUTHENTICITY AND ACCURACY

The great bulk of the biographies claim to be either autobiographical or written by someone with special access to the prisoner, such as a prison chaplain like the Ordinary of Newgate. Contemporary critics argued that even if there was contact between biographer and subject, many biographers showed scant regard for the facts of the individual's life and were motivated by considerations other than accuracy.

The main focus for such criticism was the Ordinary of Newgate's

Account, a publication that appeared after each hanging day in London, an event which could take place as many as eight times a year.[18] Critics argued both that the *Account* was inaccurate and that the Ordinary was motivated by mercenary, rather than Christian, principles. Rev. Samuel Smith, who, with George Croom, established the *Account* as a periodical publication in 1684, came in for some sharp attacks: the poet Thomas Brown alleged that Smith wrote well of prisoners who paid him and badly of those who did not.[19] Smith's successor, Dr John Allen, did little to improve matters when he was dismissed in 1700 following accusations that he had, amongst other things, extorted money from prisoners. So it was that when Paul Lorrain was appointed in 1700, both the post of Ordinary and the *Account* already had poor reputations.[20] His most famous, and most persistent, critic was Daniel Defoe. Defoe's first attack followed the publication in 1703 of a memorial sermon preached for Thomas Cook, who had been hanged for murder. In it Lorrain had celebrated Cook's repentance in prison as showing that even life-long sinners could obtain divine mercy.[21] In *A Hymn to the Funeral Sermon*, Defoe pointed out that if this were the case then there was no incentive for people to live honest lives, adding, for good measure, that Lorrain only 'Sainted' those prisoners who paid him. Later he wrote that Lorrain was 'the Object of almost every Body's Scorn; and I could never hear of above two People who spoke favourably of him, and those were the *Printer* and the *Publisher* of his *Dying Speech* Papers'.[22] Lorrain consistently rejected the allegations that he took money from prisoners, and certainly the City of London, who had been quick to sack Allen on this ground, never seems to have taken any action against him. Moreover, there is plenty of evidence in Lorrain's *Accounts* that he did not readily believe expressions of repentance, although his caution may have been the result of Defoe's attack: in 1715, just before Captain Alexander Dalzell was to be hanged for piracy, he showed signs of penitence, but, Lorrain commented, 'whether that Repentance was sincere, and not too late, is much to be doubted'.[23]

Defoe's assaults on Lorrain may have been motivated by personal dislike. Although Lorrain had been writing about the repentance of prisoners for three years, it was only after Defoe's release from Newgate prison in 1703, following a short period of imprisonment, that his attacks began, and, also, there seems a distinctly personal element in both his attacks and Lorrain's reply. So, it may be wise to treat Defoe's remarks with caution. Yet, in spite of that, others did take up the cudgels against Lorrain, and he was regularly driven to defend himself in the *Accounts*.[24] Moreover, later Ordinaries and their *Accounts* came under fire. Different Ordinaries were variously described as 'the great B – – – – p of the Cells', 'the careful Retailer of Dying Speeches' and 'a pragmatical Coxcomb, *that could not write common* English gramatically'; the *Account* was 'an incoherent Magazine of Trash and Scandal', written in 'that incomprehensible stile, by which the chaplain so wisely distinguishes himself from all other writers', based on forged dying speeches, containing 'nothing but absurdity and contradiction', and providing an example that people would emulate rather than despise.[25] In some of the criticism there was a strong religious element, emanating from, in particular, the Methodists, who had very active missions to the prisons and, as a result, came into conflict with the Ordinaries.[26] Most significant of all was the criticism which came from rivals within the book trade. The *Account* became a market leader by emphasizing the unique access which the Ordinary had to the prisoner.[27] The marketing strategies of rivals sought to counter this advantage. They tried to get their work out first, leading the Ordinaries to rush the *Accounts* into print the day after the hanging and, in the meantime, to advertise their imminent publication. Rivals also published biographies before the hanging day, as was the case with *The History Of the remarkable Life of John Sheppard* (1724), which is reprinted in this book (p. 47). They tried to demonstrate a superior connection to the condemned than that which the Ordinary had: for instance, in *A Compleat and True Account Of . . . James Carrick* (1722), Carrick, who is alleged to have written the work, claims he was a Roman Catholic and, therefore, did not confess to the Ordinary, 'so that I must request Readers not to give credit to what he shall publish concerning me, if it shall be in contradiction to what I have here related'.[28] So, although the contemporary criticism of the biographical literature cannot be ignored, much of it was directed at the Ordinary of Newgate's *Account* and seems to have been the result of personal, religious or commercial rivalry, and as such cannot be assumed to have been entirely objective.

Yet, leaving aside the rivalries within the book trade, there is other evidence which suggests that the biographies did not live up to their claims of authenticity. In 1774, after James Boswell had unsuccessfully defended John Reid on a capital charge of stealing sheep and then failed to obtain a pardon for him, he went dejectedly to see his friend Michael Nasmith. Together they drank a bottle of port, after which Boswell's mood brightened and, as he wrote in his journal, 'a curious thought struck me that I would write the case of John Reid as if dictated by himself on this the day fixed for his execution'. He did so and had it published as *The Mournful Case of Poor Misfortunate and Unhappy John Reid*. According to the subtitle, this account was 'taken from his own mouth'. After the hanging another publication appeared, *The Last Speech, Confession, and Dying Words of John Reid*, which, according to the text, had been 'given to Richard Lock, inner turnkey of the Tollbooth, Edinburgh, by . . . John Reid'. However, as Boswell noted in his journal, this had been composed by Alexander Ritchie, an Independent lay preacher.[29] Such a revealing account of the background to other 'autobiographies' is rarely available, but suspicions are aroused about both their accuracy and their authenticity by the wealth of detail and the highly literate, often flowery, style which many display.

Against all this there is other evidence which suggests that the condemned prisoners may have been involved in writing the biographies. Certainly, claims about their participation seem to have been regarded as an important selling point. As has been mentioned, the Ordinary's *Account* was built around the close link between the Ordinary and the condemned prisoner, and the title-pages of other biographies made great play of any connection with the prisoner. Of course, such claims were easily made, although not all title-pages made them. Eighteenth-century readers seem to have been sceptical about such assertions since publishers apparently went to great lengths to back them up. It was common for the publisher to include an invitation to readers to inspect the original documents upon which the text was based; and, although this would not have precluded the forging of such documents, it is interesting that publishers like John Applebee, who employed this technique on several occasions, did not use it with all their publications.[30] Other methods of authentication were also employed. Newspapers often noted that a condemned person had handed over an account at the gallows.[31] Of course, the mere fact of delivery does not guarantee the authenticity of the publication, and, in addition, it was not uncommon for such reports to appear only in newspapers which had a connection with the publishers of the particular biography.[32] William Cannicott was said to have read out a statement in court to the effect that he had delivered an account of his life to the publisher, Judith Walker.[33] Clergymen, sheriffs, constables and gaolers were variously reported to have been the recipients of holograph autobiographies. In 1732 Sarah Malcom is said to have spent a day writing her confession; this was then placed in an envelope, which was sealed by Rev. Dr Middleton and Richard Ingram, the keeper of Newgate, and handed to Dr Piddington. After she had been hanged, the envelope was opened before an assembly which consisted of Middleton, Ingram, the sheriffs of London and Middlesex and two other people. It was read, resealed and then taken to the benchers of the Inner and Middle Temples who also read it and returned it to Piddington. Only then did he publish it.[34] Incidental evidence of the authorship of a biography occasionally appears in other, rival biographies. In 1719 Paul Lorrain, the Ordinary of Newgate, noted that Edward Bird had shown him the draft of a paper he intended to have published and which, Bird hoped, would clear his name; this attribution seems the more trustworthy because Lorrain felt it was inappropriate, and, therefore, a source of criticism, for Bird to be so concerned with the world's opinion of him when he was about to leave it.[35]

This leads to the obvious question, why might prisoners have decided to co-operate in the writing of biographies? There are several possible explanations. The power of clergymen, like the Ordinaries of Newgate, and, indeed, anyone who appeared to have some degree of influence, should not be underestimated. Religious belief, fear of the unknown and the promise of life after death were, doubtless, powerful weapons in bringing many 'a poor shivering Malefactor'[36] to confession. The Ordinary's report in 1709 that John Long had 'cry'd very bitterly, wishing he had liv'd a better Life'[37] does not seem far-fetched and is often repeated. It does not take much imagination to believe that Long's mental state – and, in view of the prevalence of disease in prison, perhaps also his physical state – would have made him willing to confess, although, of course, in this condition he would have been vulnerable to suggestions about the content of the confession. Another influence on prisoners was the offer of money to maintain them in gaol, or the promise of a proper burial and protection of the corpse from the servants of the anatomy schools, who saw the hanged as a useful source of raw material.[38] Some may have confessed in the hope of obtaining a pardon: in 1690 Nicholas Carter was said to have told the Ordinary, 'if he might be spared he resolved to amend his evil Life'.[39] John Crafts was reported to have told the Ordinary in 1708 that he would not give him a detailed confession 'unless he were sure to be reprieved', and, later in the century, the highwayman William Hawke was said to have been less forthcoming in his confessions once the final decision had been taken that he should hang.[40] Gang members were well aware of the way in which the criminal justice system depended on the information supplied by criminals and some used this bargaining tool. The biographical literature is replete with works like *The Discoveries of John Poulter* (1753), reprinted in this book (p. 147), which appear to have originated in confessions made by prisoners in the hope of escaping prosecution. Some prisoners seem to have been motivated by a sense of injustice at being wrongly accused, or by a desire not so much to deny the charge as to complain about a misrepresentation of some of the facts.[41]

Finally, to return to Boswell and Reid, and to the question, what is an autobiography? Boswell had interviewed Reid on many occasions, was in possession of a statement by Reid himself and later showed the finished publication to Reid; similarly, Ritchie had regularly visited, and spoken to, Reid, and he too had shown Reid the finished work. So, although the publications were not actually written by Reid, they may well have been a summary of his case based on the interviews each writer had with him and packaged for the reading classes. Of course, this element of 'packaging' causes serious difficulties for those wishing to use the biographies. The involvement of some sort of editor was apparently not regarded as incompatible with the pamphlet being advertised as an autobiography. The title page of *A Full and Faithful Account of the Life of James Bather* (1754) notes that it was 'Published from the Author's Manuscripts; Revised and Corrected by an Impartial Hand'.[42] The publisher Cabe readily acknowledged that the manuscript provided by Thomas Daniels as the basis for *The Affecting Case of the Unfortunate Thomas Daniels* (1761) had been edited, but he claimed that this had been done not 'to give any undue colouring to facts, but simply to supply the deficiencies of the writer; whose laborious situation in life has denied him those literary advantages indispensable to the writing his story with tolerable propriety', and added that such editing had been confined to 'spelling, style, and disposition' so as to make it 'clear and fit for perusal'.[43] Of course, this repackaging for a particular audience is not simply a problem which arises when an editor is involved. Even if the involvement of the biography's subject could be demonstrated, it is still necessary to consider the relationship between the biography and the life.

THE CRIMINAL BIOGRAPHY AS LITERATURE

That a work of literature is popular when it is first published does not ensure it will be accorded any recognition by subsequent generations of scholars; indeed, the term 'popular literature' has tended to be regarded by literary critics as an oxymoron.[44] F.R. Leavis, for example, argued that the study of English literature should be restricted to a narrow range of texts on the ground that

> in the field of fiction some challenging discriminations are very much called for: the field is so large and offers such insidious temptations to complacent confusions of judgement and to critical indolence . . .

He made these 'discriminations' on the basis of his view of what was, or was not, within 'the great tradition of the English novel',[45] and criminal biographies, along with much else, were not within that 'tradition'. It is an approach which is still strongly influential in the English Departments of many universities, particularly since it was endorsed, not just by conservative critics like Leavis, but also by many on the Left who believed that popular literature was bourgeois propaganda designed to distract the masses from the true nature of their oppression and that only 'High Art' was able to stand at a critical distance from the ideas and values of the ruling class.[46] The tendency of the Leavis approach is not only to ignore the vast bulk of literature, but also to divorce from its historical context that which is studied: 'Most students of literature are taught . . . [that] the greatest art is that which timelessly transcends its historical conditions.'[47] In other words, the view is taken that an understanding of history is irrelevant to the study of literature. Texts are organized around individual writers or groups of writers, and the act of writing is presented as the result of a largely unfathomable flash of individual genius.

Although it is true that scholars extended the circle of study beyond the few texts specified by Leavis, they typically did so merely on the basis of a widened definition of what amounted to 'great literature': so, for example, where Leavis excluded the novels of Henry Fielding, others argued for their inclusion. Even those few who went further in their researches and studied texts that they did not believe to be 'great literature' did so only in order to discover 'the origin of the novel', which was regarded as the pinnacle of literary achievement. It was argued that the biographies facilitated an understanding of the genesis of certain literary techniques, such as realism, which were regarded as influential in the formation of the novel.[48] In this way criminal biographies were regarded as having value only because of their supposed relationship to the novel. As might be supposed, this has led to some fairly superficial research. For instance, the assumption that the biography was a proto-novel led to the conclusion that it must have faded away fairly rapidly with the appearance of the first novels in the early eighteenth century; yet, in fact, not only did the criminal biography not vanish at that time,[49] it continued throughout the century and, indeed, on to the present day. The discussion of the biography which sees it simply as part of a progression from picaresque literature to the novel is clearly a distortion. The important relationship which undoubtedly existed between the biography and the novel can only be studied properly within a perspective which recognizes the differences between them.

The rigidity of the Leavis approach has, however, softened, although its influence has by no means disappeared. Popular literature (the continued use of the term confirming the survival of divisions within literature) has been accorded an importance in its own right, for, as one writer recently remarked, if 'one begins to examine literature as a "communicative practice" with social and historical roots, then one cannot afford to ignore those fictional worlds which command the widest public'.[50]

The fullest treatment of the criminal biographies appears in Lincoln Faller's *Turned to Account*, although his argument draws heavily on mid-seventeenth-century texts as well as the rather different eighteenth-century ones. In a lengthy and complex discussion, he argues that there are two modes of narrative:

> The one, highly structured and univocal, seeks to reintegrate the criminal into the social and moral order, to smooth over the disruptive effects of his behavior, to digest whatever cruelties he may have committed; the other, disjunctive and ambivalent, heightens his disruptiveness, invents and amplifies cruelties, presenting a fractured, etiolated, absurd, and often frankly fictitious version of his life and character.[51]

The first mode of narrative is that of the 'familial murderer', the second is the thief. With the murderer or murderess, the biographies seek to personalize the story and to place their subjects firmly within the real world. By showing the condemned as, in the end, reaching a recognition of their sinfulness and an acceptance of their fate, the biographies supported the religious and moral status quo, thereby restoring the connection between the criminal and the rest of society 'so viciously broken' by the act of murder.

10

The biographies of thieves had a rather different purpose. Faller dismisses the idea that they were simply a means by which readers could vicariously vent their frustrations at the social constraints surrounding them by pointing out that the biographies often portray the thieves as either buffoons or brutes, neither of which traits would, presumably, have held much attraction for the readers. He does claim that there was a moral point to such biographies in that they were designed not to encourage emulation, but to deter, and he adds that they sought to distance the reader from difficult questions about the lack of comparability between crime and punishment in the eighteenth century. Through the depiction of the condemned's treatment of the gallows as a stage, the hanging becomes a matter of theatre, not morals. The heroic highway robber whose story, he argues, typically involves some attack on dishonest politicians and traders seems, at first, an attack on at least some of those who are the biography's readers. And yet Faller asserts that the texts are ambiguous in their messages, so that what a particular reader read into the text depended on her or his viewpoint: it could be seen as anti- or pro-Whig, or anti- or pro-economic individualism. Even if an attack on the reader's own values was recognized as such, it could be taken by that reader as an opportunity to defend them, especially in view of the nature of the critic: 'Such a fellow is no small gift to a guilty conscience, for he provides a golden opportunity (though you be ever so *dis*honest) to rise, laughing, to your own defense.'[52]

Finally, Faller enters into the discussion of the relationship between the criminal biography and the novel, claiming that the biography provided an opportunity for novelists to write extended narratives about 'problematic' lives. The doubts raised in readers' minds about the authenticity of criminal biographies would, he argues, have meant that a novelist such as Defoe 'had a fairly sophisticated audience waiting for him',[53] one that would have been critical in its reading of anything which, like *Moll Flanders*, purported to be a criminal biography, and this enabled the novelist to develop complex plot constructions. So, although Faller's discussion of Defoe's novels is not a part of the main text of the book, he does take some important steps towards establishing criminal biographies and novels as parts of the broad range of eighteenth-century literature in a way which restores the original breadth of meaning to the term 'literature' and which avoids subordinating one part to another on the basis of a misplaced argument about their relative importance as works of art.

THE CRIMINAL BIOGRAPHY AS HISTORY

Historians, too, have found the biographies difficult to come to terms with. While many feel comfortable – often too comfortable – with the tracts produced about crime and criminals by official inquiries and social re-formers,[54] they have been less certain about using biographies. A lot of

11

historians take as their starting point the need to sift out sources which are true/fact from those which are false/fiction, and adopting the categorization of criminal biographies as fiction, they therefore reject them. Even if it is accepted that a distinction needs to be made between fact and fiction (and the reasons for this are by no means obvious), this approach assumes what cannot be assumed, namely, that there is a standard by which fact and fiction can be separated which is both objective and immutable, that what is true today was true in the eighteenth century and, conversely, what is false now was false then. The problems with this are clear: the medieval belief that the earth was flat was as true then as our belief that it is round is today.

The rejection of the biographies as an historical source is only one approach that has been taken. Other historians adopt the opposite view by regarding them as providing an accurate reflection of reality. There are two reasons why they take such a view. First, the apparent lack of materials seems to leave them with little choice other than to put their faith in published biographies. Yet, Howson's excellent book on Jonathan Wild, *Thief-taker General* (1970),[55] shows just how much material is available to the hardworking historian and how it can be used to good effect. Second, there is the belief that the criminal biographies are accurate because they 'feel right'. Salgado summed up this attitude when he wrote about Tudor crime literature, 'What is certain is that they present, in scenes of unmatched vividness and colour, the seamy side of life in Elizabeth's London.'[56] The biographies 'feel right' because of the detail which they contain. *The History Of the remarkable Life of John Sheppard* (reprinted in this book, p. 47), which is not untypical, mentions 10 dates, refers to more than 45 streets and other places, and names or in some other way identifies over 60 people, giving the occupations of about 30 of these. And that biography is a mere nothing in its detail when compared with the extraordinary *The Discoveries of John Poulter*. Yet in both there are many obvious omissions: for instance, Poulter's biography has nothing on his life before 1749, so that the reader might be led to believe that his criminal career only began then, whereas he had been sentenced to transportation in 1746.[57]

The inclusion of detail does not mean that the story these biographies tell is an accurate reflection of reality. Indeed, the idea that any piece of writing can be this is curious because it amounts to an assertion that writers are able to take in everything and express it all on paper. It assumes that writing is a non-interventionist act, whereas what writers try to do is to produce what both they and, in their view, the potential readers will see as a coherent narrative. This involves the selection, ordering and interpretation of a vast range of available materials. No two writers will describe the same situation in the same way: as Defoe observed, 'nothing is more common, than to have two Men tell the same Story quite differing one from another, yet both of them Eye-witnesses to the Fact related'.[58] The philosopher, Karl Popper, compared the human mind – and the writer's mind is, I suppose, no different

– with a searchlight which illuminates only certain things. Similarly, the art critic, Ernst Gombrich, has written:

> We can focus on *something* in our field of vision, but never on *everything* . . . . The number of stimuli that impinge upon us at every moment – if they were countable – would be astronomical. To see at all, we must isolate and select . . . .[59]

Even if a writer attempts to describe something, the description will never be the thing itself: a description of a tree is not a tree.

Not far distant from those who believe that criminal biographies present reflections of reality are the social historians whose interest is, primarily, in the labouring poor and for the study of whom these biographies represent a rare source.[60] Wary of the problem of accepting the biographies at face value and yet unwilling to reject them totally, they have subjected them to testing against other sources, typically manuscript court records. Without question the resulting work is of great value and has provided a fresh view of the literature. However, the problems of using the literature have not been fully addressed. The verification process is open to obvious criticisms, placing, as it does, such faith in the sources which are used as verifiers. Moreover, the historian's need to employ this process before feeling able to use the literature as an historical source reinforces the traditional view that the act of distinguishing between absolutes of fact and fiction is not merely possible, but is fundamental to historiography.

Another approach to this literature has been to accept that the distinction between fact and fiction is of importance and that the biographies are fiction, but then to regard this fictional quality as giving them their value as an historical source. According to this view, while contemporary 'factual' writing on real people and events may describe external facts, it is fiction which provides the 'attitudes' or 'inner truth' of a society or a section of a society. So, it has been argued that crime literature is 'useful in its own right as a source of information about attitudes to crime'.[61] This is similar to the view – and, consequently, faces the same criticisms – that the biographies reproduce reality, the only difference being that here it is claimed that what is being reproduced is an attitude. Even leaving this aside, difficulties are met when the obvious question is asked, whose attitudes are revealed? For some writers popular literature gives a direct insight into the minds of the labouring poor;[62] for others the criminal biographies were a literature of resistance, 'a form of social protest that expressed the class resentment of many who read novels and attended executions'.[63] However, there are those who claim the reverse, that the biographies – and, indeed, all forms of popular literature – were simply a means of disseminating ruling-class propaganda amongst the subordinate classes. So, the historian, James Sharpe, has argued that crime literature 'constituted an important point of contact between official ideas on law and order and the culture of the masses'; elsewhere he has added that 'the objectives of this literature might include a desire to titilate or shock, but its underlying purpose is to reinforce the values of "straight" society.'[64]

The view that popular literature was part of the culture of the people – that is, a culture created by the labouring classes, and, as such, commonly in opposition to a separate culture of the ruling class – assumes, without providing any evidence, not only that there was such a separation in cultures, but also that the labouring people were the main readers of the biographies and had control both of the printing presses and of the means of distribution. On the other hand, the approach that argues that popular literature was pure propaganda fails to answer three questions: why it was that the literature was popular; why it took this form rather than, say, a simple list of 'do's and 'don't's; and what effect the transformation of propaganda into crime literature had. No account is taken of the readers – they are represented as mere receptacles ready for anything the ruling class may want to throw into them. Research suggests that readers may interpret texts in ways which had never occurred to the writer.[65] So, the writer and the publisher may think they are producing a text which condemns criminals, but the reader may see the criminal as a hero or heroine.

It seems not unlikely that the popularity of the literature was connected to its form: people liked reading criminal biographies, so publishers kept producing them. Even if the literature was being used as a means of propaganda by the ruling class, the need to put it into a particular form which connected with those which potential readers recognized and enjoyed must have had an effect on any message which it was intended to transmit. More generally, the disagreement as to whether the literature represents the culture *of* the people or culture *for* the people, that is, whether it takes an anti-ruling class or pro-ruling class stance, shows that identifying it with one class or one set of values is, to say the least, not easy. Curiously, it is the realization that the texts may be shot through with contradictions which provides a way out of the difficulties with them. The key is in the work of Antonio Gramsci.[66]

An important concept in Gramsci's thought is the notion of hegemony. A hegemonic class is one which not only controls the means of economic production, but also has moral and intellectual leadership over subordinate classes. Although such a class does retain control over the means of force – the army, the police and so forth – the use of such large-scale coercion is the exception rather than the norm, and only comes to the fore in times of crisis. Normally, coercion is unnecessary because, Gramsci argues, the subordinate classes subscribe to a view of the world in which only the present ruling class has the right and ability to govern, and, therefore, they do not seek to challenge that right. Although there is continuous use of coercion to suppress, stigmatize and marginalize certain social groups, this further ensures the consent of the bulk of the subordinate classes by providing them with an 'enemy within' to fear, to oppose and to make their own position appear favoured. So, Gramsci rejected the Marxist view that a ruling class imposes its own values and beliefs – its own culture – on, and to the exclusion of, that of the subordinate classes. Consent cannot be gained by such a strategy; instead the ruling class seeks to adapt the culture of the subordinate classes so that, while maintaining an apparent continuity with its old forms and practices, it is shifted so as to conform to a view of the world in which the society as presently ordered, both politically and economically, is seen as moral, natural and rational, and it dismisses alternative views as immoral, unnatural and irrational. Inevitably, the cost to the ruling class of obtaining this consent is that its own values are not being imposed in a pure form, but are themselves reshaped by the need to accommodate those of the subordinate classes. However, the amount of this reshaping is limited, so that the fundamental economic basis from which the ruling class, in the last instance, derives its power is maintained. Gramsci wrote:

> Undoubtedly the fact of hegemony presupposes that account be taken of the interests and the tendencies of the groups over which hegemony is to be exercised, and that a certain compromise equilibrium should be formed. . . . But there is also no doubt that such sacrifices and such a compromise cannot touch the essential; for though hegemony is ethical–political, it must also be economic, must necessarily be based on the decisive function exercised by the leading group in the decisive nucleus of economic activity.[67]

But the condition of hegemony is not static, because there is never complete consent; society is never totally united. Flaws in the system of beliefs and values will constantly appear, and there will also be challenges from oppositional value systems. As a result, the ruling class must constantly seek to maintain its position through the mechanisms of cultural production – the family, the churches, the schools, the media and other cultural institutions. Some of this opposition may be crushed by coercion without necessarily damaging the position of the ruling class, as, for instance, where such action can be convincingly justified as a response to problems of 'law and order' which are depicted as threatening the whole fabric of society, including the interests of the subordinate classes.[68] However, as has been said, the use by the ruling class of large-scale coercion to maintain its rule may indicate that it has lost consent; the subordinate classes no longer subscribe to the old beliefs, and this leads them to challenge the claim of the ruling class to represent their interests, and, therefore, undermines its claim to the consent of those classes. This situation will arise if, for instance, there is serious political or economic uncertainty or instability, or if the ruling class is unable to fulfil promises it has made about a fundamental issue, such as economic prosperity or victory in war. This leads to the exposure of flaws in the governing structure and its supporting ideology and also to the strengthening of oppositional ideologies as people, losing faith in the existing system, cast around for alternatives. If these problems can no longer be circumvented by the mechanisms of cultural production, then the ruling class will resort to increasingly coercive methods of maintaining their position. This will serve further to expose the illegitimacy of their rule and their loss of hegemony.

Popular literature is an important site on which the struggle for hegemony takes place. As a result popular texts can only be understood if they are seen as part of this struggle. In other words, it is important to recognize that literary texts are

> not mere images of conflicts fought out on another terrain, representations of a history which happens elsewhere; they are themselves a material part of those struggles, pitched standards around which battle is joined, instruments which help to constitute social interests rather than lenses which reflect them.[69]

This is why it is possible to see in popular literature elements of different, and opposing, ideologies. Different value systems meet and are mixed in ways that are constantly changing, but which, nevertheless, retain an articulation towards certain fundamental values. Popular literature is popular because it addresses current areas of interest and concern, namely, the tensions between different ideological positions. But the literature is not simply reflecting these tensions, it is engaging in the working out of the relations between men and women and between classes. As a result, the text exposes confusion and contradiction. Shifts in what is of current concern explain why a text which is popular loses that popularity, and, therefore, why a genre, such as the criminal biography, changes. In the next two sections consideration is given, first, to some of the issues which the biographies addressed, and, then, since hegemony is constantly being renegotiated as new issues arise and old ones fade away, the next section considers some of the ways in which the concerns of the biographies altered.

ISSUES AND TENSIONS IN CRIMINAL BIOGRAPHIES

The political, economic, social, intellectual and religious upheavals of the seventeenth and early eighteenth centuries continually threatened to rip the country apart. The uncertainties which began with the Civil War were not ended by the installation of William III as king in 1688. One of the problems which the new constitutional settlement faced was that of establishing its own legitimacy without encouraging the belief that monarchs could routinely be overthrown. This was of particular importance in view of the challenge from the dispossessed Jacobites, which did not fade away until the failure of the '45, and the unpopularity of some of the Hanoverian line. New power bases were developed. Central government expanded as its control over revenue wealth and patronage grew; expensive foreign wars led to government routinely raising loans and so made financiers politically important; the development of new ways of making money saw the continuing rise not only of people of business, but also of bankers and lawyers. The role of the established church was challenged by Methodism and religion as a whole was undercut by science, although popular religion retained its vigour.

Contemporary writers on political, social and economic theory tried to grapple with these changes. According to writers working within the civic humanist tradition, the political elite – the gentry – derived their status and authority from land. Income from land relieved the gentry of a dependence on others, particularly on government, for their livelihoods, and gave them an independence in their performance of civic duties which was unattainable by those without such advantages, and this enabled them to pursue national, rather than self-, interest. Indeed, these writers argued that the gentry had, not just a right, but also a duty to govern, and they were, therefore, critical of any neglect by the gentry of that duty. Other writers argued that notions of civic humanism did not fit in a society with a rapidly expanding commercial and financial economy. They rejected the way in which that tradition described the working of society in moral terms, with the 'good' gentry leading the rest, not for selfish gain, but for the civic good, and instead argued that the pursuit of self-interest in almost any form was what made a nation thrive. Others argued for a middle way. They struggled to accommodate economic individualism within civic humanism by arguing that the commercial benefits brought by the middle classes were essential to the nation and represented a base from which the middle classes could – indeed, should – engage in politics.[70] It is no coincidence that a concern over, and a fascination with, that symbol of social disruption, crime, emerged as a major issue at this time. The number of capital offences was rapidly increased by Parliament between the 1680s and the middle of the next century as the new political order sought to establish the roots of its power. Capital punishment was attached to offences against the post-1688 constitutional settlement, the gathering of tax revenue and property.[71]

Criminal biographies were not simply about crime and criminals. Yet the vagueness of the term 'crime' enabled the biographies to address powerfully other issues of contemporary importance. 'Crime' had no precise legal meaning, and this meant that it could be used to evoke a broad, but imprecise and, therefore, more frightening, range of fears: fear not just of losing property, but also of physical danger, of gangs and a whole criminal underworld, of moral collapse and of anarchy. These fears were then linked to other issues which were addressed in the biographies. As has been argued, by its very nature popular literature concerns itself with the examination of those values which are under strain. The ability to make such literature

17

relevant to the reader's own concerns is one important way in which it becomes popular, and, also, provides one reason why it loses its popularity as concerns change. The criminal biographies did not simply reproduce the tensions of eighteenth-century society, nor did they present neat resolutions of those tensions, instead they were actively engaged in working them through. It is useful to consider some of these tensions.

Individualism

It has been argued that, like the novel, the criminal biography was an expression of individualism which reflected the rise and dominance of the middle classes.[72] The problems with this view are, first, that the middle class had been a significant force, both in the economy and in government, well before the early eighteenth century, second, that it did not become the politically dominant class at that time, and, third, that the biographies are not an unqualified expression of the virtues of individualism. However, these texts are biographies, so the individual has a role.

To those who hold the view that individual endeavour creates the commercial wealth on which governments and peoples depend, the notion that inherited status is the only route to political power might be an anathema. Yet, the middle classes in the eighteenth century did not seek to overturn the political dominance of the landed gentry; after all, the rich were the biggest consumers. Indeed, among the middle classes, emulation rather than revolution was the more common position. Commentators, such as Defoe, expressed great concern that the desire to emulate the gentry led people to neglect their businesses. The problem was that, although financial wealth had importance, social success and political power were bound up with the acquisition of status through land ownership or marriage. Of course, those who sought status, generally, wished to maintain and even reinforce it. Moreover, since the creation of commercial wealth in this pre-technological era was believed to depend on the existence of a large and cheap workforce, the maintenance of social division was regarded as important since it was necessary to prevent the great mass of working people from shifting up the social scale and out of productive employment. So, from several viewpoints the whiff of egalitarianism inherent in notions of individualism was no more pleasing an odour to the middle classes than it was to the gentry.

The contradictions emerge in popular art and literature. The success of the industrious apprentice in Hogarth's series of engravings, *Idleness and Industry* (1747), is achieved through marriage to his employer's daughter and is measured not in terms of money, but by becoming Lord Mayor of London. In that series it is not the industrious apprentice, but the idle apprentice who is the consummate individualist, and his life ends on the gallows at Tyburn. Similarly, the criminal biographies focus on the evil consequences of extreme individualism. Ian Watt's comment about Defoe's fictional character Moll Flanders could equally be applied to the criminal biographies of the period:

> Moll Flanders . . . is a characteristic product of modern individualism in assuming that she owes it to herself to achieve the highest economic and social rewards, and in using every available method to carry out her resolve.[73]

It is not the possibility of upward mobility, as exemplified by Hogarth's industrious apprentice, which is focused on in the biographies, but rather the instability caused by individualism. The image presented is that the labouring poor only obtain upward social mobility through illegitimate means and as a result any repositioning in society is temporary.

Apprentices and 'the Great Law of Subordination'

Concern over apprentices, especially in London, was a feature of the late seventeenth and early eighteenth centuries: there were, perhaps, 20,000 by 1700, and they had a tradition of radicalism and solidarity. This seems to sit behind the link between apprentices and crime which is such a common feature of biographies in this period. A typical plot was that of the hard-working apprentice from a poor but honest background, who, through contact with 'bad company' – usually, a woman described as a 'whore' – becomes a criminal. A wave of conduct books directed at apprentices, which appeared during this period, made the same point. Their central concern was with what the printer and novelist Samuel Richardson called, in *The Apprentice's Vade Mecum* (1734), 'the present Depravity of Servants'.[74] Similarly, Defoe, writing in 1727, identified the problem as being that, 'the state of apprenticeship is not a state of servitude now, and hardly of subjection',[75] and this was the result of the breach of 'the Great Law of Subordination'. In a book of that title, written in 1724, he had argued, of apprentices, that 'more of them are ruin'd, debauch'd, and come to nothing, for want of Subordination, and being under Government, than was wont to be the Case'.[76] Vice was like a disease, and youths, especially male youths, were particularly susceptible to it. According to *The Servants Calling* (1725), 'the Young and Unexperienc'd are soonest tainted by the bad Air of Society, being aptest at Imitation'.[77] The view of the conduct books was that youths could only be protected within the disciplined environment of a properly regulated apprenticeship; similarly, although, as Sheppard is made to put it, the apprenticeship might appear to the apprentice to be 'a Yoke of Servitude' (*The History of . . . John Sheppard*; see p. 49), it is that very quality which recommends it.

The conduct books outlined what this regulated apprenticeship would involve. According to Richardson, the apprentice was not to marry, nor to gamble, nor to go to theatres or alehouses, nor to follow 'the Fopperies and Apish Fashions of the Men of mode', nor to break the sabbath. The guiding principle was: 'you have no Portion of Time during the Term of your Apprenticeship, that you can call your own; . . . you are accountable for every Hour to your master'.[78] So, although the books value the importance of the training which apprenticeship should give, they give more emphasis to this element of discipline. The other side of the coin was that the conduct books and the criminal biographies were implicitly – and sometimes explicitly – critical of the employers who failed to live up to the ideals. This connects with a reworked version of the civic humanist tradition: in urban societies, such as London, it was up to the middling classes to look beyond the short term and, through the employment relationship, to take on some of the civic obligations of government which were performed in the country by the gentry. In one of his most popular books, *The Family Instructor* (1720), Defoe wrote that 'a Master is a Parent', and as such owed a duty of care to the apprentices for 'their Souls and their Bodies';[79] he, therefore, regretted that, 'Custom has wickedly of late Years seem'd to discharge Masters of this Duty.'[80] He later wrote that, 'Servants out of government are like soldiers without an officer, fit for nothing but to rob and plunder':

> To leave a youth without government is indeed unworthy of any honest master; he cannot discharge himself *as a master*; for instead of taking care of him he indeed casts him off, abandons him, and, to put it into scripture words, he *leads him into temptation*; nay, he goes farther, to use another scripture expression, *he delivers him over to Satan*. . . . [W]hat servants can a man expect when he leaves them to their own government, not regarding whether they serve GOD or the *Devil*?[81]

Richardson made the link between these conduct books and the biographies:

> Let the *Sessions-Paper* and the *Dying-Speeches* of unhappy Criminals tell the rest: Let them inform the inconsiderate Youth, by the Confessions of the dying malefactors, how naturally, as it were Step by Step, Swearing, Cursing, Profaneness, Drunkeness, Whoredom, Theft, Robbery, Murder, and the Gallows, succeed one another![82]

The point is illustrated in *The History Of the remarkable Life of John Sheppard*: although he was previously an industrious apprentice, on meeting Elizabeth Lyon Sheppard 'contracted an ill Distemper' (p. 32), namely, an addiction, first, to vice and, later, to crime. But some blame is laid at the door of the employer. When Sheppard 'began to dispute with his Master', his master 'a mild, sober, honest Man, indulg'd him'. Another biography of Sheppard is even more explicit: there Sheppard says, of his period as an apprentice,

I believe if less Liberty had been allow'd me then, I should scarce have had so much Sorrow and Confinement after. My Master and Mistress with their Children were strict Observers of the Sabbath, but 'tis too well known in the Neighbourhood that I had too great a Loose given to my evil Inclinations, and spent the Lord's Day as I thought convenient.[83]

Similarly, in 1684 John Gower allegedly told the Ordinary of Newgate that it was through 'the Indulgence of his Master to whom he was Apprentice, that he suffered them to mispend the Sabbath-days, which was the first Step to Ruine'.[84] Nine years later, the Ordinary reported that a pickpocket called John Simons had told him that 'Had his Master . . . held a strict hand over him, he had not gone far astray from God, nor dared to have done evil Actions, but being left to his own evil Inclinations' he fell into crime.[85] William Shelton, hanged in 1739, supposedly said that 'my Master being in a bad State of Health, was not able to give me such Correction as was absolutely requisite for young Sparks in my Lax way of Living'.[86]

Having said all this, it is not difficult to see how apprentices might have read the biographies in a rather different light. To an apprentice the charge that an apprenticeship was a 'Yoke of Servitude' often rang true: apprentices were routinely exploited as sources of cheap labour and physically abused by their employers; their training was often inadequate as employers tried to ensure that they would not become trade rivals; in some industries, like carpentry, the work was very heavy and, as a consequence, a person's working life short, so that the seven years spent in an apprenticeship earning little or nothing might, understandably, be resented. The problems were added to by the breaking down in some old trades of the requirement that people serve apprenticeships, and also the development of new trades which could be practised without having served an apprenticeship. Plenty of apprentices terminated their apprenticeships by the simple expedient of running away – a course of action which might end with them in the house of correction. Hints of the apprentice's side of the story do surface in the biographies. For instance, there is a passage in *The History Of the remarkable Life of John Sheppard* in which Sheppard

> began to dispute with his Master; telling him that his way of Jobbing from House to House, was not sufficient to furnish him with a due Experience in his Trade; and that if he would not set out to undertake some Buildings, he would step into the World for better Information.

But, although many writers recognized the problems faced by apprentices, few – and certainly not those who wrote criminal biographies – suggested that apprenticeships should be scrapped. The rapidity of change during the late seventeenth and early eighteenth centuries created a conservatism, which, while not seeking to push aside those changes, did try to impress on the economically powerful the need to maintain authority. Apprentices were an easily identifiable group with a reputation for disorder, and to some extent the difficulties with them symbolized more general concerns about the breakdown of the hierarchical social order upon which not only discipline, but also economic wealth and military strength were believed to depend. The biographies engage in the negotiation between a modernized version of civic humanism, according to which economically powerful citizens have a duty to ensure social control and good government, and the philosophy of economic individualism, in which everyone pursues her or his own self-interest, although it is the advantages of the former and the disadvantages of the latter which are emphasized in the biographies: the lesson is that of the idle rather than the industrious apprentice.

Gender

To the issue of class subordination inherent in the way the biographies treat the questions of individualism and apprenticeship is added the question of gender subordination. In the biographies, although both the apprentice and the employer are partly blamed for the collapse, the need to avoid too much criticism of the apprenticeship means that the immediate cause of the breakdown of the relationship is ascribed to another cause, namely, a woman. In many of these biographies the women are one-dimensional characters, and, having broken the apprenticeship, they vanish from the narrative. Nevertheless, they are being depicted as powerful, and their power derives from their independence of any relationship of subordination to men. The power is described as illegitimate and the women as whores. Since men in the eighteenth century 'were intended (so men claimed) to excel in reason, business, action; women's fate lay in being submissive, modest, docile, virtuous, maternal and domestic',[87] then the world of crime was a world-turned-upside-down, with women dominant and men subordinate. The consequences of this empowerment of women emerge most clearly in the biography of Mary Young, reprinted in this book (p. 121). Her gang resembles a nation-state, with its own hierarchy, laws and treasury, and reveals a genius for criminal organization unparalleled by men like Sheppard and Dalton. So independence empowers women, that power results in evil, and this justifies the subordination of women.

The way in which the biographies present women also tended to undermine the view that the male offenders, merely by being written about, were being portrayed as heroes. As is more fully discussed in the introduction to *The History Of the remarkable Life of John Sheppard*, the depiction of their subordination to women, who are portrayed as 'whores' rather than women, presents these men as subhuman rather than superhuman, and this is underlined by irrational behaviour, such as their drunkenness. Implicit is the unfavourable contrast between them and those men who lived within relationships structured around the division of labour through waged work and the subordination of women. The biographies are engaging in the contemporary struggles over the definitions of 'masculinity' and 'femininity' which can also be found in, for example, changing practices at the workplace and different attitudes to marriage.

London

In view of its size, it is not surprising that London criminals dominate the biographies. To a large extent the focus in the biographies on apprentices symbolized a more general concern about the problem of youths in London. As one historian has commented:

> One of the most striking demographic characteristics of the London population was its high proportion of the young, the geographically mobile and the unmarried. The migration to London of young town and country dwellers caused its growth, a tendency reflected in the fact that among those hanged two thirds were born outside London.[88]

This immigration accelerated in the late seventeenth century and undermined the already stretched structures of London authority. The sort of face-to-face government which was at least possible in the country was never easy in a large city like London, and it became less and less so as the communities of the ruling and the ruled moved into separate, self-contained areas. The fear of the London labouring classes as unknowable and ungovernable surfaces in many works in which the city is unfavourably compared with the country: the former anarchic and unhealthy, the latter orderly and fecund. As one commentator put it: 'in London amongst the lower classes all is anarchy, drunkenness, and thievery; in the country good order, sobriety and honesty'.[89] Demographers, such as Thomas Short in his *New Observations on the Bills of Mortality* (1750), claimed that the population in London was declining, which was an alarming prospect given the belief that national wealth was directly related to the size of the working population. He argued that economic expansion, symbolized by London, was morally corrupting: the poor drank themselves to death on gin and the rich were idle parasites who made no real contribution to society.

The contrast between the city and the country features in many of the criminal biographies. According to his biography, John Adamson lived in Lynn, Norfolk, but, 'Being weary of a Country Life, and desirous of seeing *London*, he some Years ago came to Town, and having neither Friends nor Acquaintance here he was put to great straits how to live'. He turned to crime, was caught, convicted, condemned and hanged in 1739. Shortly before he died, the Ordinary of Newgate described him as 'miserably poor and nak'd' and 'a little craz'd'.[90] Of Mary Edmondson, hanged in 1759 for the murder of her aunt in Rotherhithe, it was said that she had been 'bred in a Country Place where were few or no Temptations to Debauchery or Extravagance, these Rocks upon which so many of the Female Sex are split, especially in and about *London* and *Westminster*'.[91]

London was a metaphor for the moral concerns which many had about the expansion of the economy, including those who supported that expansion. It also symbolized the division between the rulers and the ruled. In London the ruled are unknown and unknowable to the rulers, and the view of many writers, such as John Brown in *An Estimate of the Manners and Principles of the Times* (1757), was that the rulers were themselves so morally corrupted by the city that they had no desire to know the ruled. For Henry Fielding, writing in 1751, London was like 'a vast wood or forest, in which a thief may harbour with as great security as wild beasts do in the deserts of Africa or Arabia'.[92] But, of course, there was another side to all this, namely that, although London was a place of crime and disorder and a source of moral corruption, it was also the centre of wealth and power.

CHANGES IN THE LITERATURE

Those few surveys of the biographical literature which acknowledge that it changed during the eighteenth century do so only in the most perfunctory fashion. Chandler and Richetti agree that by 1730 the development of newspaper crime reporting and 'elaborate fictions', such as Defoe's *Moll Flanders* (1722), meant that 'the popularity of the separate criminal pamphlet was on the wane'.[93] This assertion is based not on historical fact, but on the belief that because more sophisticated publications were available then this 'bad art' must have gone into decline. The historian, Linebaugh, on the other hand, implies that the Ordinary of Newgate's *Account* was a relatively stable phenomenon; he declares that it 'enjoyed one of the widest markets that printed prose narratives could obtain in the eighteenth century'.[94] He fails to explain why the *Accounts* all but disappeared in the 1760s. Such a dramatic change in the fortunes of what had been a leading force in the book trade in criminal biographies needs to be considered since it suggests that some changes did occur in the literature, and since they do not seem to have occurred as early as Richetti and Chandler claim, then, presumably, the explanations they put forward need reconsidering.

One important influence was the rise to prominence of Henry Fielding and his step-brother John Fielding after 1748. As magistrates at Bow Street they were key figures in the criminal justice system in London, a position they exploited in the wake of a crime panic which gripped the capital from 1748. This began with the apprehension caused by the prospect of a rapid demobilization of the Navy and Army at the end of the War of the Austrian Succession. Apprehension seemed to turn to reality as newspapers reported stories of the involvement of soldiers and sailors in thefts, robberies and riots. As has been mentioned, London symbolized in the biographies the division between the ruled and the rulers which made the former unknowable and ungovernable by the latter. This failure of authority seemed also to be exemplified in the resort to deterrence through the use of public punishments.

The Fieldings, especially John, claimed to be able to render knowable the city and the criminals through mechanisms of surveillance, such as the use of paid officers and the collection and exchange of information. Being adept at public relations, they were able to open up and publicize their work and, at the same time, emphasize its arduous nature and its importance through their own writings, through advertisements for information on crimes and criminals, and through reports in the press of their lengthy examinations at Bow Street of victims, witnesses and suspects.[95] The Fieldings agreed with the view of the criminal lifestyle as conforming to the sort of overarching pattern described in the Ordinary of Newgate's *Account* whereby sin led to crime, but their work demonstrated that there was no inevitable link between that lifestyle and the gallows because the end result was often only arrived at by the intervention of justices like the Fieldings. Although this point should not be overstated since private involvement in the prosecution of crime was still at the centre of the criminal justice system, what the Fieldings offered as a solution to crime depended not on a tighter apprenticeship, which had, in any case, never gained acceptance amongst either the apprentices or their employers, but, instead, on a bureaucratized police structure.

Certainly, the Fieldings were keen to boast of the success of their new policing plans: in 1767 John Fielding claimed that all the gangs operating in and around London during the previous fifteen years had been broken up; the following year he declared that it was impossible for criminals 'to continue their Outrages for any Time, or, as usual, to collect themselves into large and dangerous Gangs'; and in 1770 he told a select committee of the House of Commons that no London street robber had escaped detection for twenty years.[96] He presented the pre-trial work of the justice, not what happened in the trial courts, as the central feature of crime control. Paradoxically, the reports of Old Bailey trials produced by the Gurneys from the 1740s, by presenting a much fuller picture of all the events that led to the trial, rather than the often very brief summary which had previously been published, also took the spotlight away from the trial and punishment itself. From the 1750s onwards an increasing number of the biographies included this new perspective by looking not just at the lifestyle of the subject, but also at the process of her or his detection. Indeed, a new strand of crime literature emerged in which the detection process was the main, sometimes the only, topic.[97]

This increased exposure of the criminal justice system may have been one factor behind the appearance in the crime literature of criticisms of the trial and the penal system. On a general level, the Fieldings themselves took part

25

in this with, amongst other things, their attacks on the rule that no one could be convicted on the evidence of a self-confessed felon unless that evidence was corroborated by another witness, a rule which, they argued, hindered the breaking of criminal gangs. Many of the biographies also engaged in a critique of the verdict reached in individual trials. This really got underway with the cases of Mary Blandy in 1752, Elizabeth Canning in 1753–4 and Mary Edmondson in 1759.[98] Other biographies in the second half of the eighteenth century alleged that the leniency of the penal system was a cause of higher crime: for instance, *A Genuine Account of the Life, Robberies, Trial and Execution of William Cox* (1773) urges the increased use of the death penalty on the ground that transportation allows people like Cox to continue their crimes in the penal colonies or in England, to which they are able to return easily.[99]

It is surely no coincidence that, as the literature of crime, including the biographies, became more sophisticated and more critical in its discussion of crime and the criminal justice system, the *Accounts*, with their simplistic portrayal of the progression to the gallows, began to disappear. But there were also other, longer-term pressures which reduced the importance of the *Accounts*. The improved reporting of trials, both in specialist publications like the OBSP and in the biographies, showed events as linked together through cause and effect, and the offender as an individual who is rational and responsible and whose actions can be rationally explained, rather than as directed by a divinely ordained progression from sin to the gallows.

Indeed, it can be argued that, although religion featured in many of the biographies throughout the eighteenth century, its importance, even in the Ordinary's *Account*, was actually negligible. As I argue in the introduction to the Ordinary of Newgate's *Account* of Mary Young (1741), although the biographies produced by the prison chaplain at Newgate were in one sense religious works, their commercial success rested not on this, but on their claim to accuracy and authenticity because of his unique access to the prisoners (see pp. 113–17). Market rivals, such as the biographies of Sheppard and Dalton reprinted in this book (pp. 47 and 85), did not seek to mimic the religious aspects, other than in a fairly minimal way; instead they aimed to displace the popularity of the *Accounts* by claiming greater accuracy and authenticity. This led to the piling on of more detail: more street names, names of people, dates, trial reports, letters and so forth. Even at the end of a biography when religion enters the narrative in the form of a confession and repentance, the test of that repentance depends on the accuracy and completeness of the detail in the confession. The divine is rationalized by the presentation of facts; the uncheckable relies on the checkable truth of street names: as McKeon argues in his discussion of early novels, 'a material epistemology is given the task of demonstrating a truth that is ultimately spiritual'.[100]

These are some of the ways in which the criminal biography changed during the century. It is worth emphasizing that the history of the criminal biography in the eighteenth century was not unidirectional, nor were such changes as it underwent total, sudden or the product of a simple relationship with certain events. Understanding changes in the literature is not simply a matter of identifying a time and an event as denoting a clean break with the past. Although it may be true that particular events provide a push in a certain direction, change is rarely instant and total, but more often it involves a dynamic discourse between present and past, in which the new is never entirely new and the old never entirely forgotten. Nevertheless, the point to be made is less that of how accurately the changes are described here, but that the literature should be examined within the terms of the traditions of crime literature and the commercial interests of the book trade, and also as part of the general social, economic, political, legal and intellectual context of the period.

FURTHER READING

Readers will find, as I did, that a slang dictionary is of great value: recommended are E. Partridge, *The Penguin Dictionary of Historical Slang*, Harmondsworth, Penguin, 1972 and E. Partridge, *A Dictionary of the Underworld*, London, Routledge & Kegan Paul, 1950, reprinted, Ware, Wordsworth, 1989.

For those who are unfamiliar with the history of crime and criminal law in the eighteenth century, there are a number of excellent books. Particularly recommended, because they are good surveys of their respective periods, readily available and reasonably priced, are J.A. Sharpe, *Crime in Early Modern England 1550–1750*, London and New York, Longman, 1984 and C. Emsley, *Crime and Society in England 1750–1900*, London and New York, Longman, 1987. Outstanding, but slightly more expensive, is J. Beattie, *Crime and the Courts in England 1660–1800*, Oxford, Clarendon Press, 1986. The best modern biography of an eighteenth-century criminal, and one which provides useful insights into crime during that period, is G. Howson, *Thief-taker General: The Rise and Fall of Jonathan Wild*, 1970, republished as *It Takes a Thief: the Life and Times of Jonathan Wild*, London, Cresset Library, 1987. For a general discussion of recent historical writing in this area see P. Rawlings, 'Recent writings on crime, criminal law, criminal justice, and punishment in the Early Modern Period' in W.D. Hines (ed.), *English Legal History: A Bibliography and Guide to the Literature*, New York and London, Garland Publishing, 1990. A more general discussion of the law and legal system is provided by W.R. Cornish and G. de N. Clark, *Law and Society in England 1750–1950*, London, Sweet & Maxwell, 1989.

On the general social history of the period there have been a huge number of books, but an excellent starting point is provided by R. Porter, *English Society in the Eighteenth Century*, Harmondsworth, Penguin, 1990, which also has a valuable reading list. For the economic developments see M. Berg, *The Age of Manufactures: Industry, innovation and work in Britain, 1700–1820*, London, Fontana, 1985. A good introduction to contemporary thinking on the economy and society is S. Copley (ed.), *Literature and the Social Order in Eighteenth-Century England*, London, Croom Helm, 1984.

On women see I. Pinchbeck, *Women Workers and the Industrial Revolution, 1750–1850*, London, Virago, 1981; S. Amussen, *An Ordered Society: Class and*

Gender in Early Modern England, Oxford, Clarendon Press, 1988; and A. Clark,
Women's Silence, Men's Violence: Sexual Assault in England 1770–1845, London and
New York, Pandora, 1987. Many of the biographies centre on London, for which
see M.D. George, *London Life in the Eighteenth Century*, Harmondsworth,
Penguin, 1966. It is also worth dipping into contemporary writers; particularly
recommended is D. Defoe, *Tour through the Whole Island of Great Britain*,
Harmondsworth, Penguin, 1966. On popular literature in general see V.E. Neuburg,
Popular Literature: A History and Guide, London, 1977, and on criminal biogra-
phies in particular see L. Faller, *Turned to Account: the Forms and Functions of
Criminal Biography in Late Seventeenth and Early Eighteenth-Century England*,
Cambridge, Cambridge University Press, 1987, and I.A. Bell, *Literature and Crime
in Augustan England*, London, Routledge, 1991. For reprints of some Tudor crime
literature see G. Salgādo (ed.), *Cony-Catchers and Bawdy Baskets: An Anthology of
Elizabethan Low Life*, Harmondsworth, Penguin, 1972.

The question of the origin of the novel is examined in I. Watt, *The Rise of the
Novel: Studies in Defoe, Richardson, and Fielding*, Harmondsworth, Penguin, 1963;
Watt's views have most recently been challenged in a densely argued work by M.
McKeon, *The Origins of the English Novel 1600–1740*, London, Radius, 1988. More
general surveys of popular culture in the eighteenth century include R. Malcomson,
Popular Recreations in English Society 1700–1850, Cambridge, Cambridge Univer-
sity Press, 1975 and P. Burke, *Popular Culture in Early Modern Europe*, Aldershot,
Wildwood House, 1988. There is now a huge amount of theoretical work on popular
culture, but amongst the more accessible are: R. Hoggart, *The Uses of Literacy*,
Harmondsworth, Pelican, 1958; R. Williams, *Culture and Society 1780–1950*,
Harmondsworth, Pelican, 1963; and *The Long Revolution*, Harmondsworth, Pelican,
1965; T. Bennett, G. Martin, C. Mercer and J. Woollacott (eds), *Culture, Ideology
and Social Process*, London, Open University, 1981 includes a useful discussion of
leading theorists, including Gramsci.

Finally, theoretical developments in oral history promise much of value for those
interested in criminal lives: see R. Samuel and P. Thompson (eds), *The Myths We
Live By*, London, Routledge, 1990.

NOTES

1 J. Dunton, *The Life and Errors of John Dunton Late Citizen of London*, London,
1705, p. 87. Also S. Parks, *John Dunton and the English Book Trade: A Study
of His Career with a Checklist of His Publications*, London, 1976, p. 45.
2 T. Gent, *The Life of Thomas Gent, Printer, of York*, London, 1832, pp. 140–1.
3 *Gentleman's Magazine*, 1733, vol. III, p. 137.
4 *Whitehall Evening Post*, 21 February 1754.
5 W.S. Lewis (ed.), *The Yale Edition of Horace Walpole's Correspondence*, 48
volumes, London, 1937–83, vol. 20, p. 199.
6 *Whitehall Evening Post*, 7–9 March 1786. Also *General Advertiser*, 9 March 1786.
7 The largest single collection is in the British Library.
8 Of course, a publisher may simply be trying to shift stock by pretending that a
biography is so popular that a new printing has become necessary.
9 See L. Stone, 'Literacy and education in England 1640–1900', *Past and Present*,
1969, vol. 42, pp. 69–139; R.S. Schofield, 'The measurement of literacy in pre-
industrial England' in J. Goody, (ed.), *Literacy in Traditional Societies*, Cambridge,
1968; D. Cressy, *Literacy and the Social Order: Reading and Writing in Tudor and
Stuart England*, Cambridge, 1980; R.A. Houston, 'The development of literacy:
northern England', *Economic History*, 1982, 2nd series, vol. XXXV, pp. 199–216.

10 E. Robinson (ed.), *John Clare's Autobiographical Writings*, Oxford, 1986, p. 5.

11 M. Spufford, *Small Books and Pleasant Histories: Popular Fiction and its Readership in Seventeenth-Century England*, Cambridge, 1981, chapters I–III.

12 Robinson, *John Clare's Autobiographical Writings*, pp. 2 and 5.

13 P. Burke, *Popular Culture in Early Modern Europe*, Aldershot, 1988, pp. 253–4.

14 ibid., p. 265; J.G. Rule, *The Labouring Classes in Early Industrial England, 1750–1850*, London, 1986, p. 135.

15 J.J. Richetti, *Popular Fiction Before Richardson: Narrative Patterns 1700–1739*, Oxford, 1969, p. 9.

16 On Boswell see F.A. Pottle (ed.), *Boswell's London Journal 1762–1763*, London, 1950, p. 252; M. Bailey (ed.), *Boswell's Column*, London, 1951, pp. 343–8; G.B. Hill and L.F. Powell (eds), *Boswell's Life of Johnson*, 6 volumes, London, 1934, vol. II, p. 93, vol. III, p. 532, vol. IV, p. 328. For a report of Boswell and Sir Joshua Reynolds leading the condemned onto the scaffold outside Newgate prison see *Public Advertiser*, 7 July 1785. On Walpole see: A.T. Hazen, *A Catalogue of Horace Walpole's Library*, 3 volumes, New Haven, 1969; Lewis, *Correspondence of Horace Walpole*, vol. 2, pp. 34–5, vol. 9, p. 400, vol. 13, p. 23, vol. 20, pp. 99, 101, 106, 168–9, 188, 199, vol. 24, pp. 152–4, vol. 28, pp. 192, 288, 289, vol. 30, p. 490, vol. 32, pp. 360–1, vol. 35, p. 6. Walpole also owned a portrait (now in the National Gallery of Scotland) of Sarah Malcom, who was hanged in 1732 for murder: [H. Walpole], *A Description of the Villa of Mr. Horace Walpole, youngest son of Sir Robert Walpole Earl of Orford, at Strawberry-Hill near Twickenham, Middx. With an Inventory of the Furniture, Pictures, Curiosities, &c.*, London, 1784, p. 23.

17 The British Library has three pamphlets on the case of Mary Blandy (hanged at Oxford in 1752 for murder) which originally came from Tom's Coffee-House, London. In 1708 it was said that one prisoner refused to assist in the writing of his biography because he did not wish to become 'the Sport and Ridicule of vain idle Fellows in *Coffee-Houses*': *The Life and Penitent death of John Mawgridge, Gent. Who was Executed for the Murder of Captain Cope. Penn'd from his own Account of himself, and approv'd of by him, before his Death*, London, 1708, p. 2.

18 See the introduction to The Ordinary of Newgate's *Account*: Mary Young (1741), pp. 113–19.

19 T. Brown, 'An Elegy on that most Orthodox and Painstaking Divine, Mr. *Sam. Smith*, Ordinary of *Newgate*, who dy'd of a Quinsey, on St. Bartholomew's Day, the 24th of *August*. 1698', in T. Brown, *The Works of Mr. Thomas Brown*, 5 volumes, London, 5th edn, 1720–1, vol. IV, pp. 41–3; T. Brown, 'An Epitaph upon that profound and learned Casuist, the late Ordinary of *Newgate*', in ibid., vol. IV, pp. 43–5.

20 On Allen see *An Account of a New and Strange Discovery; That was made by John Sheirly, alias Davis, & Joseph Fisher, The same Day of their Execution, Relating to the Ordinary of Newgate: With a True Copy of the Petition, that was Presented to the Lord Mayor, by the Prisoners of Newgate, concerning the same with many other remarkable Particulars*, London, 1700; *Capt. Charles Newy's Case, Impartially Laid Open*, London, 1700; *Mr. Allen's Vindication; or, Remarks upon a late Scandalous pamphlet, Entituled; A strange and New discovery, &c.*, London, 1700; *The Life and Conversation Of the Pretended Captain Charles Newey; Together with some Remarks upon A Scurrilous and Scandalous Pamphlet, called Newey's Case*, London, 1700.

21 P. Lorrain, *Walking with God: Shewn in a Sermon Preach'd at the Funeral of Mr. Thomas Cook, In the Parish-Church of St. James Clerkenwell, Aug. 13, 1703*, London, 1703.

22 [D. Defoe], *A Hymn to the Funeral Sermon*, London, 1703; [D. Defoe], *A Trip through London: containing Observations on Men and Things*, London, 8th edn, 1728, pp. 50–1. Also [D. Defoe?], *The History of the Press Yard*, London, 1717, pp. 46–53; [D. Defoe], *A Trip through the Town. Containing Observations on the Humours and Manners of the Age*, London, 4th edn, 1735, p. 24; *Mercurius Politicus*, March 1718, p. 159. For Lorrain's reply see [P. Lorrain], *Remarks On the Author of the Hymn to the Pillory. With an Answer to the Hymn to the Funeral Sermon*, London, 1703. Generally, see R.R. Singleton, 'Defoe, Moll Flanders and the Ordinary of Newgate', *Harvard Library Bulletin*, 1976, vol. 24, pp. 407–13.

23 Ordinary of Newgate's *Account*, 5 December 1715. See also ibid., 23 March 1708/9.

24 ibid., 4 May 1705, 24 June 1709, 5 December 1715. See also *A Copy of William Gregg's Paper Delivered by him, to the Sheriffs of London and Middlesex, and Paul Lorrain Ordinary of Newgate, at Tyburn, the Place he was executed for High Treason, on Wednesday the 28th of April 1708. Printed from the Original, and Published by Authority*, London, 1708.

25 *Parker's Weekly Journal*, September 1732, quoted in Ordinary of Newgate's *Account*, 9 October 1732, p. 18; *Account of the Life, Adventures and Transactions of Robert Ramsey, alias Sir Robert Gray. From his Birth to his Execution at Tyburn, on Wednesday, the Thirteenth of January 1741–2*, London, 1742, p. 30; *The Matchless Rogue. Or, An Account of the Life of Tom Merriman*, London, 1725, p. 86; *Some Observations on the Trial of Mr. Thomas Carr, who was Executed at Tyburn, January 18, 1737. With Some Remarks on the Partial and Contradictory Account given of him by the Ordinary of Newgate*, London, 1737, pp. 1–2 and 8–9; *Select Trials at the Sessions-House in the Old-Bailey, for Murder, Robberies, Rapes, Sodomy, Coining, Frauds, Bigamy, and other Offences. To which are added, Genuine Accounts of the Lives, Behaviour, Confessions and Dying Speeches of the most eminent Convicts*, 4 volumes, London, 1742, vol. I, p. 325, also, pp. 81 and 312–19; *The Life, Travels, Exploits, Frauds and Robberies, of Charles Speckman, alias Brown, Who was Executed at Tyburn, on Wednesday the 23d of November, 1763*, London, 1763, p. 53, also, p. 50 (reprinted in this book, p. 185); B. Swift, *Tyburn to the Marine Society. A Poem*, London, 1759, p. 27. See also *Manuscripts of the Earl of Egmont: Diary of Viscount Percival, Afterwards First Earl of Egmont*, 3 volumes, London, 1920–3, vol. I, p. 11; *A Full, True and Impartial Account of all the Robberies Committed in City, Town, and Country, For several Years past by William Hawkins. In Company with Wilson, Butler, Fox, and others not yet Taken*, London, 1722, p. 42; *A Compleat and True Account Of all the Robberies committed by James Carrick, John Malhoni, and their Accomplices, In Dublin, Cork, Limerick, Waterford, and other Places in Ireland. As also on the Highway in England, and in the Streets of the Highway in England, and in the Streets of London and Westminster, and Places adjacent*, London, 1722, pp. 1 and 24; *Daily Journal*, 7 September 1724; H. Fielding, *The History of the Life of the Late Mr. Jonathan Wild the Great*, London, 1743; Philo-Patria, *A Letter to Henry Fielding, Esq. Occasioned by his Enquiry into the Causes of the late Increase of Robberies, &c.*, London, [1751], pp. 12–14; C. Jones, *Some Methods Proposed Towards putting a Stop to the Flagrant Crimes of Murder, Robbery, and Perjury*, London, 1752, p. 9; Lewis (ed.), *Correspondence of Horace Walpole*, vol. 10, pp. 5–6 and 113; *Memoirs of the Life of John Matthieson, Executed for a Forgery on the Bank of England, on Wednesday the 28th of July, 1779*, London, 1779, pp. 40–1.

26 *Some Account of the Life and Death of Matthew Lee, executed at Tyburn,*

October 11, 1752, In the 20th Year of his Age, London, 2nd edn, 1752. But see
J. Lackington, *Memoirs of the Forty-Five First Years of the Life of James
Lackington, the present Bookseller in Chiswell-street, Finsbury-square*, London,
7th edn, 1794, pp. 170–1; *Monthly Review*, 1788, p. 26. For other religious
critiques: *An Answer to a Narrative or the Ordinary of Newgate's Account*,
London, 1718, quoted in P. Linebaugh, 'The Ordinary of Newgate and his
Account' in J.S. Cockburn (ed.), *Crime in England 1550–1800*, London, 1977,
pp. 246–69, at p. 255; R. Fowler, *The Copy of a Letter sent to Matthew
Henderson, While under Sentence of Death in Newgate, for the barbarous
Murder of his Mistress, the Lady Dalrymple*, London, 1745, p. 11n. and *passim*;
W. Cudworth, *A Copy of a Letter sent to the Revd. Mr. K – – – . Concerning
Repentance*, London, 1752, pp. 3–4 and 6.

27 Ordinary of Newgate's *Account*, 24 May 1684.
28 *A Compleat and True Account Of . . . Carrick*, p. 24.
29 W.K. Wimsatt and F.A. Pottle (eds), *Boswell for the Defence 1769–1774*,
    London, 1960, pp. 306, 310, 318, 331 and *passim*.
30 Ordinary of Newgate's *Account*, 14 September 1741, pp. 7–15; *Miss Mary
    Blandy's own Account of the Affair between Her and Mr. Cranstoun*, London,
    1752; [Rev. W. Wilson], *A Full and Genuine Account of the Lives, Characters,
    Behaviour, last Dying Words and Confessions, of the Four Malefactors, that were
    executed on Friday the 6th Day of this Instant April 1739, at Kennington-
    Common*, London, 1739.
31 For example, *Whitehall Evening Post*, 7 February 1754, 5 June 1754, possibly
    referring to *Memoirs of the Life and remarkable Exploits of the noted Dennis
    Neale, alias John Clarke, otherwise call'd the Second Turpin, who was executed
    at Tyburn on Monday the 4th of February, 1754, for robbing on the Highway*,
    London, 1754.
32 See the introduction to *The History Of the remarkable Life of John Sheppard*,
    p. 43.
33 *A Genuine Account of the Life and Actions of William Cannicott, Who was
    Executed at Tyburn, on Monday, September 20, 1756, For the Murder of his Wife,
    on Tuesday the 20th of July, 1756. Written by Himself, while Confined in
    Newgate*, London, 1756, p. 11.
34 *A True Copy of the Paper, Delivered the Night before her Execution, by Sarah
    Malcom, to the Rev. Mr. Piddington, Lecturer of St. Bartholomew the Great.
    March 6th, 1732–3*, London, 1732, pp. 3–5. See also *Meditations and Letters
    wrote by the late William Alexander, During his Confinement in Newgate; Who
    was convicted of Forgery, at the last Assizes at Newcastle, and executed the 17th
    Nov. 1783; Published from his own Manuscripts. To which are added His Last
    Dying Speech, Some Account of his Behaviour, &c.*, Newcastle, [1783], pp. iv and
    15; *The True Copy of the Original Paper signed by Mr. Richard Noble, Which
    he designed for his Last Speech, deliver'd to Mr. Cook Curate of Kingston and
    Ordinary of Surry; Another to Mr. Boughton Vicar of Kingston; and a Third to
    the reverend Mr. L'Herondel; with A particular Account of his Behaviour some
    Days before his Execution, by all the aforesaid Clergy-men*, London, 1713. But
    see *Some Observations on the Trial of Mr. Thomas Carr*.
35 Ordinary of Newgate's *Account*, 23 February 1718/19, p. 4. The publication
    referred to was presumably *Mr. Bird's Case. The nature and circumstances of this
    prosecution, will appear from the malice as well as character of my prosecutors*,
    London, [1719]. See also Ordinary of Newgate's *Account*, 18 May 1743, which
    refers to *The Life and Adventures of Gilbert Langley, formerly of Serle-street,
    near Lincoln's Inn, Goldsmith*, London, 1743; and the introduction to *The Life,
    Travels, Exploits, Frauds and Robberies, of Charles Speckman*, pp. 181–2.

36 *Memoirs of the Right Villainous John Hall, The late Famous and Notorious Robber. Penn'd from his own Mouth sometime before his Death*, London, 4th edn, 1714, p. 27.

37 Ordinary of Newgate's *Account*, 16 December 1709. See also ibid., 26 January 1690, 28 February 1694, 28 September 1694, 18 May 1709, 16 September 1709, 22 December 1711.

38 P. Linebaugh, 'The Tyburn riot against the surgeons', in D. Hay, E.P. Thompson and P. Linebaugh (eds), *Albion's Fatal Tree: Crime and Society in Eighteenth-Century England*, Harmondsworth, 1977, pp. 65–117.

39 Ordinary of Newgate's *Account*, 26 January 1690 (see also the report on John Benlose, ibid.). See also ibid., 28 September 1694.

40 Ordinary of Newgate's *Account*, 24 September 1708; Rev. J. Villette, *A Genuine Account of the Behaviour, Confession, and Dying-Words of William Hawke and William Jones, Who were Executed at Tyburn on the 1st of July, 1774*, London, 1774, pp. 20–1. But see *The Life, Trial, &c. of William Hawke, The notorious Highwayman containing an Account of all the remarkable Robberies he committed before and since his Return from Transportation; with the Manner in which he was apprehended, and his Behaviour during the Time he was under Sentence of Death*, London, 1774, p. 24. See also Ordinary of Newgate's *Account*, 24 September 1704.

41 For example, *Mr. Bird's Case. The nature and circumstances of this prosecution, will appear from the malice as well as character of my prosecutors; A Narrative Of all the Robberies, Escapes, &c. of John Sheppard*, London, 1724; Ordinary of Newgate's *Account*, 14 September 1741, report on James Hall; J. Bather, *A Full and Faithful Account of the Life of James Bather, late Boatswain of the Nightingale Brig. Thomas Benson, Esq; Owner. Written by Himself*, London, [1754]; *A Genuine Account of the Life and Actions of William Cannicott; The Genuine Memoirs of Joshua Crompton; Written by Himself in the Cells of Guildford, After his unhappy Conviction for Forgery on the Bank of England; Who was executed on Gangley Common near Guildford, on Thursday the 20th of August, 1778*, London, 1778, p. 4.

42 *A Full and Faithful Account of the Life of James Bather.*

43 *The Affecting Case of the Unfortunate Thomas Daniels, who was Tried at the sessions held at the Old Bailey, September 1761, for the Supposed Murder of his Wife; by Casting her out of a Chamber Window: And for which he was sentenced to die, but received his Majesty's most Gracious and Free Pardon*, London, 1761, p. 5. See also the introduction to Ordinary of Newgate's *Account*: Mary Young (1741), p. 113. Hack writers would presumably have worked up the manuscripts: Thomas St Leger, who was hanged in 1745, claimed to have written criminal biographies before turning to smuggling: Ordinary of Newgate's *Account*, 26 July 1745. See also *The True and Genuine Account of the Confession (Whilst under Sentence of death) of Thomas Jones, and James Welch, For the barbarous Rape and Murder of Sarah Green, as Taken from the Mouth of Nicholls (the Evidence against them) and by them attested to be the Truth*, London, 1751, p. 10.

44 T. Davis, 'Education, ideology and literature' in T. Bennett, G. Martin, C. Mercer and J. Woollacott (eds), *Culture, Ideology and Social Process*, London, 1983, pp. 251–60.

45 F.R. Leavis, *The Great Tradition*, Harmondsworth, 1977, p. 8.

46 L. Althusser, 'A letter on Art in reply to Andre Daspre' in *Lenin and Philosophy and Other Essays*, trans. B. Brewster, London, 2nd edn, 1977, pp. 203–8, at p. 204.

47 T. Eagleton, *Marxism and Literary Criticism*, London, 1976.

48 F.W. Chandler, *The Literature of Roguery*, 2 volumes, Boston, 1907.

49 ibid., vol. I, p. 164; Richetti, *Popular Fiction Before Richardson*, pp. 29–30.

50 C. Pawling, 'Introduction: popular fiction: ideology or utopia?' in *Popular Fiction and Social Change*, London, 1984, p. 2.
51 L. Faller, *Turned to Account: the Forms and Functions of Criminal Biography in Late Seventeenth and Early Eighteenth-Century England*, Cambridge, 1987, p. 195.
52 ibid., p. 188.
53 ibid., p. 199.
54 See, for example, L. Radzinowicz, *A History of English Criminal Law and its Administration from 1750*, 5 volumes, London, 1948–86, vol. I.
55 G. Howson, *Thief-Taker General: The Rise and Fall of Jonathan Wild*, London, 1970. See also D. Barlow, *Dick Turpin and the Gregory Gang*, London, 1973.
56 G. Salgado, *The Elizabethan Underworld*, London, 1977, p. 22.
57 See the introduction to *The Discoveries of John Poulter*, p. 139.
58 Quoted in M. McKeon, *The Origins of the English Novel 1600–1740*, London, 1988, p. 121.
59 Quoted in J. Hall, *The Sociology of Literature*, London, 1979, p. 32.
60 For instance, P. Linebaugh, 'Tyburn: a study of crime and the labouring poor in London during the first half of the eighteenth century', unpublished Ph.D. thesis, Warwick University, 1975.
61 T.C. Curtis and F.M. Hale, 'English thinking about crime, 1530–1620', in L.A. Knafla (ed.), *Crime and Criminal Justice in Europe and Canada*, Waterloo, Canada, 1981.
62 L. Lowenthal, *Literature, Popular Culture and Society*, New Jersey, 1961, p. xii.
63 L.J. Davis, *Factual Fictions: The Origins of the English Novel*, New York, 1983.
64 J. Sharpe, '"Last dying speeches": religion, ideology and public execution in seventeenth-century England', *Past and Present*, 1985, vol. 107, pp. 144–67, at p. 162; J. Sharpe, *Crime in Early Modern England 1550–1700*, London, 1984, p. 165. This links with the discussion of criminal justice in D. Hay, 'Property, authority and the criminal law' in D. Hay *et al.* (eds), *Albion's Fatal Tree*, pp. 17–63.
65 Hall, *The Sociology of literature*, p. 22.
66 For an introduction to the work of Gramsci see C. Mouffe (ed.), *Gramsci and Marxist Theory*, London, 1979; Bennett *et al.* (eds), *Culture, Ideology and Social Process*, pp. 185–260. See also E.P. Thompson, 'Eighteenth-century English society: class struggle without class?', *Social History*, 1978, vol. III, p. 151; 'Patrician society, plebian culture', *Journal of Social History*, 1974, vol. VII, p. 395.
67 Bennett *et al.* (eds), *Culture, Ideology and Social Process*, pp. 197–8.
68 For a twentieth-century study illustrating this, see S. Hall, C. Critcher, T. Jefferson, J. Clarke and B. Roberts, *Policing the Crisis*, London, 1979.
69 T. Eagleton, *The Rape of Clarissa*, quoted in T. Bennett and J. Woollacott, *Bond and Beyond: The Political Career of a Popular Hero*, London, 1987, p. 277.
70 S. Copley (ed.), *Literature and the Social Order in Eighteenth-Century England*, London, 1984.
71 P. Rawlings, 'Recent writings on crime, criminal law, criminal justice, and punishment in the Early Modern Period' in W.D. Hines (ed.), *English Legal History: A Bibliography and Guide to the Literature*, London, 1990, pp. 62–112, at pp. 84–7.
72 I. Watt, *The Rise of the Novel: Studies in Defoe, Richardson, and Fielding*, Harmondsworth, 1963.
73 ibid., p. 98.
74 [S. Richardson], *The Apprentice's Vade Mecum: or, Young Man's Pocket Companion*, London, 1734, p. v.

75 [D. Defoe], *The Complete English Tradesman in Familiar Letters; Directing him in all the several Parts and Progressions of Trade*, 2 volumes, London, 2nd edn, 1727, vol. I, p. 15.
76 [D. Defoe], *The Great Law of Subordination consider'd; or, the Insolence and Unsufferable Behaviour of Servants in England duly enquir'd into*, London, 1724, p. 7.
77 *The Servants Calling; with some Advice to the Apprentice*, London, 1725, p. 71.
78 Richardson, *Apprentice's Vade Mecum*. Also, *Servants Calling*, p. 69.
79 [D. Defoe], *The Family Instructor, In Three Parts*, London, 8th edn, 1720, p. 222.
80 ibid., p. 232.
81 [Defoe], *Complete English Tradesman*, vol. I, p. 160.
82 [Richardson], *Apprentice's Vade Mecum*, p. 4.
83 *Narrative Of . . . John Sheppard*, p. 5.
84 Ordinary of Newgate's *Account*, 23 May 1684.
85 ibid., 8 May 1693.
86 ibid., 9 October 1732, p. 14.
87 R. Porter, *English Society in the Eighteenth Century*, Harmondsworth, 1990, p. 23.
88 Linebaugh, 'Tyburn riot against the surgeons', pp. 79–80.
89 J. Shebbear, *An Essay on the Origin, Progress and Establishment of National Society*, London, 1776.
90 Ordinary of Newgate's *Account*, 14 March 1739, p. 6.
91 *The Case of Mary Edmonson. By a Gentleman of the Law*, London, 1759, p. 4.
92 H. Fielding, 'An Enquiry into the Causes of the Late Increase of Robbers, &c.' in T. Roscoe (ed.), *The Works of Henry Fielding*, pp. 759–93, at p. 780. See also J. Fielding, *A Plan for A Preservatory and Reformatory, For the Benefit of Deserted Girls, and Penitent Prostitutes*, London, 1758, p. 4.
93 See above, note 49.
94 Linebaugh, 'The Ordinary of Newgate and his *Account*', p. 250.
95 J. Styles, 'Sir John Fielding and the problem of criminal investigation in eighteenth-century England', *Transactions of the Royal Historical Society*, 1983, 5th series, vol. 33, pp. 127–49.
96 T. Purland, *Alsatian Eccentricities, 1700–1780*, 2 volumes of newspaper cuttings in the British Library, item 755; *Parliamentary History*, vol. 16, cols 929–43, at col. 930; Sir J. Fielding, *Extracts from such of the Penal Laws, as Particularly relate to the Peace and Good Order of this Metropolis*, London, new edition, 1768, p. vi.
97 For example, *A Genuine Narrative of the Lives, Characters and Trials Of the four following Malefactors: viz. James Cotes, for a Highway-Robbery; Richard William Vaughan; William Stevens; and William Boodger*, London, 1758; *An Account of John Westcote, Late Porter To the Right Honourable The Earl of Harrington. In which is laid down An Effectual Method For preventing Theft and Robbery*, London, [1765]; James Bevell, *An Authentic Narrative of the Methods by which the Robbery committed in The House of the Right Honourable the Earl of Harrington, in the Stable-Yard, St. James's, was discovered. With Some Remarkable Anecdotes, and Original Letters sent to Sir John Fielding on the Occasion*, London, [1765]; *The Genuine Memoirs of Joshua Crompton; Written by Himself in the Cells of Guildford, After his unhappy Conviction for Forgery on the Bank of England; Who was executed on Gangley Common near Guildford, on Thursday the 20th of August, 1778*, London, 1778; *The Trial of Thomas Smith, and John Kennedy, for a Highway Robbery, committed on the Body of John Matthews, in the Parish of Rickmansworth, Herts. on Sunday Evening the 13th of May last. As also, A particular Account of the Circumstances*

attending the discovery thereof, and of the Persons of the Robbers, Uxbridge, 1787. See also J. Hewitt, *The Proceedings of J. Hewitt, Alderman, And one of his Majesty's Justices of the Peace, for the City and County of Coventry, in the Year 1756. Being a particular Account of the Gang of Coiners, apprehended in the Counties of Oxford, Warwick, and Stafford, pursued by the Author*, Birmingham, 1783; J. Hewitt, *A Journal of the Proceedings of J. Hewitt, Senior Alderman Of the City of Coventry, And one of His Majesty's Justices of the Peace for the said City and County, In his Duty as Magistrate*, 2 volumes, Birmingham, 2nd edn, 1790.

98 H. Fielding, *An Enquiry Into the Causes of the Late Increase of Robbers, &c.*, London, 1751, Sect. IX. On the Blandy case see W. Roughead, *Trial of Mary Blandy*, Edinburgh, 1904. On the Canning case see A. Machen, *The Canning Wonder*, London, 1926; B. Wellington, *The Mystery of Elizabeth Canning*, New York, 1940; L. de la Torre, *Elizabeth is Missing or, Truth Triumphant*, London, 1947; J. Treherne, *The Canning Enigma*, London, 1989. For other examples see *The Case of Mary Edmonson. By a Gentleman of the Law*, London, 1759; *The Case and Memoirs of the Late Rev. James Hackman. And of his Acquaintance with the late Miss Martha Reay*, London, 1779; E. Inge and T. Webb, *A Defence and Substance of the Trial of John Donellan, Esq; who was convicted for the Murder of Sir Theodosius Boughton, Bart. at the Assizes held at Warwick, On Friday the 30th of March 1781*, London, 1781. A large number of pamphlets were published during and after the conviction of the Perreau brothers in 1775, some of which challenged the veracity of Caroline Rudd's crucial evidence for the prosecution: *Mr. Daniel Perreau's Narrative of his unhappy case*, London, 1775; *Observations on the Trial of Mr. Robt. Perreau*, London, 1775; *A Solemn Declaration of Mr. Daniel Perreau*, London, 1776.

99 See also *The Life of Patrick Madan*, London, 1781; *An Account of John Westcote*, p. 21.

100 McKeon, *Origins of the English Novel*, p. 99.

I
THE HISTORY OF ...
JOHN SHEPPARD (1724)

1

INTRODUCTION

John Sheppard's skill as a thief seems to have been fairly ordinary, but he had an aptitude for escaping from prison and this made him famous. He was born in Spitalfields in March 1702 and was hanged, for housebreaking, at Tyburn in November 1724. In September 1724, after an escape from Newgate Prison, he was described by the prison authorities as 'about 23 Years of Age, about 5 Foot 4 Inches high, very slender, of a pale Complection, has lately been very sick, did wear a light Bobb Wigg, light colour'd Coat and white Waistcoat, has an Impediment in his Speech, and is a Carpenter by Trade.'[1] According to another report at about the same time, he 'appears to be very young, having a perfect Boy's Countenance and Stature, and not like one of 22 Years',[2] a description which is confirmed by Sir James Thornhill's portrait of him.

Although the newspapers of the time loved to refer to him as 'the famous House breaker',[3] neither he nor his crimes attracted any significant media attention until after his first escape from Newgate on 31 August 1724, and even then one of the main London newspapers, the *Daily Post*, did not begin to print reports about him until after his recapture.[4] It may have been that the degree of attention which was given to his escapes from Newgate was as a result of what the *London Journal* had referred to earlier in the summer as 'this Dearth of News'.[5] Certainly, both attempted and successful escapes from prisons, including Newgate, were common. In June 1724 Peter Curtis and John Parkinson dug a large hole in the wall of the condemned cell in Newgate in their attempt, and in July Thomas Fox actually escaped;[6] in the following October, whilst Sheppard was still at liberty after his second escape, a number of felons in Newgate tried a mass break-out;[7] and in November Sheppard's comrade, Joseph Blake, and a forger called Abraham Duval or Deval damaged the condemned cell so badly during their escape attempt that all the prisoners had to be removed and put elsewhere.[8]

In any event, Sheppard's fame was at its peak from September to November 1724, that is, during the period of his two escapes from Newgate and up to the time he was hanged. Crowds of the gentry and aristocracy flocked to see and to talk to him in Newgate, Sir James Thornhill, the royal painter, sketched him, George II ordered prints depicting his escapes, and a leading actor in a play about him called *Harlequin in Newgate* went to study him in person. As the *Daily Journal* reported, he had become a major tourist attraction: 'The Country People as come to London flock daily to see three great Curiosities as this Town at present affords, viz. The two young Lyons stuff'd at the Tower; the Ostrich on Ludgate-Hill; and the famous John Sheppard in Newgate.' The gaolers were said to have made £200 from the visitors.[9] Sheppard featured in ballads, ballad operas, plays, satires, prints and biographies, and almost twenty years later one commentator remarked, 'I don't remember any Felon in this Kingdom, whose Adventures have made so much Noise as *Sheppard*'s.'[10] Indeed, he was still 'spoken of and sung with applause' by children in the streets of London at the end of the century,[11] and William Ainsworth's popular novel, *Jack Sheppard* (1839), assured the continuation of his fame into the next century and beyond.[12]

To a large extent Sheppard's fame was a product of newspaper reporting – perhaps the first instance of newspapers building up a popular image of an individual. His first escape from Newgate was reported by the newspapers as a dextrous piece of work in which he had been aided by two women. He was quickly recaptured, but he escaped again during the night of 16 October 1724. The newspapers now put his abilities onto a different level of skill. This time the involvement of outside help was positively refuted and magical explanations advanced. According to the *Evening Post*, 'This Escape has astonish'd the World, and 'tis demonstrable, that he had not the least Assistance from any Persons whatsoever',[13] while the *Weekly Journal, or Saturday's Post* reported that the escape 'hath struck the Keepers with such Amazement, that they think he was assisted, in this last Enterprize, by the Devil himself'.[14] Other newspapers noted the 'great Astonishment' of the Newgate officers and 'the great Admiration of all People' for Sheppard's escape.[15] His recapture at night on 31 October, while drinking brandy at a chandler's shop in his old neighbourhood of Drury Lane, did not lead the newspapers to view his skills as in any way diminished. For instance, the *Daily Post* concluded its report of his recapture with Sheppard defying the gaolers to hold him 'with all their Irons, Art and Skill'.[16] All the newspapers recorded in great detail the elaborate precautions which the gaolers took to prevent another escape, but the reports are underpinned by the idea of Sheppard's omnipotence. So, although he was said to have been chained to the floor by '300 Pounds of Weight of Irons', it was noted that this alone was not sufficient and there were also 'two Persons . . . appointed to watch him Night and Day'.[17] The expectation of a third escape was kept alive by false stories of his having actually escaped again,[18] and reports that he had offered to demonstrate his escapology skills to the judges of the Court of the King's Bench.[19]

It is within this context of newspaper reporting that *The History Of the remarkable Life of John Sheppard* must be read, for a key element in the construction of the narrative is the way in which it is a response to Sheppard's popular fame. His escapes are, apparently, portrayed very much in the same way as they were in the newspapers; indeed, if anything, their supernatural element is heightened by being introduced very early on. He enters, with ease, the home of his master and mistress, Mr and Mrs Wood, in spite of being locked out, 'such was the power of his early Magick' (p. 4); after starting on a life of crime and being arrested he makes what is referred to as a 'Miraculous' escape from New Prison (p. 10); his first escape from Newgate reveals him as 'a Creature something more than Man, a *Protoeus*, Supernatural' (p. 47). His 'magic' enables him not only to escape from prisons, but also to overthrow the authority of those whom he previously served as an apprentice or employee. Those employers who oppose him or who have testified against him, such as Kneebone, live in fear when he escapes from Newgate and as a result are 'put to great Expence and Trouble to Guard themselves against this dreadful Villain' (p. 24). His power is such that 'none durst attempt him' (p. 22), so while Kneebone is cowering in his fortified house, Sheppard is out drinking brandy and eating oysters in a nearby alehouse (p. 22).

The History also describes a frenzy among the labouring poor over Sheppard's exploits. Amongst them no work is done because they are 'all engag'd in Controversies and Wagers, about *Sheppard*' (p. 27). So it is that the portrayal in *The History* of Sheppard as a supernatural being seems to subscribe to the general mood of the newspapers and, perhaps, of the people. But this image is built up only to be demolished. There is a telling episode early in the biography when Sheppard steals a suit from Barton. Barton is described as 'a Master Taylor, a Man of Worth and Reputation', in other words, the epitome of a successful member of the middling classes who had been Sheppard's employers. Sheppard has the suit altered for his own use (pp. 10–11). This act at first seems to symbolize his assumption of the role of the master, but what it actually reveals is the shallowness of his power. Putting on the suit which does not fit him hints at the lack of substance in his power.

Undoubtedly, *The History* sought to gain a market by exploiting the excitement of Sheppard's escapades, but ultimately he is portrayed as sub-human and rather pathetic. After meeting Elizabeth Lyon and leaving the 'good and careful patronage' of his master, Wood, he is no longer a human with the power to reason, but an animal reacting to brute passions. He is 'a *Dog*', 'the slippery *Ele*' and 'a *Lost Sheep*'. His inability to reason like a human being is revealed by his failure to take even the most elementary precautions against capture: after his escape from New Prison he returns to his old neighbourhood, 'like a *Dog* to *his Vomit*', and is, therefore, easily recaptured. Overall, his crimes and his escapes are portrayed as rather pointless, and the message that no one can overturn or escape from the 'natural' social order is clear. All of which was doubtless reassuring to the middling-class readers who, while presumably enjoying the excitement of the tale, ultimately identified not with Sheppard, but with the fears and vulnerability of the Woods and of Kneebone.

Other biographies of Sheppard present similar points of view. For instance, one, which was probably published in 1725, said that he was pitied by 'both *Rich* and *Poor, Noble* and *Ignoble*', and added that,

> the Boldness in his Attempts, and the Presence of Mind he always had to release himself out of Difficulties, made him pitied even by his Enemies, and those very Persons whom he had injured, could not but say, it was pity such an ingenious Fellow should be a Thief; which puffed him up with so much Ambition, that he even took a Pleasure in telling of his Rogueries, and usually sent the Company away, who came to see him in his Chains, with as much Pleasure as Admiration.[20]

In the long term, the subtleties of *The History* did not undermine the myth of Sheppard. Indeed, since the interest in him was the reason for the publication, it was in the continuation of that interest that its hope for popular success lay, and, of course, merely writing about Sheppard ensured that the biography reinforced his fame. Moreover, Sheppard's recapture and death after *The History* had been published led its astute publisher, John Applebee, to replace it with another, up-to-date, although rather inferior product, *A Narrative Of all the Robberies, Escapes, &c. of John Sheppard.*

The History is also a classic illustration of a plot structure which has been mentioned in the General Introduction to this book. A male apprentice from a poor background meets a woman who turns him from his apprenticeship and into crime. Before meeting Lyon, Sheppard was an excellent worker 'and had the Character of a very sober and orderly Boy' (p. 2). It is his 'fatal Acquaintance' with Lyon which 'laid the Foundation of his Ruin' (p. 2). The theme is that youths, like Sheppard, are vulnerable to the temptations of vice, symbolized by Lyon, and their only protection is 'the good and careful Patronage' of a master within the context of a disciplined apprenticeship. There is implicit criticism of Wood, who fails to maintain adequate control over Sheppard, but such criticism is only made significant because of the implicit view that social control could best be achieved by the middling classes. In this way even the element of criticism asserts the importance of their hegemony. This plot structure reveals a tension between shifts in capitalism and class and concern about social order. The development of *laissez-faire* capitalism was clearly opposed to, first, what were seen as the stifling effects of apprenticeship on the free market, in which the balancing of supply and demand was all-important, and, second, the desire of the middling classes to improve their status by emulating the gentry while at the same time reducing their contact with their employees. On the other hand, for some apprenticeship seemed to offer the hope of social order controlled by an employer who combined that role with those of parent and spiritual adviser.

Women, such as Elizabeth Lyon, play an important part in biographies of this type. Lyon's role in Sheppard's life is a reversal of what was regarded as the proper and natural role of women, in that it was she who dominated Sheppard, rather than the other way around. Her independence, autonomy and dominance over Sheppard are seen as unnatural and, therefore, as symbols of her corruption. Unlike Sheppard, Lyon is presented as almost totally devoid of any traces of human nature. She personifies evil, and as such mirrors the role which many took to be Eve's in the Garden of Eden, namely, that the Devil turned her to evil and then left it up to her to persuade Adam to break God's command.[21] The biography reproduces this set of relationships. Lyon takes Sheppard from honest work and leads him into crime: Lyon/women embodied the evil which tempted Sheppard/men from the 'good and careful Patronage' of the middle-class employer (Wood/God).

BIBLIOGRAPHICAL NOTES

a contemporary wrote of having seen 'six or seven different Histories of [Sheppard's] Life',[22] and the leading publisher of criminal biographies at that time, John Applebee, was at the forefront of this rush. No doubt sensing the market, he published *The History* just after Sheppard's second escape from Newgate, and then produced the first edition of *A Narrative Of all the Robberies, Escapes, &c. of John Sheppard* on the day Sheppard was hanged. A notice confirming the authenticity of *A Narrative* was published in the *Daily Journal* – a newspaper in which Applebee was involved – two days before Sheppard's death, purportedly signed by Sheppard and witnessed by Lewis Houssart, who was also in the condemned cell.[23] The *Daily Journal* and, apparently, *Parker's London News, or the Impartial Intelligencer*, reported one of Applebee's marketing coups. On the day of the hanging, when Sheppard 'arrived at the Tree, he sent for Mr. Applebee, a Printer, into the Cart, and in the View of several thousands of People, deliver'd to him' a printed copy of *A Narrative*.[24]

Scholars have argued that there was a connection between Defoe and Applebee, that it was Defoe who took delivery of the pamphlet at Tyburn, and that he wrote both *The History* and *A Narrative*, as well as essays on Sheppard for *Applebee's Original Weekly Journal*. There is no real evidence to support any of this. It seems unlikely that someone in their sixties, as Defoe was, would have relished the prospect of getting into the middle of what was certain to be a large and rather volatile crowd.[25] Furthermore, a glance at the two texts reveals quite a difference in the quality of the writing which does at least suggest that there were two writers.

A biography of Sheppard seems also to have been included in another of Applebee's publications, the Ordinary of Newgate's *Account*. However, although this was advertised as published in November 1724, it does not seem to have survived. It is likely that it was based on the work referred to in the title-page of *The History* as written by Rev. Wagstaffe, the deputy for the absent Ordinary, Thomas Purney. Presumably Wagstaffe's account was originally intended for publication in the *Account* which appeared in early September, following the original day appointed for Sheppard to be hanged. However, the *Authentic Memoirs of the Life and Surprising Adventures of John Sheppard* says that the *Account* of Sheppard was published on 17 November 1724, by Purney, and, according to *The History of the Lives and Actions of Jonathan Wild,* Purney did return from the country to visit Sheppard before he was hanged.

Moore, in his bibliography of Defoe's works,[26] includes both *The History* and *A Narrative* without providing evidence for such an ascription. He also dates *A Narrative* as the earlier of the two, which is certainly wrong: *A Narrative* was advertised in eight editions, the first being published on 16 November 1724;[27] whereas *The History* was advertised in three editions, the first appearing on 19 October 1724, the second on 24 October and the third some time before 2 November. The last advertisement for *The History* appeared on 13 November, the day before the publication of Applebee's more up-to-date biography, *A Narrative,* was announced as imminent.[28]

Apart from those already mentioned, there were several other biographies of Sheppard published in 1724–5: *A Narrative of the Life and Robberies, and further Surprising Escapes of John Sheppard. To which is prefix'd, exact Draughts of the several Locks he broke, and the Breaches he made in the Rooms through which he pass'd, when he made his Escape out of Newgate; with a particular account of his being Retaken, and an exact Draught of the Manner he is now fetter'd down in the Stone Room in Newgate,* London, T. Turner, 1724. This was advertised in the *Evening Post,* 14 November 1724, but I have been unable to trace a copy. *Authentic Memoirs of the Life and Surprising Adventures of John Sheppard; Who was Executed at Tyburn, November the 16th, 1724. By way of Familiar Letters from a Gentleman in Town, to his Friend and Correspondent in the Country,* London, J. Marshall, 1724. The text itself suggests that it was published on 17 November. J. Thurmond, *Harlequin Sheppard. A Night Scene in Grotesque Characters: As it is Perform'd at the Theatre-Royal in Drury Lane,* London, J. Roberts and A. Dodd, 1724, Introduction, pp. 5–12. *The History of the Lives and Actions of Jonathan Wild, Thief-Taker. Joseph Blake alias Bleuskin, Foot-Pad. And John Sheppard, Housebreaker,* London, Edw. Midwinter, [1725?]. J. Villette, *The Annals of Newgate, or the Malefactor's Register,* 4 volumes, London, 1776, vol. I, pp. 253–72, prints a biography, the source of which is unclear, although perhaps Villette's post as Ordinary of Newgate gave him access to the lost Ordinary of Newgate's *Account* of Sheppard.

For modern biographies see H. Bleackley and S.M. Ellis, *The Trial of Jack Sheppard,* Edinburgh, 1933. C. Hibbert, *Road to Tyburn,* London, 1969. G. Howson, *Thief-taker General: The Rise and Fall of Jonathan Wild,* London, 1970, *passim.*

NOTES

1 *Daily Post,* 4 September 1724; *Daily Journal,* 4 September 1724; *Evening Post,* 10 September 1724; *Daily Courant,* 4 September 1724, 20 October 1724.
2 *Parker's London News,* 11 November 1724.
3 *London Journal,* 7 November 1724; *British Journal,* 7 November 1724; *Weekly Journal or British Gazetteer,* 7 November 1724.
4 Although see *The Original London Post,* 27 February 1724.
5 *London Journal,* 22 August 1724.
6 *Daily Post,* 15 June 1724. They failed and were hanged the next day: *Daily Post,* 16 June 1724. For Fox's escape see GLRO, MJ/SBB/823/1724 July, p. 68.
7 *Daily Journal,* 14 October 1724.
8 *British Journal,* 14 November 1724. Twelve years later Daniel Maden escaped twice from the condemned hold in Newgate, only to be recaptured and eventually hanged, but, although he attracted a certain amount of attention, it

was nothing like that accorded to Sheppard: *London Evening Post*, 25 May 1736, 29 May 1736, 15 June 1736, 18 September 1736, 25 September 1736, 28 September 1736, 7 October 1736, 16 October 1736, 30 October 1736, 2 November 1736.

9 *Daily Journal*, 4 November 1724, 18 November 1724; *London Journal*, 7 November 1724, 14 November 1724; *Parker's London News*, 4 November 1724; *Weekly Journal or British Gazetteer*, 7 November 1724; *British Journal*, 7 November 1724, 14 November 1724. There had been two ostriches which, unlike Sheppard, were, at 27 hands, very tall, but, like him, at least metaphorically, 'They will eat Iron, of which they are very fond': *Daily Journal*, 21 September 1724.

10 *Select Trials, at the Sessions-House in the Old-Bailey, for Murder, Robberies, Rapes, Sodomy, Coining, Frauds, Bigamy, and other Offences. To which are added Genuine Accounts of the Lives, Behaviour, Confessions and Dying Speeches of the most eminent Convicts*, 4 volumes, London, 1742, vol. I, p. 146. Among the major theatrical pieces based on Sheppard's life were *The Prison Breaker, or the Adventures of John Sheppard*, London, 1725, which was performed at the Theatre Royal in Lincoln's Inn Fields; this was later rewritten, with songs added, by Thomas Walker as *The Quaker's Opera* and performed at St Bartholomew's Fair with Walker in the role of Sheppard. Also J. Thurmond, *Harlequin Sheppard. A Night Scene in Grotesque Characters as it is Performed at the Theatre Royal in Drury Lane*, London, 1724 (see *Select Trials*, vol. I, p. 147). Satirical pieces included *An Epistle from Jack Sheppard to the Late L − − D C − − − − −LL − R of E − − − − −D* [London, 1725?], a satire on Lord Macclesfield. Two prints showing Sheppard's confinement and his escape on 15 October were published by Thomas Bowles and John Bowles in late October: *Daily Journal*, 26 October 1724; *Daily Post*, 28 October 1724. These were probably the prints bought by George II (*Daily Journal*, 3 November 1724), although other prints were published (*Daily Post*, 4 November 1724). Bowles and Bowles themselves produced another print after Sheppard's recapture: *Daily Journal*, 6 November 1724.

11 Francis Place Manuscripts, British Library, Add. Mss 27,827.

12 W.H. Ainsworth, *Jack Sheppard: A Romance*, 3 volumes, London, 1839.

13 *Evening Post*, 17 October 1724.

14 *Weekly Journal, or Saturday's Post*, 17 October 1724.

15 *British Journal*, 17 October 1724; *Weekly Journal, or British Gazetteer*, 17 October 1724. Also *London Journal*, 24 October 1724.

16 *Daily Post*, 2 November 1724. Also *London Journal*, 7 November 1724.

17 *Daily Journal*, 2 November 1724, 3 November 1724; *Daily Post*, 14 November 1724.

18 *Daily Post*, 14 November 1724; *Evening Post*, 14 November 1724; *Parker's London News*, 16 November 1724.

19 *Daily Journal*, 11 November 1724.

20 *The History of the Lives and Actions of Jonathan Wild, Thief-Taker. Joseph Blake alias Bleuskin, Foot-Pad. And John Sheppard, Housebreaker*, London, [1725?], preface.

21 [D. Defoe], *The History of the Devil*, London, 1726, pp. 489–90.

22 *Select Trials*, vol. I, p. 146. See H. Bleackley and S.M. Ellis, *The Trial of Jack Sheppard*, London, 1933, pp. 127–30.

23 *Daily Journal*, 14 November 1724.

24 *Daily Journal*, 17 November 1724. The report in *Parker's London News*, 18 November 1724, is ambiguous: it says that Sheppard 'left a printed Pamphlet with Mr. *App bee*, (as he himself tells us in his Daily-Journal) and desired (Right Irish dear joy) that it might be forthwith printed and published, tho' it was

already done to hand': *Parker's London News*, 20 November 1724. Elsewhere Applebee was enigmatically referred to as Sheppard's 'sole Executor': *Authentic Memoirs of the Life and Surprising Adventures of John Sheppard: Who was Executed at Tyburn, November the 16th, 1724. By way of Familiar Letters from a Gentleman in Town, to his Friend and Correspondent in the Country*, London, 1724.

25 A huge crowd had gathered a few days earlier for the King's Bench hearing at which Sheppard's death sentence was confirmed, and a number were injured in the crush: *Daily Journal*, 11 November 1724. As it turned out there was a riot at Tyburn after Sheppard's death (see p. 74, note 65), and according to the *London Journal*, 21 November 1724, 'Never was there a greater Crowd assembled on any Occasion'.

26 J.R. Moore, *A Checklist of the Writings of Daniel Defoe*, Hamden, Connecticut, 2nd edn, 1971, items 466 and 468, pp. 193–5.

27 *Daily Journal*, 14 November 1724, 16 November 1724, 17 November 1724, 19 November 1724, 20 November 1724, 23 November 1724, 2 December 1724.

28 *Daily Journal*, 17 October 1724, 26 October 1724, 2 November 1724, 13 November 1724.

2

THE
HISTORY
Of the remarkable LIFE of
JOHN SHEPPARD,
containing
A particular Account of his many
ROBBERIES and ESCAPES,
Viz.

His robbing the Shop of Mr. *Bains* in White-Horse-Yard of 24 Yards of Fustian. Of his breaking and entering the House of the said Mr. *Bains*, and stealing in Goods and Money to the Value of 20 l. Of his robbing the House of Mr. *Charles* in *May Fair* of Money, Rings, Plate, &c. to the Value of 30 l. Of his robbing the House of Mrs. *Cook* in *Clare-Market*, along with his pretended Wife, and his Brother, to the Value of between 50 and 60 l. Of his breaking the Shop of Mr. *Philips* in *Drury-Lane*, with the same Persons, and stealing Goods of small Value. Of his entering the House of Mr. *Carter*, a Mathematical Instrument Maker in *Wytch street*, along with *Anthony Lamb* and *Charles Grace*, and robbing of Mr. *Barton*, a Master Taylor who lodged therein, of Goods and Bonds to the Value of near 300 l. Of his breaking and entering the House of Mr. *Kneebone*, a Woollen-Draper, near the *New Church* in the *Strand*, in Company of *Joseph Blake* alias *Blewskin* and *William Field*, and stealing Goods to the Value of near 50 l. Of his robbing of Mr. *Pargiter* on the Highway near the Turnpike, on the Road to *Hampstead*, along with the said *Blewskin*, Of his robbing a Lady's Woman in her Mistress's Coach on the same Road. Of his robbing also a Stage Coach, with the said *Blewskin*, on the *Hampstead* Road. Likewise of his breaking the Shop of Mr. *Martin* in *Fleet-street*, and stealing 3 silver Watches of 15 l. Value. ALSO

A particular Account of his rescuing his pretended Wife from St. *Giles*'s Round-House. Of the wonderful Escape himself made from the said Round-House. Of the miraculous Escape he and his said pretended Wife made together from *New-Prison*, on the 25th of *May* last. Of his surprizing Escape from the Condemn'd Hold of *Newgate* on the 31st of *August*: Together with the true manner of his being retaken; and of his Behaviour in *Newgate*, till the most astonishing and never to be forgotten Escape he made from thence, in the Night of the 15th of October. The Whole taken from the most authentick Accounts, as the Informations of divers Justices of the Peace, the several Shop-keepers above-mention'd, the principal Officers of *Newgate* and *New-Prison* and from the Confession of *Sheppard* made to the Rev. Mr. *Wagstaff*, who officiated for the Ordinary of *Newgate*.

LONDON: Printed and Sold by JOHN APPLEBEE in *Black-Fryers*, J. ISTED, at the *Golden-Ball* near *Chancery-Lane* in *Fleet street*, and the Booksellers of *London* and *Westminster*. (Price One Shilling.)

TO THE
CITIZENS
OF
London and *Westminster.*

GENTLEMEN,

EXperience has confirm'd you in that everlasting Maxim, *that there is no other way to protect the* Innocent, *but by Punishing the* Guilty.

Crimes ever were, and ever must be unavoidably frequent in such populous Cities as yours are, being the necessary Consequences, either of the Wants, *or the Depravity, of the lowest part of the* humane Species.

At this time the most flagrant Offences, as Burning *of* Dwellings; Burglaries, *and* Highway Robberies *abound; and* Frauds *common* Felonies, *and* Forgeries *are practic'd without Number; thus not only your Properties, but even your very Lives are every way struck at.*

The Legislative Power *has not been wanting in providing necessary and wholesome Laws against these* Evils, *the executive part whereof (according to your great Privileges) is lodged in your own Hands: And the Administration hath at all times applyed proper Remedies and Regulations to the Defects which have happen'd in the* Magistracy *more immediately under their Jurisdiction.*

Through the just and salutary Severities of the Magistrates, *publick excessive* Gaming *has been in a manner* Surpress'd, *and some late Examples of divine Vengeance have overtaken certain of the most notorious lewd* Prostitutes *of the* Town, *which together with the laudable endeavours of the great and worthy* SOCIETIES,[1] *has given no small check to that enormous and spreading* Vice.

But here's a Criminal *bids Defiance to your* Laws, *and* Justice *who declar'd and has manifested that the* Bars *are not made that can either keep him* OUT, *or keep him* IN, *and accordingly hath a second time fled from the very* BOSOM OF DEATH.

His History *will astonish! and is not compos'd of Fiction, Fable, or Stories plac'd at* York, Rome, *or* Jamaica, *but* Facts *done at your* Doors, *Facts unheard of, altogether new, Incredible, and yet Uncontestable.*

He is gone once more upon his wicked Range in the World. Restless Vengeance is pursuing, and Gentlemen *'tis to be hop'd that she will be assisted by your Endeavours to bring to Justice this notorious Offender.*

THE
LIFE
OF
JOHN SHEPPARD, &c.

THIS *John Sheppard,* a Youth both in Age and Person, tho' an old Man in Sin; was Born in the Parish of *Stepney* near *London,* in the Year 1702,[2] a

Son, Grandson, and great Grandson of a *Carpenter*: His Father died when he was so very Young that he could not recollect that ever he saw him. Thus the burthen of his Maintenance, together with his Brother's and Sister's,[3] lay upon the Shoulders of the Widow Mother, who soon procured an Admittance of her Son *John* into the *Work-House* in *Bishopsgate-street*, where he continued for the space of a Year and half, [p. 2] and in that time received an Education sufficent to qualifie him for the Trade his Mother design'd him, *viz.* a *Carpenter:* Accordingly he was recommended to Mr. *Wood* in *Witch-street* near *Drury-Lane*,[4] as a Master capable of entertaining and instructing her Son: They agreed and Bound he was for the space of seven Years; the Lad proved an early profficient, had a ready and ingenious Hand, and soon became Master of his Business, and gave entire Satisfaction to his Masters Customers, and had the Character of a very sober and orderly Boy. But alas unhappy Youth! before he had compleated six Years of his Apprenticeship, he commenced a fatal Acquaintance with one *Elizabeth Lyon*,[5] otherwise call'd, *Edgworth Bess*, from a Town of that Name in *Middlesex* where she was Born, the reputed Wife of a Foot Soldier, and who lived a wicked and debauch'd Life; and our young *Carpenter* became Enamour'd of her, and they must Cohabit together as Man and Wife.

Now was laid the Foundation of his Ruin; *Sheppard* grows weary of the Yoke of Servitude, and began to dispute with his Master; telling him that his way of Jobbing from House to House, was not sufficient to furnish him with a due Experience in his Trade; and that if he would not seek out to undertake some Buildings, [p. 3] he would step into the World for better Information. Mr. *Wood* a mild, sober, honest Man, indulg'd him; and Mrs. *Wood* with Tears, exhorted him against the Company of this lewd Prostitute: But her Man prompted and harden'd by his HARLOT, D – – – n'd *her Blood*, and threw a Stick at his Mistress, and beat her to the Ground. And being with his Master at Work at Mr. *Britt*'s the *Sun* Ale-house near *Islington*, upon a very trivial Occasion fell upon his Master, and beat and bruised him in a most barbarous and shameful Manner.[6] Such a sudden and deplorable Change was there in the Behaviour of this promising young Man. Next ensued a neglect of Duty, both to God and his Master, lying out of Nights, perpetual Jarrings, and Animosities; these and such like, were the Consequences of his intimacy with this she *Lyon*; who by the sequel will appear to have been a main loadstone in attracting of him up to the fatal Tree.[7]

Mr. *Wood* having Reason to suspect, that *Sheppard* had robb'd a Neighbour, began to be in great Fear and Terror for himself. And when his Man came not Home in due season at Nights bar'd him out; but he made a mere jest of the Locks and Bolts, and enter'd in, and out at Pleasure; and when Mr. *Wood* and his Wife have had all the Reason in the World to believe him Lock't [p. 4] out, they have found him very quiet in his Bed the next Morning, such was the power of his early Magick.

Edgworth Bess having stol'n a Gold Ring from a Gentleman, whom she had pick'd up in the Streets, was sent to St. *Giles*'s Roundhouse; *Sheppard* went immediately to his Consort, and after a short Discourse with Mr. *Brown* the Beadle, and his Wife, who had the Care of the Place, he fell upon the poor old Couple, took the Keys from them, and let his Lady out at the Door in spight of all the Out-cryes, and Opposition they were capable of making.

About *July* 1723,[8] He was by his Master sent to perform a Repair, at the House of Mr. *Bains*, a Peice-Broker in *White-Horse Yard*; he from thence stole a Roll of Fustian, containing 24 Yards, which was afterwards found in his Trunk. This is supposed to be the first Robbery he ever committed, and it was not long e're he Repeated another upon this same Mr. *Bains*, by breaking into his House in the Night-time, and taking out of the *Till* seven Pounds in Money, and Goods to the value of fourteen Pounds more. How he enter'd this House, was a Secret till his being last committed to *Newgate*, when he confess'd that he took up the Iron Bars at the Cellar Window, and after he had done his Business, he nailed them down again, so that [p. 5] Mr. *Bains* never believed his House had been broke; and an innocent Woman a Lodger in the House lay all the while under the weight of a suspicion of committing the Robbery.

Sheppard and his Master had now parted, ten Months before the expiration of his Apprenticeship, a woeful parting to the former; he was gone from a good and careful Patronage, and lay expos'd to, and comply'd with the Temptations of the most wicked Wretches this Town could afford as *Joseph Blake*, alias *Blewskins, William Field, Doleing, James Sykes*, alias *Hell* and *Fury*,[9] which last was the first that betray'd, and put him into the Hands of Justice, as will presently appear.

Having deserted his Masters Service, he took Shelter in the House of Mr. *Charles* in *May-Fair*, near *Piccadilly*, and his Landlord having a Necessity for some Repairs in his House, engag'd one Mr. *Panton* a *Carpenter* to Undertake them, and *Sheppard* to assist him as a Journeyman; but on the 23d of *October*, 1723, e're the Work was compleat, *Sheppard* took Occasion to rob the People of the Effects following, *viz.* seven Pound ten Shillings in Specie, five large silver Spoons, six plain Forks ditto, four Tea-Spoons, six plain Gold Rings, and a Cypher Ring; four Suits of Wearing Apparel, besides Linnen, to a considerable [p. 6] value. This Fact he confess'd to the Reverend Mr. *Wagstaff* before his Escape from the Condemn'd Hold of *Newgate*.

Sheppard had a Brother, nam'd *Thomas*, a *Carpenter* by Profession, tho' a notorious *Thief* and *House-breaker* by Practice. This *Thomas* being committed to *Newgate* for breaking the House of Mrs. *Mary Cook* a *Linnen-Draper*, in *Clare-street, Clare-Market*, on the 5th of *February* last, and stealing Goods to the value of between 50, and 60 *l*. he impeach'd his Brother *John Sheppard*, and *Edgworth Bess* as being concerned with him in the Fact; and these three were also Charg'd with being concern'd together, in breaking the House of Mr. *William Phillips* in *Drury-Lane*, and stealing divers Goods, the Property of Mrs. *Kendrick* a Lodger in the House, on the 14th of the said *February*:[10] All possible endeavours were us'd by Mrs. *Cook*, and Mr. *Phillips*, to get *John Sheppard* and *Edgworth Bess* Apprehended, but to no purpose, till the following Accident.

Sheppard was now upon his wicked Range in *London*, committing Robberies every where at Discretion; but one Day meeting with his

Acquaintance, *James Sykes*, alias *Hell* and *Fury*, sometimes a Chair-man, and at others a Running Foot-man. This *Sykes* invited him to go to one *Redgate*'s, a Victualling-house near the *Seven Dials*, to [p. 7] play at *Skettles*, *Sheppard* comply'd, and *Sykes* secretly sent for Mr. *Price* a Constable in St. *Giles*'s *Parish*, and Charg'd him with his Friend *Sheppard* for the Robbing of Mrs. *Cook*, &c. *Sheppard* was carried before Justice *Parry*, who order'd him to St. *Giles*'s Round-house till the next Morning for farther Examination: He was Confin'd in the Upper part of the Place, being two Stories from the Ground, but e're two Hours came about, by only the help of a Razor, and the Stretcher of a Chair, he broke open the Top of the Round house, and tying together a Sheet and Blanket, by them descended into the Church-yard and Escap'd, leaving the Parish to Repair the Damage, and Repent of the Affront put upon his Skill and Capacity.

On the 19th of *May* last in the Evening, *Sheppard* with another Robber named *Benson*, were passing thro' *Leicester-fields*, where a Gentleman stood accusing a Woman with an attempt to steal his Watch, a Mobb was gathered about the Disputants, and *Sheppard*'s Companion being a *Master*, got in amongst them and pick'd the Gentleman's Pockets in good earnest of the Watch; the Scene was surprisingly chang'd, from an imaginary Robbery to a real one; and in a moment ensued an Out-cry of *stop Thief*, *Sheppard* and *Benson* took to their Heels, and *Sheppard* was seiz'd by a Serjeant of [p. 8] the Guard at *Leicester* House, crying out *stop Thief* with much earnestness. He was convey'd to St. *Ann's Round House* in *Soho*, and kept secure till the next Morning, when *Edgworth Bess* came to visit him, who was seiz'd also; they were carried before Justice *Walters*, when the People in *Drury-Lane* and *Clare-Market* appeared, and charged them with the Robberies aforemention'd: But *Sheppard* pretending to Impeach certain of his Accomplices, the Justice committed them to *New-Prison*, with intent to have them soon removed to *Newgate*, unless there came from them some useful Discoveries.[11] *Sheppard* was now a second time in the hands of Justice, but how long he intended to keep in them, the Reader will soon be able to Judge.

He and his MATE were now in a strong and well guarded Prison, himself loaded with a pair of double *Links* and *Basils*[12] of about fourteen pounds weight, and confined together in the safest Appartment call'd *Newgate Ward*; *Sheppard* conscious of his Crimes, and knowing the *Information* he had made to be but a blind Amusement that would avail him nothing; he began to Meditate an Escape. They had been thus detained for about four Days, and their Friends having the Liberty of seeing them, furnish'd him with Implements proper for his Design, accordingly Mr. *Sheppard* goes to work, and [p. 9] on the 25th of *May* being *Whitson Monday* at about two of the Clock in the Morning, he had compleated a practicable breach, and sawed of his Fetters; having with unheard of Diligence and Dexterity, cut off an Iron Bar from the Window, and taken out a Muntin, or Bar of the most solid Oak of about nine Inches in thickness, by boring it thro' in many Places, a work of great Skill and Labour; they had still five and twenty Foot to descend from the Ground; *Sheppard* fasten'd a Sheet and Blanket to the Bars, and causes Madam to take off her Gown and Petticoat, and sent her out first, and she being more Corpulent than himself, it was with great Pain

51

and Difficulty that he got her through the Interval, and observing his Directions, was instantly down, and more frighted than hurt; the *Phylosopher* follow'd, and lighted with Ease and Pleasure; But where are they Escap'd to? Why out of one Prison into another. The Reader is to understand, that the *New Prison* and *Clerkenwell Bridewell* lye Contiguous to one another, and they are got into the Yard of the latter, and have a Wall of twenty-two Foot high to Scale, before their Liberty is perfected; *Sheppard* far from being unprepared to surmount this Difficulty, has his Gimblets and Peircers ready, and makes a Scaleing-Ladder. The Keepers and Prisoners of both [p. 10] Places are a sleep in their Beds; he Mounts his *Bagage*, and in less than ten Minutes carries both her and himself over this Wall, and compleats an entire Escape. Altho' his Escape from the Condemn'd Hold of *Newgate*, has made a far greater Noise in the World, than that from this Prison hath. It has been allow'd by all the Jayl-Keepers in *London*, that one so Miraculous was never perform'd before in *England*; the broken Chains and Bars are kept at *New Prison* to Testifie, and preserve the Memory of this extraordinary Villain.[13]

Sheppard not warn'd by this Admonition, returns like a *Dog to his Vomit*, and comes Secretly into his Master *Wood*'s Neighbourhood in *Witch-street*, and concerts Measures with one *Anthony Lamb*, an Apprentice to Mr. *Carter* a Mathematical Instrument-maker, for Robbing of Mr. *Barton* a Master Taylor; a Man of Worth and Reputation, who Lodg'd in Mr. *Carter's* House. *Charles Grace*, a graceless Cooper was let into the Secret, and consented, and resolved to Act his Part.[14] The 16th of *June* last was appointed, *Lamb* accordingly lets *Grace* and *Sheppard* into the House at Mid-Night; and they all go up to Mr. *Barton*'s Appartment well arm'd with Pistols, and enter'd his Rooms, without being disturb'd. *Grace* was Posted at Mr. *Barton*'s Bedside with a loaded Pistol, and positive Orders to shoot him [p. 11] through the Head, if in case he awak'd. *Sheppard* being engag'd in opening the Trunks and Boxes, the mean while. It luckily happen'd for Mr. *Barton*, that he slept Sounder than usual that Night, as having come from a Merry-making with some Friends; tho' poor Man little Dreaming in what dreadful Circumstances. They carried off in Notes, and Bonds, Guineas, Cloaths, Made and Unmade, to the value of between two and three Hundred Pounds; besides a Padesuoy[15] Suit of Cloaths, worth about eighteen or twenty Pounds more; which having been made for a Corpulent Gentleman, *Sheppard* had them reduc'd, and fitted for his own Size and Wear, as designing to Appear and make a Figure among the *Beau Monde*. *Grace* and *Sheppard*, having disposed of the Goods at an Ale-house in *Lewkenors Lane* (a Rendezvous of Robbers and Ruffians) took their Flight, and *Grace* has not been since heard of. *Lamb* was apprehended, and carried before Justice *Newton*, and made an ample Confession; and there being nothing but that against him at his Tryal, and withal, a favourable Prosecution, he came off with a Sentence of Transportation only. He as well as *Sheppard* has since confirm'd all the above particulars, and with this Addition, *viz*. That it was Debated among them to have Murder'd all the People in the House, save one Person.

[p. 12] About the latter End of the same Month, *June*, Mr. *Kneebone*, a Woollen-Draper near the New Church in the *Strand*, receiv'd a Caution from the Father of *Anthony Lamb*, who intimated to Mr. *Kneebone* that his House was intended to be broke open and robb'd that very Night. Mr. *Kneebone* prepar'd for the Event, ordering his Servants to sit up, and gave Directions to the Watchman in the Street to observe his House: At about two in the Morning *Sheppard* and his Gang were about the Door, a Maid-Servant went to listen, and heard one of the Wretches, say, *Da – – n him, if they could not enter that Night, they would another, and would have* 300 *l. of his,* (meaning) Mr. *Kneebone's* Money. They went off, and nothing more was heard of them till *Sunday* the 12th Day of *July* following, when *Joseph Blake,* alias *Blewskins, John Sheppard,* and *William Field* (as himself Swears) came about 12 o'Clock at Night, and cut two large Oaken-Bars over the Cellar-Window, at the back part of the House in *Little-Drury-Lane,* and so entered; Mr. *Kneebone,* and his Family being at Rest, they proceeded to open a Door at the Foot of the Cellar-Stairs, with three Bolts, and a large Padlock upon it, and then came up into the Shop and wrench'd off the Hasp, and Padlock that went over the Press, and arriv'd at their desir'd Booty; [p. 13] they continu'd in the House for three Hours, and carry'd off with them One Hundred and eight Yards of Broad Woollen Cloth, five Yards of blue Bays, a light Tye-Wig, and Beaver-Hat, two Silver Spoons, an Handkerchief, and a Penknife. In all to the value of near fifty Pounds.[16]

The *Sunday* following, being the 19th of *July, Sheppard* and *Blewskins* were out upon the *Hampstead* Road, and there stopt a Coach with a Ladies Woman in it, from whom they took but Half-a-Crown; all the Money then about her; the Footman behind the Coach came down, and exerted himself; but *Sheppard* sent him in hast up to his Post again, by threat of his Pistol.

The next Night being the 20th of *July,* about Nine, they Robb'd Mr. *Pargiter,* a Chandler of *Hamstead,* near the Halfway-House; *Sheppard* after his being taken at *Finchley* was particularly examin'd about this Robbery. The Reverend Mr. *Wagstaff* having receiv'd a Letter from an unknown Hand with two Questions, to be propos'd to *Sheppard, viz.* Whether he did Rob *John Pargiter,* on *Monday* the 20th of *July,* about Nine at Night, between the *Turnpike* and *Hamstead;* How much Money he took from him? Whither *Pargiter* was Drunk, or not, and if he had Rings or Watch about him, when robb'd? which, Request was comply'd with, and *Sheppard* [p. 14] affirm'd, that Mr. *Pargiter* was very much in Liquor, having a great Coat on; neither Rings on his Fingers or Watch, and only three Shillings in his Pocket, which they took from him, and that *Blewskins* knock him down twice with the Butt-end of his Pistol to make sure Work, (tho' Excess of drink had done that before) but *Sheppard* did in kindness raise him up as often.[17]

The next Night, *July* 21, they stopt a Stage-Coach, and took from a Passenger in it, Twenty-two Shillings, and were so expeditious in the Matter, that *not two Words were made about the Bargain.*

Now Mr. *Sheppard's* long and wicked Course seemingly draws towards a Period. Mr. *Kneebone* having apply'd to *Jonathan Wild,* and set forth Advertisements in the Papers, complaining of his Robbery. On *Tuesday* the 22d of *July* at Night *Edgworth Bess* was taken in a Brandy-shop, near *Temple-Bar* by *Jonathan Wild;* she being much terrify'd, discover'd where

Sheppard was: A Warrant was accordingly issued by Justice *Blackerby*, and the next Day he was Apprehended, at the House of *Blewskin's* Mother, in *Rose-Mary-Lane*, by one *Quilt*, a Domestick of Mr. *Wild's* though not without great opposition, for he clapt a loaded Pistol to *Quilt's* Breast, and attempted to shoot him, but the Pistol miss'd fire; he was brought back to *New Prison*, confin'd in the [p. 15] Dungeon;[18] and the next Day carried before Justice *Blackerby*. Upon his Examination he Confess'd the three Robberies on the Highway aforemention'd, as also the Robbing of Mr. *Bains*, Mr. *Barton*, and Mr. *Kneebone*, he was committed to *Newgate*, and at the Sessions of *Oyer* and *Terminer*, and Goal delivery, holden at the *Old-Baily*, on the 12th, 13th and 14th of *August*, he was try'd upon three several Indictments,[19] *viz.* First for breaking the House of *William Philips*.

John Sheppard, of the Parish of St. *Martin* in *the Fields*, was indicted for breaking the House of *William Philips*, and stealing divers Goods, the 14th of *February* last. But there not being sufficient Evidence against the Prisoner, he was acquitted.

He was also indicted a Second Time, of St. *Clement Danes*, for breaking the House of *Mary Cook*, the 5th of *February* last, and stealing divers Goods: But the Evidence against the Prisoner being defficient as to this Indictment also, he was acquitted.

He was also indicted the Third Time, of St. *Mary Savoy*, for breaking the House of *William Kneebone*, in the Night-Time, and stealing 108 Yards of Woollen Cloth, the 12th of *July* last. The Prosecutor depos'd, That the Prisoner had some Time since been his Servant, and when he went to Bed, the Time mention'd in the In[p. 16]dictment, about 11 a-Clock at Night, he saw all the Doors and Windows fast; but was call'd up about four in the Morning, and found his House broke open, the Bars of a Cellar-Window having been cut, and the Bolts of the Door that comes up Stairs drawn, and the Padlock wrench'd off, and the Shutter in the Shop broken, and his Goods gone; whereupon suspecting the Prisoner, he having committed ill Actions thereabouts before, he acquainted *Jonathan Wild* with it, and he procur'd him to be apprehended. That he went to the Prisoner in *New Prison*, and asking how he could be so ungrateful to rob him, after he had shown him so much Kindness? The Prisoner own'd he had been ungrateful in doing so, informing him of several Circumstances as to the Manner of committing the Fact, but said he had been drawn into it by ill Company. *Jonathan Wild*, depos'd, The Prosecutor came to him, and desir'd him to enquire after his Goods that had been stolen, telling him he suspected the Prisoner to have been concern'd in the Robbery, he having before committed some Robberies in the Neighbourhood. That inquiring after him, and having heard of him before, he was inform'd that he was an Acquaintance of *Joseph Blake*, alias *Blewskins*, and *William Field*: Whereupon he sent for *William Field*, who came to him; upon [p. 17] which he told him, if he would make an ingenuous Confession, he believ'd he could prevail with the Court to make him an Evidence. That he did make a Discovery of the Prisoner, upon which he was apprehended, and also of others since convicted, and gave an Account of some Parcels of the Cloth, which were found accordingly. *William Field* depos'd, That the Prisoner told him, and

Joseph Blake, that he knew a *Ken*[20] where they might get something of Worth. That they went to take a View of the Prosecutor's House, but disprov'd of the Attempt, as not thinking it easy to be perform'd: But the Prisoner perswaded them that it might easily be done, he knowing the House, he having liv'd with the Prosecutor. That thereupon he cut the Cellar Bar, went into the Cellar, got into the Shop, and brought out three Parcels of Cloth, which they carried away. The Prisoner had also confest the Fact when he was apprehended, and before the Justice. The Fact being plainly prov'd, the Jury found him guilty of the Indictment.

Sentence of Death was pronounc'd upon him accordingly. Several other Prosecutions might have been brought against him, but this was thought sufficient to rid the World of so Capital an Offender: He beg'd earnestly for Transportation, to the [p. 18] most extream Foot of his Majesty's Dominions; and pleaded Youth, and Ignorance as the Motive which had precipitated him into the Guilt; but the Court deaf to his Importunities, as knowing him, and his repeated Crimes to be equally flagrant, gave him no satisfactory Answer: He return'd to his dismal Abode the Condemn'd Hold, where were Nine more unhappy Wretches in as dreadful Circumstances as himself. The Court being at *Windsor*, the Malefactors had a longer Respite than is usual; during that Recess, *James Harman, Lumley, Davis*[21] and *Sheppard* agreed upon an Escape, concerted Measures, and provided Instruments to make it effectual; but put off the Execution of their Design, on Account the two Gentlemen having their hopes of Life daily renewed by the favourable Answers they receiv'd from some considerable Persons; but those vanishing the day before their Execution, and finding their Sentence irreversible, they two dropt their hopes, together with the Design, they form'd for an Escape, and so in earnest prepar'd to meet Death on the Morrow, (which they accordingly did.) 'Twas on this Day Mr. *Davis* gave *Sheppard* the Watch Springs, Files, Saws, &c. to Effect his own Release; and knowing that a Warrant was Hourly expected for his Execution with Two others, on the *Friday* following; he [p. 19] thought it high time to look about him, for he had waited his Tryal, saw his Conviction, and heard his Sentence with some patience; but finding himself irrespitably decreed for Death, he could sit passive no longer, and on the very Day of the Execution of the former; whilst they were having their Fetters taken off, in order for going to the Tree,[22] that Day he began to saw, *Saturday* made a progress; but *Sunday* omitted, by Reason of the Concourse in the *Lodge*: *Edgworth Bess* having been set at Liberty, had frequent Access to him, with others of his Acquaintance. On *Monday* the Death *Warrant* came from *Windsor*, appointing that he, together with *Joseph Ward*, and *Anthony Upton* should be Executed on the *Friday* following, being the 4th of *September*.[23] The Keepers acquainted him therewith, and desir'd him to make good use of that short Time. He thank'd them, said *he would follow their Advice*, and *prepare*. *Edgworth Bess*, and another Woman had been with him at the Door of the Condemn'd Hold best part of the Afternoon, between five and six he desir'd the other Prisoners, except *Stephen Fowles*[24] to remain above, while he offer'd something in private to his Friends at the Door; they comply'd, and in this interval he got the Spike asunder, which made way for the Skeleton to pass with his Heels foremost, by the Assistance of *Fowles*, whom [p. 20] he most ungenerously betray'd to the Keepers after his being retaken, and the Fellow was as severely punish'd for it.

Having now got clear of his Prison, he took Coach disguis'd in a Night Gown at the corner of the *Old Baily*, along with a Man who waited for him in the Street (and is suppos'd to be *Page* the Butcher) ordering the Coachman to drive to *Black-Fryers Stairs*, where his prostitute gave him the Meeting, and they three took Boat, and went a Shoar at the *Horse-Ferry* at *Westminster*, and at the *White-Hart* they went in, Drank, and stay'd sometime; thence they adjourn'd to a Place in *Holbourn*, where by the help of a Saw he quitted the Chains he had brought with him from *Newgate*; and then like a Freeman took his Ramble through the City and came to *Spittle-Fields*,[25] and there lay with *Edgeworth Bess*.

It may be easy to imagine what an alarm his Escape gave to the Keepers of *Newgate*, three of their People being at the farther End of the *Lodge*, engag'd in a Discourse concerning his wonderful Escape from *New-Prison*, and what Caution ought to be us'd, lest he should give them the slip, at that very Instant as he perfected it.[26]

On *Tuesday* he sent for *William Page* an Apprentice to a Butcher in *Clare-Market*, who came to him, and being Pennyless, he desir'd *Page* to give him what Assistance he [p. 21] could to make his way, and being a Neighbour and Acquaintance, he comply'd with it; but e'er he would do any thing, he consulted a near Relation, who as he said, encourag'ed him in it; nay, put him upon it, so meeting with this Success in his Applicaton to his Friend, and probable an Assistance in the Pocket, he came to *Sheppard* having bought him a new blue *Butcher*'s Frock, and another for himself, and so both took their Rout to *Warnden* in *Northamptonshire*, where they came to a Relation of *Page*'s, who receiv'd and Entertain'd them kindly, the People lying from their own Bed to Accommodate them. *Sheppard* pretending to be a *Butcher*'s Son in *Clare-Market*, who was going farther in the Country to his Friends, and that *Page* was so kind as to Accompany him; but they as well as their Friend became tir'd of one another; the *Butchers* having but one Shilling left, and the People poor, and Consequently unable to Subsist two such Fellows, after a stay of three or four Days, they return'd, and came for *London*, and reach'd the City on *Tuesday* the 8th of *September*, calling by the way at *Black-Mary's-Hole*, and Drinking with several of their Acquaintance, and then came into *Bishopsgate street*, to one *Cooley's* a *Brandyshop*; where a *Cobler* being at Work in his Stall, stept out and Swore *there was* Sheppard, *Sheppard* hearing him, departed immediately. In [p. 22] the Evening they came into *Fleet-street*, at about Eight of the Clock, and observing Mr. *Martin's* a Watchmaker's Shop to be open, and a little Boy only to look after it: *Page* goes in and asks the Lad whether Mr. *Taylor* a *Watchmaker* lodg'd in the House? being answer'd in the Negative, he came away, and Reports the Disposition of the Place: *Sheppard* now makes Tryal of his old Master-peice; fixeth a Nail Peircer into the Door post, fastens the Knocker thereto with Packthread, breaks the Glass, and takes out three *Silver Watches* of 15 l. value, the Boy seeing him take them, but could not get out to pursue him, by reason of his Contrivance. One of the Watches he Pledg'd for a Guinea and Half.[27] The same Night they came into *Witch-street*, *Sheppard* going into his *Masters* Yard, and calling for his Fellow 'Prentice, his Mistress heard, knew his Voice, and was dreadfully frightened; he next went to the *Cock* and *Pye Ale-House* in *Drury-Lane*, sent for a *Barber* his Acquaintance, drank Brandy and eat Oysters in the view of several People. *Page* waiting all the while at the Door, the whole Neighbourhood being alarm'd, yet none durst attempt him, for fear of Pistols, &c. He had vow'd Revenge upon a poor Man as kept a Dairy-Cellar, at the End of *White-Horse-Yard* who having seen him at *Islington* after his Escape, and engag'd not to speak [p. 23] of it, broke his Promise; wherefore *Sheppard* went to his Residence took the Door off the Hinges and threw it down amongst all the Mans Pans, Pipkins, and caus'd a Deluge of Cream and Milk all over the Cellar.

This Night he had a narrow Escape, one Mr. *Ireton* a Sheriffs Officer seeing him and *Page* pass thro' *Drury-Lane*, at about Ten o'Clock pursu'd 'em, and laid hold of *Page* instead of *Sheppard*, who got off, thus *Ireton* missing the main Man, and thinking *Page* of no Consequence, let him go after him.[28]

Edgworth Bess had been apprehended by *Jonathan Wild*, and by Sir *Francis Forbes* one of the Aldermen of *London*, committed to the *Poultry-Compter*,[29] for being aiding and assisting to *Sheppard* in his Escape; the Keepers and others terrify'd and purg'd her as much as was possible to discover where he was, but had it been in her Inclination, it was not in her Power so to do, as it manifestly appear'd soon after.[30]

The People about the *Strand*, *Witch-street* and *Drury-Lane*, whom he had Robb'd, and who had prosecuted him were under great Apprensions and Terror, and in particular Mr. *Kneebone*, on whom he vow'd a bloody Revenge; because he refus'd to sign a Petition in his behalf to the *Recorder* of *London*.[31] This Gentleman was forc'd to keep arm'd [p. 24] People up in his House every Night till he was Re-taken, and had the same fortify'd in the strongest manner. Several other Shop-keepers in this Neighbourhood were also put to great Expence and Trouble to Guard themselves against this dreadful Villain.

The Keepers of *Newgate*, whom the rash World loaded with Infamy, stigmatiz'd and branded with the Title of Persons guilty of Bribery; for Connivance at his Escape, they and what Posse in their Power, either for Love or Money did Contribute their utmost to undeceive a wrong notion'd People. Their Vigilance was remarkably indefatigable, sparing neither Money nor Time, Night nor Day to bring him back to his deserv'd Justice. After many Intelligences, which they endeavour'd for, and receiv'd, they had one which prov'd very Successful. Having learnt for a certainty that their Haunts was about *Finchly Common*, and being very well assur'd of the very House where they lay; on *Thursday* the 10th of *September*, a posse of Men, both of Spirit and Conduct, furnish'd with Arms proper for their Design, went for *Finchley*, some in a Coach and Four, and others on Horseback. They dispers'd themselves upon the *Common* afore-said, in order to make their View, where they had not been long e're they came in Sight of *SHEPPARD* in Company of [p. 25] *WILLIAM PAGE*, habited like two *Butchers* in new blue Frocks, with white Aprons tuck'd round their Wastes.

Upon *Sheppard's* seeing *Langley* a Turnkey at *Newgate*, he says to his Companion *Page, I see a Stag*; upon which their Courage dropt; knowing that now their dealing way of Business was almost at an End; however to make their Flight as secure as they could, they thought it adviseable to take to a Foot-path, to cut off the pursuit of the *Newgate* Cavalry; but this did not prove most successful, *Langley* came up with *Page* (who was hindermost) and Dismounting with Pistol in Hand, commands *Page* to throw up his Hands, which he trembling did, begging for Life, desiring him to *Fisk* him, *viz.* (search him,) which he accordingly did, and found a broad Knife and File; having thus disarm'd him, he takes the *Chubb* along with him in quest of the slippery *Ele, Sheppard*; who had taken Shelter in an old Stable, belonging to a Farm-House; the pursuit was close, the House invested, and a Girl seeing his Feet as he stood up hid, discover'd him. *Austin* a Turnkey first attach'd his Person, *Langley* seconded him, *Ireton* an Officer help'd to Enclose, and happy was the hindermost who aided in this great Enterprise. He being shock'd with the utmost Fear, told them he [p. 26] submitted, and desir'd they would let him live as long as he could, which they did, and us'd him mildly; upon searching him they found a broad Knife with two of the Watches as he had taken out of Mr. *Martin's* Shop, one under each Armpit; and now having gain'd their Point, and made themselves Masters of what they had often endeavoured for, they came with their *Lost Sheep* to a little House on the *Common* that sold Liquors, with this Inscription on the Sign, *I have brought my Hogs to a fair Market*; which our two unfortunate *Butchers* under their then unhappy Circumstances, had too sad Reason to apply to themselves. *Sheppard* had by this time recover'd his Surprize, grew calm and easy, and desir'd them to give him Brandy, they did, and were all good Friends, and Company together.[32]

They adjourn'd with their Booty to another Place, where was waiting a Coach and Four to Convey it to Town, with more Speed and Safety; and Mr. *Sheppard* arriv'd at his old Mansion, at about two in the Afternoon. At his a-lighting, he made a sudden Spring; He declar'd his Intention was to have slipt under the Coach, and had a Race for it; he was put into the Condemn'd-Hold, and Chain'd down to the Floor with double *Basels* about his Feet, [p. 27] *&c. Page* was carried before Sir *Francis Forbes* and committed to the same Prison for Accompanying and aiding *Sheppard* in his Escape. The prudence of Mr. *Pitt* caus'd a Separation between him and his Brother the first Night, as a Means to prevent any ensuing Danger, by having two Heads, which (according to our Proverbial Saying) *are better than one.*

The Joy the People of *Newgate* conceiv'd on this Occasion is inexpressible, *Te Deum* was Sung in the *Lodge*, and nothing but Smiles, and Bumpers, were seen there for many Days together. But *Jonathan Wild* unfortunately happen'd to be gone upon a wrong Scent after him to *Sturbridge*,[33] and Lost a Share of the Glory.

His Escape and his being so suddenly Re-taken made such a Noise in the Town, that it was thought all the common People would have gone Mad about him; there being not a *Porter* to be had for Love nor Money, nor getting into an Ale-house, for *Butchers*, *Shoemakers*, and *Barbers*, all engag'd in Controversies, and Wagers, about *Sheppard*. *Newgate* Night and Day surrounded with the Curious from St. *Giles*'s and *Rag-Fair*, and *Tyburn Road* daily lin'd with Women and Children; and the *Gallows* as carefully watch'd by Night, lest he [p. 28] should be hang'd *Incog*. For a Report of that nature, obtain'd much upon the Rabble; In short, it was a Week of the greatest Noise and Idleness among Mechanicks that has been known in *London*, and *Parker* and *Pettis*, two *Lyricks*, subsisted many Days very comfortably upon *Ballads* and *Letters* about *Sheppard*. The vulgar continu'd under great Doubts and Difficulties, in what would be his Case, and whether the *Old Warrant*, or a *New One* must be made for his Execution, or a New Tryal, &c. were the great Questions as arose, and occasion'd various Reasonings and Speculation, till a News Paper, call'd the *Daily Journal* set them all to Rights by the Publication of the Account following, viz.

'*J. Sheppard* having been Convicted of Burglary, and Felony, and received Sentence of Death, and afterwards Escap'd from *Newgate*; and being since Re-taken; we are assur'd that it must be prov'd in a *Regular*, and *Judicial* way, that he is the same Person, who was so Convicted and made his Escape, before a Warrant can be obtain'd for his Execution; and that this Affair will be brought before the Court at the *Old Baily* the next Sessions.'

This was enough; People began to grow calm and easy and got *Shav'd*, and their Shoes *finish'd*, and Business returned into its former Channel, the Town resolving to wait the *Sessions* with Patience.[34]

[p. 29]The Reverend Mr. *Wagstaff*, who officiated in the absence of the *Ordinary*, renew'd his former Acquaintance with Mr. *Sheppard*, and examin'd him in a particular manner concerning his Escape from the Condemn'd Hold: He sincerely disown'd, that all, or any, belonging to the Prison were privy thereto; but related it as it has been describ'd. He declar'd that *Edgworth Bess*, who had hitherto pass'd for his *Wife*, was not really so: This was by some thought to be in him Base, and Ungenerous in that, as she had Contributed towards his Escape, and was in Custody on that Account, it might render her more liable to Punishment, than if she had been thought his Wife; but he endeavour'd to acquit himself, by saying, that she was the sole Author of all his Misfortunes; That she betray'd him to *Jonathan Wild*, at the time he was taken in *Rosemary-Lane*; and that when he was contriving his Escape, she disobey'd his orders, as when being requir'd to attend at the Door of the Condemn'd-Hold by Nine, or Ten in the Morning to facilitate his Endeavours, she came not till the Evening, which he said, was an ungrateful Return for the care he had taken in setting her at Liberty from *New-Prison*; and thus Justify'd himself in what he had done, and said he car'd not what became of her.

[p. 30]He was also Examined about Mr. *Martin's* Watches; and whether *Page* was privy to that Robbery; he carefully guarded himself against uttering any thing that might affect him, peremptorily declar'd him Innocent of that, as well as of being privy to his Escape, and said, that he only out of Kindness, as being an old Companion, was resolv'd to share in his Fortunes after he had Escap'd.[35]

He was again continually meditating a second Escape, as appear'd by his own Hardiness, and the Instruments found upon him, on *Saturday* the 12th, and *Wednesday* the 16th of *September*, the first Time a small File was found conceal'd in his Bible, and the second Time two Files, a Chisel and an Hammer being hid in the Rushes of a Chair; and whenever a Question was mov'd to him, when, or by what Means those Implements came to his Hands; he would passionately fly out, and say, *How can you? you always ask me these, and such like Questions;* and in a particular manner, when he was ask'd, Whether his Companion *Page* was an Accomplice with him, either in the affair of the Watches, or any other? (he reply'd) *That if he knew, he would give no direct Answer,* thinking it to be a Crime in him to detect the Guilty.

[p. 31]It was thought necessary by the Keepers to remove him from the Condemn'd-Hold to a Place, call'd the *Castle*, in the Body of the Goal, and to Chain him down to two large Iron Staples in the Floor; the Concourse of People of tolerable Fashion to see him was exceeding Great, he was always Chearful and Pleasant to a Degree, as turning almost every thing as was said into a Jest and Banter.[36]

Being one *Sunday* at the Chapel, a Gentleman belong to the *Lord Mayor*, ask'd a Turnkey, Which was *Sheppard*, the Man pointed to him? Says *Sheppard, yes Sir, I am the Sheppard, and all the Goalers in the Town are my Flock, and I cannot stir into the Country, but they are all at my Heels* Baughing, *after me,* &c.

He told Mr. *Robins*, the *City Smith, That he had procur'd him a small Job, and that whoever it was that put the Spikes on the Condemn'd-Hold was an honest Man, for a better peice of Metal,* says he, *I never wrought upon in my Life.*

He was loth to believe his frequent Robberies were an Injury to the Publick, for he us'd to say, That *if they were ill in one Respect, they were as good in another, and that* [p. 32] *though he car'd not for Working much himself, yet he was desirous that others should not stand Idle, more especially those of his own Trade, who were always Repairing of his Breaches.*

When serious, and that but seldom, he would Reflect on his past wicked Life. He declar'd to us, that for several Years of his Apprenticeship he had an utter abhorrence to Women of the Town, and us'd to pelt them with Dirt when they have fell in his way; till a *Button-Mould-Maker* his next Neighbour left off that Business, and set up a Victualling-house in *Lewkenhors-Lane*, where himself and other young Apprentices resorted on *Sundays*, and at all other Opportunities.[37] At this House began his Acquaintance with *Edgworth Bess*. His Sentiments were strangely alter'd, and from an Aversion to those Prostitutes, he had a more favourable Opinion, and even Conversation with them, till he Contracted an ill Distemper, which as he said, he cur'd himself of by a Medicine of his own preparing.

He inveigh'd bitterly against his Brother *Thomas* for putting him into the Information, for Mrs. *Cook's* Robbery, and pretended that all the Mischiefs that attended him was owing to that Matter. He acknowledg'd that he was concern'd in that [p. 33] Fact, and that his said Brother broke into his Lodgings, and stole from him all his Share and more of the acquir'd Booty.

He oftentimes averr'd, that *William Field* was no ways concern'd in Mr. *Kneebone's* Robbery; but that being a Brother of the Quill,[38] *Blewskin* and himself told him the particulars, and manner of the Facts, and that all he Swore against him at his Tryal was False, and that he had other Authority for it, than what came out of their (*Sheppard* and *Blewskin*) Mouths, who actually committed the Fact.

And moreover, that *Field* being acquainted with their Ware-house (a Stable) near the *Horse-Ferry* at *Westminster*, which *Sheppard* had hir'd, and usually reposited therein the Goods he stole. He came one Night, and broke open the same, and carried off the best part of the Effects taken out of Mr. *Kneebone's* Shop.

Sheppard said he thought this to be one of the greatest Villanies that could be acted, for another to come and Plunder them of Things for which they had so honourably ventur'd their Lives, and wish'd that *Field*, as well as his Brother *Tom* might meet with forgiveness for it.

[p. 34]He declar'd himself frequently against the Practice of *Whidling*, or *Impeaching*, which he said, had made dreadful Havock among the *Thieves*, and much lamented the depravity of the *Brethren* in that Respect; and said that if all were but such *Tight-Cocks* as himself, the *Reputation* of the *British Thievery* might be carried to a far greater height than it had been done for many Ages, and that there would then be but little Necessity for Jaylors and Hangmen.

These and such like were his constant Discourses, when Company went up with the Turnkeys to the *Castle* to see him, and few or none went away without leaving him Money for his Support; in which he abounded, and did therewith some small Charities to the other Prisoners; however, he was abstemious and sparing enough in his Diet.[39]

Among the many Schemes laid by his Friends, for the preserving himself after his Escape, we were told of a most Remarkable one, propos'd by an ingenious Person, who advis'd, that he might be Expeditiously, and Secretly convey'd to the Palace at *Windsor*, and there to prostrate his Person, and his Case at the Feet of a most Gracious Prince, and his Case being so very singular and new, it might in great proba[p. 35]bility move the Royal Fountain of unbounded Clemency; but he declin'd this Advice, and follow'd the Judgment and Dictates of *Butchers*, which very speedily brought him very near the Door of the *Slaughter-house*.

On the 4th of *September*, the Day as *Joseph Ward*, and *Anthony Upton* were Executed, there was publish'd a whimsical Letter, as from *Sheppard*, to *Jack Ketch*, which afforded Diversion to the Town, and Bread to the Author, which is as followeth, *viz.*

SIR,

"I Thank you for the Favour you intended me this Day: I am a Gentleman, and allow you to be the same, and I hope can forgive Injuries; fond Nature prompted, I obey'd, Oh, propitious Minute! and to show that I am in Charity, I am now drinking your Health, and a *Bon Repo* to poor *Joseph* and *Anthony*. I am gone a few Days for the Air, but design speedily to embark; and this Night I am going upon a Mansion for a Supply; it's a stout Fortification, but what Difficulties can't I encounter, when, dear *Jack*, you find that Bars and [p. 36] Chains are but trifling Obstacles in the way of your Friend and Servant"

From my Residence in   JOHN SHEPPARD.
Terra Australi *incognito.*

P.S. Pray my Service to Mr. *Or – di – y* and to Mr. *App – ee.*[40]

On *Saturday* the 10th of *October, Anthony Lamb,* and *Thomas Sheppard,* with 95 other Felons were carried from *Newgate* on Shipboard, for Transportation to the Plantations;[41] the last begg'd to have an opportunity given him of taking his final Leave of his Brother *John*; but this was not to be Granted, and the greatest Favour that could be obtain'd, was that on the *Sunday* before they had an Interview at the *Chapel,* but at such a distance, that they neither saluted, or shook Hands, and the Reason given for it, was that no Implements might be convey'd to *Sheppard* to assist him in making an Escape.

This Caution seem'd to be absolutely necessary, for it appear'd soon after that *Sheppard* found Means to release himself from the Staples to which he was Chain'd in the *Castle,* by unlocking a great Padlock with a Nail, which he had pickt up on the Floor, and endeavour'd to pass up the [p. 37] Chimney, but was prevented by the stout Iron Bars fix'd in his way, and wanted nothing but the smallest File to have perfected his Liberty. When the Assistants of the Prison, came as usual with his Victuals, they began to examine his Irons; to their great Surprize they found them loose, and ready to be taken off at Pleasure. Mr. *Pitt* the Head Keeper, and his Deputies were sent for, and *Sheppard* finding this Attempt entirely frustrated, discover'd to them by what means he had got them off; and after they had search'd him, found nothing, and Lock'd and Chain'd him down again: He took up the Nail and unlock'd the Padlock before their Faces; they were struck with the greatest Amazement as having never heard, or beheld the like before. He was then Hand-Cuff'd, and more effectually Chain'd.[42]

The next Day, the Reverend Mr. *Purney Ordinary* of the Place came from the Country to visit him, and complain'd of the sad Disposition he found him in, as Meditateing on nothing, but Means to Escape, and declining the great Duty incumbent upon him to prepare for his approaching Change. He began to Relent, and said, that since his last Effort had prov'd not Successful, he would entertain no more Thoughts of that Nature, but entirely Dispose, and Resign [p. 38] himself to the Mercy of Almighty God, of whom he hop'd still to find forgiveness of his manifold Offences.

He said, that *Edgworth Bess* and himself kept a little Brandy-shop together in *Lewkenhors-Lane,* and once sav'd about Thirty Pounds; but having such an universal Acquaintance amongst Theives, he had frequent calls to go *Abroad,* and soon quitted that Business, and his Shop.

On *Friday* the 2d, of *October* his old Confederate *Joseph Blake* alias *Blewskin,* was apprehended and taken at a House in St. *Giles*'s Parish by *Jonathan Wild,* and by Justice *Blackerby* committed to *Newgate. William Field* who was at his Liberty, appearing and making Oath, that *Blewskin* together with *John Sheppard* and himself, committed the Burglary and Felony in Mr. *Kneebone*'s House, for which *Sheppard* was Condemn'd.

The Sessions commencing at the *Old-Bailey* on *Wednesday* the 14th of

October following, an Indictment was found against *Blewskin* for the same, and he was brought down from *Newgate* to the *Old-Bailey* to be Arraign'd in order to his Tryal; and being in the Yard within the Gate before the Court; Mr. *Wild* being there Drinking [p. 39] a glass of Wine with him, he said to Mr. *Wild*, *You may put in a word for me, as well as for another Person?* To which Mr. *Wild* reply'd, I cannot do it. *You are certainly a dead Man, and will be tuck'd up very speedily,* or words to that effect: Whereupon *Blewskin* on a sudden seiz'd Mr. *Wild* by the Neck, and with a little Clasp Knife he was provided with he cut his Throat in a very dangerous Manner; and had it not been for a *Muslin* Stock twisted in several Plaits round his Neck, he had in all likelyhood succeeded in his barbarous Design before *Ballard* the Turnkey, who was at Hand, could have time to lay hold of him; the Villain triumph'd afterwards in what he had done, Swearing many bloody Oaths, that if he had murder'd him, he should have died with Satisfaction, and that his Intention was to have cut off his Head, and thrown it into the Sessions House Yard among the Rabble, and Curs'd both his Hand and the Knife for not Executing it Effectually.

Mr. *Wild* instantly had the Assistance of three able Surgeons, *viz.* Mr. *Dobbins*, Mr. *Marten* and Mr. *Coletheart*, who sew'd up the Wound, and order'd him to his Bed, and he has continu'd ever since, but in a doubtful State of Recovery.[43]

[p. 40]The Felons on the Common Side of *Newgate*, also animated by *Sheppard's* Example, the Night before they were to be Shipt for Transportation, had cut several Iron Bars assunder, and some of them had saw'd off their Fetters, the rest Huzzaing, and making Noises, under pretence of being Joyful that they were to be remov'd on the Morrow, to prevent the Workmen being heard; and in two Hours time more, if their Design had not been discover'd, near One Hundred Villains had been let loose into the World, to have committed new Depredations; nothing was wanted here but *Sheppard's* great Judgment, who was by himself in the strong Room, call'd the *Castle*, meditating his own Deliverance, which he perfected in the manner following.[44]

On *Thursday* the 15th of this Instant *October*, at between One and Two in the Afternoon, *William Austin*, an Assistant to the Keepers, a Man reputed to be a very diligent, and faithful Servant, went to *Sheppard* in the strong Room, call'd the *Castle*, with his Necessaries, as was his Custom every Day. There went along with him Captain *Geary*, the Keeper of *New Prison*, Mr. *Gough*, belonging to the *Gate-house* in *Westminster*, and two other Gentlemen, who had the Curiosity to see the Prisoner, [p. 41] *Austin* very strictly examined his Fetters, and his Hand-Cuffs, and found them very Safe; he eat his Dinner and talk'd with his usual Gayety to the Company: They took leave of him and wish'd him a good Evening. The Court being sitting at the *Old-Bailey*, the Keepers and most of their Servants were attending there with their Prisoners: And *Sheppard* was told that if he wanted any thing more, then was his Time, because they could not come to him till the next Morning: He thank'd them for their Kindness, and desir'd them to be *as early as possible.*

The same Night, soon after 12 of the Clock Mr. *Bird*, who keeps a

Turners-shop adjoyning to *Newgate*, was disturb'd by the Watchman, who found his Street Door open, and call'd up the Family, and they concluding the Accident was owing to the Carelessness of some in the House, shut their Doors, and went to Bed again.

The next Morning *Friday*, at about eight Mr. *Austin* went up as usual to wait on *Sheppard*, and having unlock'd and unbolted the double Doors of the Castle, he beheld almost a Cart-load of Bricks and Rubbish about the Room, and his Prisoner gone: The Man ready to sink, came trem[p. 42]bling down again, and was scarce able to Acquaint the People in the *Lodge* with what had happen'd.

The whole Posse of the Prison ran up, and stood like Men depriv'd of their Senses: Their surprize being over, they were in hopes that he might not have yet entirely made his Escape, and got their Keys to open all the strong Rooms adjacent to the *Castle*, in order to Trace him, when to their farther Amazement, they found the Doors ready open'd to their Hands; and the strong Locks, Screws and Bolts broken in pieces, and scatter'd about the Jayl. Six great Doors (one whereof having not been open'd for seven Years past) were forc'd, and it appear'd that he had Descended from the Leads of *Newgate* by a Blanket (which he fasten'd to the Wall by an Iron Spike he had taken from the Hatch of the *Chapel*) on the House of Mr. *Bird*, and the Door on the Leads having been left open, it is very reasonable to conclude he past directly to the Street Door down the Stairs; Mr. *Bird* and his Wife hearing an odd sort of a Noise on the Stairs as they lay in their Bed, a short time before the Watchman alarm'd the Family.

[p. 43]Infinite Numbers of Citizens came to *Newgate* to behold *Sheppard's* Workmanship, and Mr. *Pitt* and his Officers very readily Conducted them up Stairs, that the World might be convinc'd there was not the least room to suspect, either a Negligence, or Connivance in the Servants. Every one express'd the greatest Surprize that has been known, and declar'd themselves satisfy'd with the Measures they had taken for the Security of their Prisoner.[45]

One of the Sheriffs came in Person, and went up to the *Castle* to be satisfy'd of the Situation of the Place, &c. Attended by several of the City Officers.

The Court being sat at the *Sessions-House*, the Keepers were sent for and Examin'd, and the Magistrates were in great Consternation, that so horrid a Wretch had escap'd their Justice.[46] It being intended that he should have been brought down to the Court the last Day of the *Sessions*, and order'd for Execution in two or three Days after; if it appear'd that he was the Person Condemn'd for the breaking Mr. *Kneebone's* House, and included in the Warrant for Execution, &c.

[p. 44]Many of the Methods by which this miraculous Escape was effected, remain as yet a Secret, there are some indeed too Evident, the most reasonable Conjecture that has hitherto been made, is, that the first Act was his twisting and breaking assunder by the strength of his Hands a small Iron Chain, which together with a great Horse Padlock, (as went from the heavy Fetters about his Legs to the Staples) confin'd him to the Floor, and with a Nail open'd the Padlock and set himself at Liberty about the Room: A large flat Iron Bar appears to have been taken out of the Chimney, with the Assistance whereof 'tis plain he broke thro' a Wall of many Foot in Thickness, and made his way from the *Castle* into another strong Room Contiguous, the Door of it not having been open'd since several of the *Preston* Prisoners were Confin'd there about seven Years ago:[47] Three Screws are visibly taken off of the Lock, and the Doors as strong as Art could make them, forc'd open. The Locks and Bolts, either wrench'd or Broke, and the Cases and other Irons made for their Security cut assunder: An Iron Spike broke off from the Hatch in the *Chapel*, which he fix'd in the Wall and fasten'd his Blanket to it, to drop on the Leads of Mr. *Bird*'s House, his Stockings were found on the [p. 45] Leads of *Newgate*; 'tis question'd whether sixty Pounds will repair the Damage done to the Jayl.

It will perhaps be inquir'd how all this could be perform'd without his being heard by the Prisoners or the Keepers; 'tis well known that the Place of his Confinement is in the upper part of the Prison, none of the other Felons being Kept any where near him; and 'tis suppos'd that if any had heard him at Work, they would rather have facilitated, than frustrated his Endeavours. In the Course of his Breaches he pass'd by a Door on his Left belonging to the *Common-Side* Felons,[48] who have since Curs'd him heartily for his not giving them an opportunity to kiss his Hand, and lending them a favourable lift when his Hand was in; but that was not a Work proper for Mr. *Sheppard* to do in his then Circumstances.

His Fetters are not to be found any where about the Jayl, from whence 'tis concluded he has either thrown them down some Chimney, or carried them off on his Legs, the latter seems to be Impracticable, and would still render his Escaping in such Manner the more astonishing; and the only Answer that is given to the whole, at *New[p. 46]gate* is, *That the* Devil *came in Person and assisted him.*

He undoubtedly perform'd most of these Wonders in the darkest part of the Night, and without the least Glimpse of a Candle; in a word, he has actually done with his own Hands in a few Hours, what several of the most skilful Artists allow, could not have been acted by a number of Persons furnish'd with proper Implements, and all other Advantages in a full Day.

Never was there any thing better Tim'd, the Keepers and all their Assistants being obliged to a strict Attendance on the Sessions at the *Old-Bailey*, which held for about a Week; and *Blewskin* having confin'd *Jonathan Wild* to his Chamber, a more favourable opportunity could not have presented for Mr. *Sheppard*'s Purposes.

The Jaylors suffer'd much by the Opinion the ignorant Part of the People entertain'd of the Matter, and nothing would satisfie some, but that they not only Conniv'd at, but even assisted him in breaking their own Walls and Fences, and that for this Reason too, *viz.* That he should be at Liberty to instruct and train up others in his Method of House-Breaking; and replenish the Town with a new set of Rogues, to [p. 47] supply the Places of those Transported beyond Sea.

This is indeed a fine way of Judging, the well-known Characters of Mr. *Pitt*, and his Deputies, are sufficient to wipe of such ridiculous Imputations; and 'tis a most lamentable Truth, that they have often-times had in their

Charge Villains of the deepest Die; Persons of Quality and great Worth, for whom no Entreaties, no Sums how large soever have been able to interfere between the doleful Prison, and the fatal Tree.

The Officers have done their Duty, they are but Men, and have had to deal with a Creature something more than Man, a *Protœus*, Supernatural, Words cannot describe him, his Actions and Workmanship which are too visible, best testifie him.

On *Saturday* the 17th, *Joseph Blake*, alias *Blewskin*, came upon his Tryal at the *Old-Bailey*: *Field* gave the same Evidence against him, as he had formerly done against *Sheppard*; and the Prisoner making but a triffling Defence, the Jury found him Guilty of Burglary and Felony. The Criminal when the Verdict was brought in, made his Obeyances to the Court, *and thank'd them for their Kindness.*[49]

It will be necessary that we now return to the Behaviour of Mr. *Sheppard*, some few Days before his last Flight.

Mr. *Figg* the famous Prize Fighter comeing to see him, in *NEWGATE*, there past some pleasant Raillery between them; and after Mr. *Figg* was gone, *Sheppard* declared he had a Mind to send him a formal Challenge to Fight him at all the Weapons in the strong Room; and that let the Consequence be what it would, he should call at Mr. *Figg*'s House in his way to Execution, and drink a merry Glass with him by way of Reconciliation.[50]

A young Woman an Acquaintance of his Mother, who wash'd his Linnen and brought him Necessaries, having in an Affray, got her Eyes beaten Black and Blue; says *Sheppard* to her, *How long hast thou been Married?* Replyes the Wench, *I wonder you can ask me such a Question, when you so well know the Contrary:* Nay, says *Sheppard* again, Sarah *don't deny it, for you have gotten your CERTIFICATE in your Face.*

Mr. *Ireton* a Bailiff in *Drury-Lane* having pursued *Sheppard* after his Escape from the Condemn'd-Hold with uncommon Dili[p. 49]gence; (for the safety of that Neighbourhood which was the chief Scene of his Villainies) *Sheppard* when Re-taken, declared he would be even with him for it, and if ever he procur'd his Liberty again, *he would give all his Prisoners an ACT OF GRACE.*[51]

A Gentleman in a jocose way ask'd him to come and take a Dinner with him, *Sheppard* reply'd, *he accepted of the Invitation, and perhaps might take an opportunity to wait on him*; and there is great Reason to believe he has been as good as his Word.

He would complain of his Nights, as saying, *It was dark with him from Five in the Evening, till Seven in the Morning*; and being not permitted to have either a Bed or Candle, his Circumstances were dismal; and that he never slept but had some confus'd Doses, he said he consider'd all this with the Temper of a Philosopher.

Neither his sad Circumstances, nor the solemn Exhortations of the several Divines who visited him, were able to divert him from this ludicrous way of Expression; he said, *They were all Ginger-bread Fellows,*[52] and came rather out of Curiosity, than Charity; and to form *Papers* and *Ballads* out of his Behaviour.

A *Welch* Clergyman who came pretty often, requested him in a particular Manner to refrain Drinking; (tho' indeed there was no necessity for that Caution) *Sheppard* [p. 50] says, Doctor, *You set an Example and I'll follow*; this was a smart Satyr and Repartee upon the *Parson*, some Circumstances consider'd.

When he was visited in the *Castle* by the Reverend Mr. *Wagstaff*, he put on the Face only of a Preparation for his End, as appear'd by his frequent Attempts made upon his Escape, and when he has been press'd to Discover those who put him upon Means of Escaping, and furnish'd him with Implements, he would passionately, and with a Motion of striking, say, *ask me no such Questions, one File's worth all the Bibles in the World.*

When ask'd if he had not put off all Thoughts of an Escape and Entertain'd none but those of Death, would Answer by way of Question, not directly, whether they thought it possible, or probable for him to Effect his Release, when Manacled in the manner he was. When mov'd to improve the few Minutes that seem'd to remain of his Life; he did indeed listen to, but not regard the Design and Purport of his Admonition, breaking in with something New of his own, either with respect to his former Accomplices, or Actions, and all too with Pleasure and Gayety of Expression.

When in *Chapel*, he would seemingly make his Responses with Devotion; but [p. 51] would either Laugh, or force Expressions (when as an Auditor of the Sermon) be of Contempt, either of the Preacher, or of his Discourse.

In fine, he behav'd so, in Word, and Action, (since re-taken) that demonstrated to the World, that his Escape was the utmost Employ of his Thoughts, whatever Face of Penitence he put on when visited by the Curious.

An Account of SHEPPARD'S
  Adventures of five Hours immediately
  after his Escape from *Newgate*, in a Letter to his Friend.
    DEAR FRIEND![53]

OVER a Bottle of Claret *you'll give me leave to* declare it, *that I've fairly put the* Vowels *upon the good Folks at* Newgate, i.o.u. *When I'm able, I may, or may not discharge my* Fees,[54] *'tis a* Fee-simple, *for a Man in my Condition to acknowledge; and tho' I'm safe out of* Newgate, *I must yet have, or at least, affect, a* New Gate *by Limping, or Turning my Toes in by making a right* Hand *of my* Feet. *Not to be long, for I hate Prolixity in all Business:* In short, *after* Filing, Defileing, Sawing, *when no Body* Saw, Climbing (*this* Clime *in*) *it prov'd a good* Turner *of my Affairs, thro' the House of a* Turner. *Being quite past, and safe* [p. 52] *from Estreat on Person or Chattels, and safe in the* Street, *I thought Thanks due to him who cou'd Deliver hence; and immediately (for you must know I'm a* Catholick) *to give Thanks for my Deliverance, I slept amongst the* Grey-Fryers *to come and joyn with me, in saying a* Pater-Noster, *or so, at* Amen-Corner. *The Fryers being* Fat *began to* Broil, *and soon after* Boild *up into a Passion to be disturb'd at that time of Night. But being got Loose and having no Time to Lose, I gave them good Words, and so the Business was done. From thence I soon slip'd through* Ludgate, *but was damnably fearful of an* Old Bailey *always lurking thereabout, who might have brought me to the* Fleet[55] *for being too* Nimble, *besides, I was wonderfully apprehensive of receiving some unwelcome* Huggings *from the* W – – – – – n[56] *there; therefore with a step and a stride I soon got over* Fleet-ditch, *and (as in Justice I ought) I prais'd the* Bridge *I got over. Being a* Batchelor, *and not being capable to manage a* Bridewell[57] *you know. I had no Business near St.* Brides, *so kept the right hand side, designing to* Pop *into the* Alley *as usual; but fearing to go thro' there, and* harp *too much on the same* String, *it gave an* Allay *to my* Intention, *and on I went to* Shoe-lane *end but there meeting with a* Bully Hack[58] *of the Town, he wou'd have shov'd me down, which my Spirit resenting, tho' a brawny* Dog, *I soon* Coller'd *him, fell* Souse *at him, [p. 53] then with his own* Cane *I* strapp'd *till he was force to* Buckle *too, and hold his* Tongue, *in so much he durst not say his* Soul *was his own, and was glad to pack of at* Last, *and turn his* Heels *upon me: I was glad he was gone you may be sure, and* dextrously *made a* Hand *of my* Feet *under the* Leg-Tavern; *but the very* Thoughts *of* Fetter-Lane *call'd to mind some Passages, which made me avoid the* Passage *at the end of it, (next to the Coffee House you know) so I soon whip'd over the way, yet going along two wooden* Loggerheads *at St.* Dunstan's, *made just then a damn'd Noise about their* Quarters, *but the sight of me made perfectly* Hush *in a* Minute; *now fearing to goe by* Chance-a-wry-Lane,[59] *as being upon the* Watch *my self and not to be debarr'd at* Temple-Bar; *I stole up* Bell-Yard, *but narrowly escap'd being* Clapper-claw'd[60] *by two Fellows I did not like in the Alley, so was forc'd to goe round with a design to* Sheer-off *into* Sheer-Lane, *but the* Trumpet *sounding at that very time, alarm'd me so, I was forc'd to* Grope *my way back through* Hemlock-Court, *and take my Passage by* Ship-Yard *without the Bar again; but there meeting with one of our trusty Friends, (all Ceremonies a-part) he told me under the* Rose *I must expect no* Mercy *in St. Clement's Parish, for the* Butchers *there on the* Back *on't would* Face *me, and with their* Cleavers *soon bring me down on my* marrow Bones; [p. 54] you may believe I soon hasten'd thence, but by this time being Fainty and nigh Spent, I put forward, and seeing a* Light *near the* Savoy-Gate, *I was resolv'd not to make* Light *of the Opportunity, but call'd for an hearty Dram of* Luther *and* Calvin, *that is,* Mum *and* Geneva[61] *mix'd; but having Fasted so long before, it soon got into my Noddle, and e'er I had gone twenty steps, it had so intirely* Stranded *my Reason, that by the time I came to* Half-Moon-Street *end, it gave a* New-Exchange *to my Senses, and made me quite* Lunatick.

However, after a little Rest, I stole down George-Passage *into* Oaf-Alley *in* York-Buildings, *and thence (tho' a vile Man) into* Villiers-Street, *and so into the* Strand *again, where having gone a little way,* Hefford's Harp *at the Sign of the* Irish Harp, *put me a Jumping and Dancing to that degree, that I could not forbear making a* Somerset *or two before* Northumberland-House. *I thought once of taking the* Windsor *Coach for my self* John Sheppard, *by the Name of* Crook – – *but fearing to be* Hook'd *in before my Journey's End, I stept into* Hedge-Lane, *where two* Harlots *were up in the* Boughs *(it seems)* Branching *out their Respects to one another, through their Windows, and People beginning to gather thereabout, I ran* Pelmel[62] to Piccadilly, *where meeting, by meer Chance a* Bakers *Cart going to* [p. 55] Turnham-Green, *I being not* Mealy *Mouth'd, nor the Man being* Crusty *I* wheel'd *out of Town*.

I did call at Hammersmith, *having no occasion directly. I shall stay two or three Days in that Neighbourhood, so, if you Direct a Letter for Mr.* Sligh Bolt, *to be left with Mrs.* Tabitha Skymmington *at* Cheesewick, *it's Safety will* Bear Water *by any* Boat, *and come* Current, *with the* Tyde *to*

Dear BOB

Yours from the Top
of *Newgate* to the Bottom
J. SHEPPARD.

P.S. If you see *Blewskin*, tell him I am well, and hope he receiv'd my last – – – I wou'd write by the *Post* if I durst, but it wou'd be, certainly *Postpon'd* if I did, and it would be *stranger* too, to trust a Line by a *Stranger*, who might *Palm* upon us both and never Deliver it to *Hand*.

I send this by a *Waterman*, (I dare trust) who is very Merry
upon me, and says he wou'd not be in my *Jacket*.[63]
Saturday Octob. 17, 1724.

[p. 56]We shall conclude with what had been often observ'd by many Persons to *Sheppard; viz.* That it was very Imprudent in him to take Shelter in the City, or the adjacent Parts of it, after his Escape from the Condemn'd Hold; and withal to commit a *Capital Offence*, almost within Sight of *Newgate*, when his Life and all was in such Danger. His Reply was general, *viz.* That it was his Fate: But being ask'd a particular Reason for his not taking a longer Rout[64] than the City, and the Neighbouring parts: pleaded Poverty as his Excuse for Confinement within those Limits; at the same time urging, that had he been Master at that time of five Pounds, *England* should not have been the Place of his Residence, having a good Trade in his Hands to live in any populated Part of the World.[65]

FINIS.

ERRATA.

IN Page 3, 1. 22, read *this Eminence of Guilt*, instead of *to the fatal Tree*.

NOTES

1 'Societies' here refers to the societies for the reformation of manners which flourished from the late seventeenth century to the late 1730s. They published morally uplifting pamphlets and prosecuted people for offences such as drunkenness and prostitution. Defoe, an early supporter of the societies, became a critic of their failure to prosecute the gentry: 'Your Annual Lists of Criminals appeare,/ But no Sir *Harry* or Sir *Charles* is there' (*Review*, 7 April 1709, Edinburgh edn). He argued that without a good example from such people it was pointless to expect the morals of the poor to improve. The societies were revived in 1757 with the support of Sir John Fielding, the Bow Street magistrate, and John Wesley, but they collapsed in 1763, following a civil action for damages; a similar society appeared in 1787 with William Wilberforce as its leading light. On the early societies see G.V. Portus, *Cartis Anglicana or, An Historical Inquiry into those Religious and Philanthropic Societies that flourished in England between*

the Years 1678 and 1740, London, 1912; D.W.R. Bahlman, *The Moral Revolution of 1688*, New Haven, 1957; E.J. Bristow, *Vice and Vigilance: Purity Movements in Britain since 1700*, Dublin, 1977; T.C. Curtis and W.A. Speck, 'The societies for the reformation of manners: a case study in the theory and practice of moral reform', *Literature and History*, 1976, vol. 3, pp. 45–64; J. Woodward, *An Account of the Societies for the Reformation of Manners in London and Westminster, And other Parts of the Kingdom*, London, 1699; [D. Defoe], *Reformation of Manners. A Satyr*, London, 1702; [D. Defoe], *More Reformation. A Satyr upon Himself*, London, 1703.

2 John Sheppard was baptized on 4 March.

3 His sister died young and his surviving brother was Thomas Sheppard, who was baptized 28 February 1698.

4 Witch, or Wych, Street was lost, and most of the rest of the area around Drury Lane in which the narrative is set was radically altered, during the nineteenth-century construction of the Aldwych. In other accounts Sheppard was said to have been a servant to William Kneebone (as was his mother), whose house he later broke into, and to have been apprenticed first to a cane chairmaker in Hounsditch, but he died and so Sheppard was apprenticed to Wood in April 1717: OBSP, 12–14 August 1724; *A Narrative of all the Robberies, Escapes, &c. of John Sheppard*, London, 1724, p. 4; *The History of the Lives and Actions of Jonathan Wild, Joseph Blake alias Bleuskin, Foot-Pad. And John Sheppard, Housebreaker*, London, 3rd edn, [1725?], pp. 105–6; *Parker's London News, or the Impartial Intelligencer*, 18 November 1724.

5 For Lyon see note 65. According to J. Villette, *The Annals of Newgate; or, Malefactor's Register*, 4 volumes, London, 1776, vol. I, p. 255, Lyon was only one of Sheppard's 'intimates', his other favourite being a woman called Maggot, and it was she who encouraged him to commit the robbery on Bains (referred to at p. 50).

6 For another version of these events see *A Narrative . . . of John Sheppard*, p. 5. There it is alleged that the quarrel at Islington was over Wood's poor treatment of Sheppard and a fellow worker, and that the stick, allegedly thrown at Mrs Wood, was actually aimed at Elizabeth Lyon and her husband, the soldier. The premature termination of apprenticeships by apprentices absconding was not uncommon: see the General Introduction, p. 21.

7 See erratum at the end of the text, p. 69.

8 According to *A Narrative . . . of John Sheppard*, pp. 6–7, the two thefts from Bains took place 'about the latter End of *July* 1723' and on 1 August. Villette, *Annals of Newgate*, vol. I, p. 255, says that Sheppard's first theft was from the Rummer Tavern in Charing Cross.

9 For these people see G. Howson, *Thief-taker General: The Rise and Fall of Jonathan Wild*, London, 1970.

10 For the trial of Thomas Sheppard see OBSP, 8–10 July 1724. The offence is reported to have taken place on 5 February 1724; Thomas – who had, apparently, been arrested trying to sell the stolen goods – was indicted with 'John Sheppard, not yet taken'. He was acquitted of burglary, but convicted of felony and sentenced to be transported. When eventually arrested, John was arraigned on three charges, one of which was breaking into the house of Phillips, but he was acquitted on that count: OBSP, 12–14 August 1724; Villette, *Annals of Newgate*, vol. I, p. 257. Thomas had previously been burnt in the hand in 1723 following two trials for the theft of tools: OBSP 28–30 August 1723; Villette, *Annals of Newgate*, vol. I, pp. 256–7.

11 Those who were being held as potential witnesses for the Crown were – probably

wisely in view of the communal nature of prisons – kept at New Prison, while their comrades, who were being held for felonies, were put in Newgate.

12 Leg irons.

13 There seems to have been no exactly contemporaneous newspaper report of this escape, although it is referred to (without any details) in reports of Sheppard's first escape from Newgate: *The Original London Post, or Heathcote's Intelligencer*, 27 July 1724; *The Weekly Journal, or British Gazetteer*, 5 September 1724. According to a later biography the escape occurred on Whitsun Monday 1724: J. Thurmond, *Harlequin Sheppard. A Night Scene in Grotesque Characters: As it is Perform'd at the Theatre-Royal in Drury Lane*, London, 1724, p. 7. The keeper of New Prison claimed for assistance from the Middlesex justices for repairing the damage caused by Sheppard. Various keepers of New Prison had complained of its ruinous condition from at least as early as December 1720, when John Marwick warned that escapes were likely; the warning was repeated by Marwick in 1722 and by his successor, John Geary, in the following year. Geary and his successor, Joshua Walker, continued the complaints into 1725, the year after Sheppard's escape, and on into the next decade. The key problem was, who was going to pay for the repairs? Prisons were run for profit by their keepers, so they wished to avoid expenditure; on the other hand, the Middlesex Quarter Sessions, under whose jurisdiction the New Prison came, were equally keen to resist the idea that the local ratepayers should bear the whole cost: GLRO, MJ/SBB/789/1720 December, p. 54; MJ/SBB/1721 April, p. 67 (but, MJ/SBB/795/1721 October, ff. 126–8); MJ/OC/2/1722 July, fo. 30; MJ/OC/2/1723 August, fo. 84, 85; MJ/OC/2/1723 December, ff. 100–1; MJ/SP/1724 October/64, fo. 102; MJ/OC/2/1724 October, fo. 124; MJ/OC/2/1725 April, ff. 10–11; MJ/OC/2/1725 June, ff. 22–3; MJ/OC/2/1725 August, fo. 28; MJ/OC/2/1725 October, ff. 84–5; MJ/SP/1732 July/50; MJ/SP/1732 October/88. Generally, W.J. Sheehan, The London prison system, 1666–1795, unpublished Ph.D. thesis, University of Maryland, 1975; C. Harding, W. Hines, R. Ireland, P. Rawlings, *Imprisonment in England and Wales: A Concise History*, London, 1985.

14 For this robbery see OBSP, 8–10 July 1724, trial of Lamb. Lamb tried to withdraw his confession at the trial on the ground that 'he was terrified into his Confession'. He was transported to Maryland in 1724: OBSP, 8–10 July 1724; P.W. Coldham, *English Convicts in Colonial America*, 2 volumes, New Orleans, 1974–6, vol. I, p. 160.

15 That is, paduasoy.

16 See OBSP, 12–14 August 1724, trial of Sheppard; OBSP, 14–21 October 1724, trial of Blake. According to Kneebone's evidence Sheppard had been his servant, and he had suspected Sheppard of the crime, 'he having committed ill Actions thereabouts before'.

17 The robbery was reported to have taken place near the Half Way House on the road to Hampstead. Two soldiers, Benjamin and Francis Brightwell, were charged with the offence and tried at the same sessions as John Sheppard, but were acquitted after providing alibis and bringing a number of character witnesses, including William Hughes, a clergyman, who said of Francis, 'there was not such another Granadier [Grenadier] in the Universe, he carrying a large Share of exquisite Learning under his Granadiers Cap.' It was later reported of Francis that the allegation 'broke his Heart', and he died a week after the trial: *Parker's London News*, 29 July 1724, 31 July 1724; OBSP, 12–14 August 1724; *Daily Journal*, 21 September 1724 (which also mentions Sheppard's 'confession' of the offence to Wagstaffe).

18 *The Original London Post, or Heathcote's Intelligencer*, 27 July 1724. Quilt Arnold (*History of the Lives and Actions of Jonathan Wild*, p. 114) and his wife

themselves had been on trial at the Old Bailey in 1723, and, although he was acquitted, she was sentenced to transportation: OBSP, 16–18 October 1723. Jonathan Wild was a receiver of goods and a gang leader, who, playing both sides, also collected rewards offered for the capture of certain criminals: Howson, *Thief-taker General*.

19 See OBSP, 12–14 August 1724, which seems to have been the source of this account of the trial. For more detail of the Kneebone charge see OBSP, 14–21 October 1724, trial of Blake.

20 A ken is slang for a house.

21 James Harman and John Davis had been convicted of highway robbery in July and were hanged on 28 August: *Daily Journal* 11 July 1724, 29 August 1724, 31 August 1724.

22 Prisoners were handed over by the Newgate officers in the Press Yard of the prison. Their fetters were removed, their arms were tied and a halter placed around their necks. They were then put into the cart and taken to Tyburn.

23 Joseph Ward had been condemned for three robberies and Anthony Upton for a burglary, and both were hanged on 4 September: OBSP, 12–14 August 1724; *Daily Post* 5 September 1724.

24 Fowles had been condemned for shoplifting: OBSP, 12–14 August 1724.

25 Spitalfields.

26 For reports of Sheppard's escape see *Daily Journal*, 1 September 1724, 2 September 1724; *Evening Post* 1 September 1724; *Parker's London News*, 2 September 1724, 4 September 1724; *Weekly Journal, or British Gazetteer*, 5 September 1724; *British Journal*, 5 September 1724. For the advertisement offering a reward for Sheppard's recapture see *Daily Post*, 4 September 1724; *Daily Journal*, 4 September 1724; *Evening Post*, 10 September 1724.

27 Thomas Martin advertised for information about the theft which took place on 8 September: *Daily Post*, 10 September 1724. See *Parker's London News*, 11 September 1724; *The London Journal*, 12 September 1724; *Weekly Journal, or British Gazetteer*, 12 September 1724; *Daily Journal*, 14 September 1724; OBSP, 4–9 December 1724, trial of Page.

28 At Page's trial, Ireton said that on the night of the theft from Martin's shop he had lost a handkerchief and had accused William Page, who happened to be standing nearby; Page denied any knowledge of the matter, but told him that Sheppard was in the area. Ireton gave chase in vain, Sheppard having hidden under a coach: OBSP, 4–9 December 1724; *History of the Lives and Actions of Jonathan Wild*, p. 119.

29 A small prison in which arrested persons were held temporarily.

30 According to newspaper reports, which described her as Sheppard's wife, Lyon was arrested on 1 September, the day after his escape: *Daily Journal*, 3 September 1724; *Daily Post*, 3 September 1724; *Weekly Journal or British Gazetteer*, 5 September 1724; see note 65.

31 It was regarded as useful for someone seeking mercy to obtain the support of the victim.

32 See *Daily Post*, 11 September 1724; *Daily Journal*, 11 September 1724; *Evening Post*, 10 September 1724, 12 September 1724; *Parker's London Weekly*, 11 September 1724, 14 September 1724; *The London Journal*, 12 September 1724; *Weekly Journal or British Gazetteer*, 12 September 1724; *British Journal*, 12 September 1724; OBSP, 4–9 September 1724, trial of Page.

33 Possibly Stourbridge.

34 The newspapers were in some confusion over what was to be done with Sheppard. Initially, it was reported by the *Weekly Journal, or British Gazetteer* that he could not be hanged because the Recorder, Sir William Thompson, and

his Deputy, Mr Sergeant Ragby, whose warrant was needed, were absent in Bath. The *Daily Journal* said that the warrant had to come from Windsor where the King was staying, and that a messenger had been sent there in order to obtain 'his Speedy Execution', with Monday 14 September being put forward as the likely date, although later the same newspaper said there would be some delay because the warrant had to be signed in Middlesex. It was then reported that there would be a delay not because of the absence of officials, but because formal proof of Sheppard's identity had to be made in court: *Weekly Journal or British Gazetteer*, 19 September 1724, 26 September 1724; *Daily Journal*, 11 September 1724; 21 September 1724.

35 See *Daily Journal*, 11 September 1724, 14 September 1724, 21 September 1724.

36 According to *Daily Journal*, 12 September 1724 (also *London Journal*, 19 September 1724), a file was found in a Bible by the keepers on 12 September, although others (*Evening Post*, 15 September 1724; *Parker's London News, or the Impartial Intelligencer*, 16 September 1724) report Wagstaff as having found it and that it was given him by his brother, Thomas. For the discoveries on 16 September see *Daily Journal*, 17 September 1724, in which it is said that, 'when he perceiv'd his last Effort to escape thus discovered and frustrated, his wicked and obdurate Heart began to relent, and he shed abundance of Tears' (also *Evening Post*, 17 September 1724).

37 According to *A Narrative ... of John Sheppard*, pp. 5–6, the public house was the Black Lyon Ale-house in Drury Lane and was owned by Joseph Hind. Lewkenhor's or Lewkener's or Lutenor's or Newtoner's Lane was just off Drury Lane: see *The Life and Actions of James Dalton*.

38 That is, like Quilt Arnold, an employee of Jonathan Wild, the thief-taker.

39 Since anything above a bare minimum – and sometimes even that – had to be purchased, prisoners depended to a large extent on various charities and gifts from friends, relatives and visitors. See Harding *et al.*, *Imprisonment in England and Wales*.

40 Published in *Daily Journal*, 4 September 1724; *Weekly Journal, or British Gazetteer*, 5 September 1724; *Parker's London News, or the Impartial Intelligencer*, 7 September 1724. For other such 'letters' see *Daily Journal*, 7 September 1724, 30 October 1724; *Applebee's Original Weekly Journal*, 31 October 1724; *Weekly Journal, or British Gazetteer*, 24 October 1724, 31 October 1724, 14 November 1724; *Parker's London News, or Impartial Intelligencer*, 14 September 1724, 2 November 1724, 11 November 1724. 'App-ee' is Applebee, the publisher.

41 *Daily Journal*, 14 October 1724. Generally, see A.R. Ekrich, *Bound for America: the Transportation of British Convicts to the Colonies, 1718–75*, Oxford, 1987.

42 In many respects this resembles the report in the *Daily Journal*, 9 October 1724 (see also *Evening Post*, 10 October 1724), although according to that the attempted escape took place on 7 October. See also *Parker's London News, or the Impartial Intelligencer*, 12 October 1724.

43 Wild did recover, only to be hanged in the following year: *Daily Post*, 3 October 1724, 15 October 1724; *Daily Journal*, 3 October 1724, 5 October 1724, 7 October 1724, 15 October 1724, 19 October 1724, 22 October 1724; OBSP, 14–21 October 1724, 13–15 May 1725; Howson, *Thief-taker General*.

44 It seems that the attempted escape took place on 9 October.

45 *A Narrative ... of John Sheppard*, pp. 19–29; *Evening Post*, 17 October 1724; *Daily Journal*, 17 October 1724; *Daily Post*, 17 October 1724; *Weekly Journal, or British Gazetteer*, 17 October 1724; *Weekly Journal, or Saturday's Post*, 17 October 1724, 24 October 1724; *British Journal*, 17 October 1724; *London Journal*, 17 October 1724, 24 October 1724.

46 This, presumably, prompted the offer of a reward of twenty guineas: *Daily Post*,

20 October 1724; *Daily Journal*, 20 October 1724. Gaol keepers were liable to prosecution if their prisoners escaped. William Pitt, the Keeper of Newgate (1707–32), must have been particularly sensitive about escapes. He had been suspended in 1717 following the escape of some Jacobite prisoners and, although he was acquitted and reinstated, complaints about him persisted for the rest of his period in office. In July 1724 the Keepers were fined £50 for allowing an escape. GLRO, MJ/SBB/823/1724 July, p. 68; Sheehan, *The London Prison System, 1666–1795*, pp. 204–10 and chapter IX.

47 *The History of the Press Yard: Or, a Brief Account of the Customs and Occurrences that are put in Practice, and to be met with in that Antient Repository of Living Bodies, called, His Majesty's Gaol of Newgate in London*, London, 1717.

48 Newgate prisoners were put in either the Common-Side or the Master's Side; which it was depended on their ability to pay.

49 OBSP, 14–21 October 1724.

50 James Figg (died 1734) taught boxing and fighting techniques at his academy in Marylebone Fields, and advertised regularly in the newspapers; Hogarth designed an advertising card for him. It was reported that Figg provided Sheppard with wine in Newgate on the day of his death: *Dictionary of National Biography*; *Parker's London News, or the Impartial Intelligencer*, 18 November 1724.

51 An Act of Grace was a free and general pardon occasionally given by Act of Parliament to whole categories of prisoners. Such a statute might be passed, for instance, on the coronation of a monarch or the birth of an heir to the throne.

52 Showy, but worthless people.

53 This 'letter' is chiefly concerned with making puns on names of places in London.

54 Fees were paid by prisoners to gaolers before their release.

55 Fleet Prison, a prison for debtors.

56 Thomas Huggins, or Bainbridge, or Bambridge was the Warden of the Fleet Prison in the 1720s. At the end of the decade he was accused of cruelty and tried for murdering a prisoner; it was his activities that led to a Parliamentary inquiry into the debtors' prisons: see Harding *et al.*, *Imprisonment in England and Wales*.

57 A large house of correction in London (a prison for petty offenders).

58 One who provides violent support for another in pursuit of some criminal act.

59 A pun on Chancery Lane.

60 To thrash soundly.

61 Mum was a beer originally brewed in Brunswick; geneva was another word for gin.

62 A play on pell-mell and Pall Mall.

63 This last phrase probably means the waterman promised not to give him away.

64 Route.

65 Sheppard was recaptured at about midnight on Saturday 31 October 1724, after having been seen drinking brandy in a shop (according to one report he was in a chandler's shop owned by a Mrs Campbell, drinking with someone called Nicks, a Drury Lane butcher, although elsewhere it is said that he was seen in a butcher's shop near Newtoner's Lane (see note 37) – before he went into a brandy shop with a woman referred to as Frisky Moll) by a boy described as 'belonging to Mr. Bradford, a Headborough in Drury Lane'. Sheppard was taken on 10 November 1724 to the Court of King's Bench where he was formally identified and the sentence of death was confirmed. He was hanged on the following Monday, 16 November, 'and died with much Difficulty' (hanging, being by strangulation, sometimes took a long time). It was said that Applebee provided a hearse for the corpse, but the crowd, thinking that the employees of the surgeons were trying to take his body for anatomy lessons, rioted and it was

only after the military intervened that he was buried. The advertised reward of twenty guineas for Sheppard's recapture was paid on 14 November. Lyon was held in the Compter prison, from the time of her arrest in October, after Sheppard's first escape from Newgate, until late December 1724 when she was released. She was eventually transported in 1726 to Maryland for housebreaking; the report of the trial referred to her as a 'Relict of the memorable *Jack Sheppard*'. Page was convicted in December 1724 at the Old Bailey and transported to the Rappahannock River in Virginia in 1725 for his part in the thefts from Martin's shop and for helping Sheppard after his escape. See *Daily Journal*, 21 October 1724, 2 November 1724, 9 November 1724, 11 November 1724, 12 November 1724, 13 November 1724, 17 November 1724, 18 November 1724, 10 December 1724; *Daily Post*, 2 November 1724, 9 November 1724, 11 November 1724, 16 November 1724, 17 November 1724, 18 November 1724; *Evening Post*, 3 November 1724, 10 November 1724, 12 November 1724, 17 November 1724, 19 November 1724; *Weekly Journal, or British Gazetteer*, 7 November 1724; *British Journal*, 7 November 1724, 14 November 1724, 21 November 1724; *Parker's London News, or the Impartial Intelligencer*, 4 November 1724, 18 November 1724, 20 November 1724; *London Journal*, 7 November 1724, 21 November 1724; *A Narrative . . . of John Sheppard*; *Authentic Memoirs of the Life and Surprising Adventures of John Sheppard*; OBSP, 4–7 December 1724; OBSP, 2–7 March 1726; Coldham, *English Convicts*, vols I, p. 112, II, p. 239.

II

THE LIFE AND ACTIONS OF JAMES DALTON (1730)

3

INTRODUCTION

James Dalton was, according to this biography, born in 1700; he was hanged
at Tyburn in 1730. The only physical description we have of him is that,
during the last year of his life, he was said to have been 'a little Man'.[1] The
lives of James Dalton and John Sheppard were connected through Jonathan
Wild, the thief-taker and thief-organizer, and his 'creatures', most notably
William Field, the petty criminal and informer, who survived Wild and who
appears in both biographies. From 1720 to 1730 Dalton made perhaps as
many as six appearances at the Old Bailey, either as a defendant or, to avoid
prosecution, as a witness for the Crown. But it was in 1728 that he gained
real notoriety when he escaped prosecution by informing against a large
number of his comrades – some contemporaries said it was as many as
twelve – and by appearing as the chief witness at the trials of six of them.
This biography says that he went abroad soon afterwards in order to escape
vengeance. In any event he was back in England by, probably, late 1729,
and was soon in prison again, this time for an attempted robbery on the
famous physician, Dr Mead. He was sentenced in 1730 to a prison-term for
that offence, but shortly afterwards he was tried, condemned and hanged
for robbing John Waller. However, there was some doubt as to whether
this offence actually took place, and, indeed, Waller was later convicted of
bringing false charges of robbery against others in order to obtain the
large rewards offered. Waller may have worked on his own, but it is
tempting to speculate that those who had seen Dalton escape in 1728 at the
expense of their friends or relatives, approved of, and maybe even assisted
in, the prosecution. Certainly, an unknown woman had thrown a bottle at
him when he was on trial for attempting to rob Mead.

The Life and Actions of James Dalton was published against the background of an apparent belief in the late 1720s that crime was rapidly
increasing. Although there seem rarely to have been any periods in history
when crime was not thought to be on the increase, there was at this time a
more vivid expression of this fear than was normal in newspapers and
pamphlets. Some, perhaps only partly in jest, linked this situation to the
death of Jonathan Wild, who had been hanged in 1725:

Then you'll repent, too late then in vain
Will you wish to have your *Jonathan* again!

Wild had pleased those whose property had been stolen by restoring it to them through his connections with criminals. Moreover, through those same connections, he had provided the gallows with the steady flow of victims that was so important to a criminal justice system which had only a primitive police force and which, therefore, relied on the deterrent effects of a carefully stage-managed and public hanging.[2] But, whatever the cause of the concern over crime, the situation led the government to issue a proclamation in 1728 offering a large reward for the conviction of London street robbers. It seems likely that the gang of which Dalton was a member was responsible for a series of robberies early in that year which, because their victims included leading figures such as the financier Sir Gilbert Heathcote, may have been the immediate trigger for the proclamation. The gang was quickly broken up, partly as a result of Dalton's assistance to the authorities, and in May 1728 Dalton's fame was assured when an 'autobiography' was published titled, *A Genuine Narrative of all the Street Robberies Committed since October last, by James Dalton.*

So it was that when *The Life and Actions of James Dalton* appeared two years later in 1730, it built on the existing image of Dalton as a notorious robber. Not surprisingly, the events of 1728 are of central importance, but the impeachments, which gave Dalton his notoriety, are dealt with in an interesting way. Although the information he gave to the authorities and the trials in which he was the star witness were major events in his life, they are passed over fairly quickly. Even when they are mentioned their importance is played down and Dalton's role in them is justified. So, the biography has Dalton declaring that, 'for the Preservation of my own Life, [I] was obliged to turn Evidence', adding that, although six were hanged as a result, 'I protest that they were every one guilty of the Crimes they suffered for'. The biography then tries to turn Dalton into something of a hero by noting that, although he was pressured by thief-takers, he refused to give false evidence against Richard Nicholls. On the other hand, this mood is not allowed to dominate too much, for at the end of the same paragraph the biography has him complaining that although he should have received £840 in rewards for convicting six robbers, he got only £40.

Like the Sheppard biography, *The Life and Actions of James Dalton* maintains some sense of time passing and of geographical location. The bulk of the action described in the biography takes place within a fairly restricted area just north of the Thames, around West Smithfield and High Holborn. However, interspersed with this sense of confinement are incidents in which the horizons become global as he travels – generally following a criminal conviction – to Spain, Portugal, Holland, the West Indies and the North American colonies. These parts of the biography broaden the range of exciting incidents beyond crime and into adventures of travel, mutiny and escape. At the same time, they connect with contemporary concerns about transportation, which had become a common form of punishment after the passing of the Transportation Act in 1718. It was devised as an alternative to hanging, which was thought to be too severe for petty offences, and whipping, which was thought to be too lenient.[3] However, transportation was hidden from the public view, so that, like imprisonment, it fitted uneasily into a criminal justice system whose other main forms of punishment for serious crime – hanging, whipping and the pillory – relied heavily on their roles as public spectacles. *The Life and Actions of James Dalton* implicitly raises doubts about transportation: the lack of a punitive regime in the colonies; the apparent ease with which offenders returned from transportation before the term had expired; and the failure of the criminal justice system to identify those who returned.

The biography also implicitly raises questions about the way in which the criminal justice system relied on criminals. Wild was dead, but nothing seemed to have changed. It appeared that people, like Dalton, could commit a series of robberies over a number of years with impunity, in spite of being known to the authorities and appearing in court on numerous occasions, because they were aware that their information was of great value to a system which lacked any formally organized police structure and could, therefore, be used as a bargaining counter if ever they were arrested. Similarly, the role of Field showed how the criminal justice system was dependent on the input of people who simultaneously worked on both sides of the criminal law and who could not only ensure their freedom from prosecution, but, like Wild, could also make money out of the rewards offered. All of this begged questions about the organization of a state in which a corrupt criminal justice system played such an important role. Moreover, a system which depended on such fundamentally uncertain methods of detection provided little protection for people as they travelled about London. This does not mean that any solutions are hinted at, or even that the problem is clearly enunciated. Paradoxical it may have been, but this state of affairs was, it seemed, the only option. Certainly, the idea of a more efficiently organized police force – if, indeed, that is any sort of solution to crime – was not on the agenda.

As has been indicated in the introduction to *The History Of the remarkable Life of John Sheppard* (pp. 39–43), criminal biographies were not solely concerned with crime. The criminal incidents often provided the medium through which other issues were raised, such as the role of women and the relationship between different social classes. There are more women in Dalton's biography than in that of Sheppard, but, at first sight, they seem to play a less important role. Some of the women are treated as luxury goods, on which, when it is available, money is spent in much the same way as it might be on drink. But, unlike the situation in *The History Of the remarkable Life of John Sheppard*, these women do not seem to have been the reason why Dalton turned to crime in the first place. Indeed it is only after he begins to steal as a child that he consorts with 'Prostitutes' or 'Lewd Women'. However, having met such women he spends all his money on them: so, for instance, Dalton remarks that, after leaving home with money stolen from his father-in-law in his pocket, '[I] then falling in Company with two ill Women, I soon spent all the Money'; similarly, in *A Genuine Narrative . . . James Dalton* (1728) it was said that, 'All the money they got by these practices [street robbery] was spent among the common women of the town'. The implication is that further crime is required to feed his carnal desires which are both too expensive and time-consuming to be supplied by 'honest' work. Moreover, this view of 'lewd women' as addictive fits in not only with the presentation in the Sheppard biography, but also with other biographies, causing one commentator to remark, some years later, that, 'Every Robber, at least the most notorious [obtains money through crime] to spend it in *Debauchery*'.[4] *The Life and Actions of James Dalton* also introduces another type of woman, who is, nevertheless, analogous to Lyon. Ann, or Hannah, Britton, the receiver of stolen goods, is independent and in control of her relationship with Dalton. For instance, Dalton and Speedman steal a barrel of anchovies and give them to Britton; they then go out to commit a robbery and on returning order some of the anchovies for supper. To Dalton's disgust, she charges them a penny each, but they agree to pay. Later, it is on Britton's instructions that they turn to housebreaking.

In the eighteenth century the receiver was regarded as occupying a position of importance in the structure of criminal enterprise. It was commonplace to argue that without receivers there could be no crime,[5] and Britton's role supports this view. At the same time, people who acted as receivers in such biographies were typically those regarded as marginal, such as Jews and independent women. So, as in the biography of Sheppard, women acquire power by stepping outside what is taken to be the natural order, in which women are subordinate to, and dependent upon, men. As a result of its 'unnatural' origins, the power acquired by such women through their independence from men is depicted as producing evil results. In the Dalton biography a third type of woman appears, namely, those whom he marries. In his relationships with his wives he is very much in control, and, typically, the marriage is a means used by him to exploit the women for his own short-term gratification or gain. For instance, he agrees, in exchange for two guineas, to marry his first wife on the understanding that the arrangement is solely for the purpose of legitimating the baby she is carrying; he uses the situation to rape her and probably infect her with 'the Foul Disease'. On another occasion, he marries a woman in America, but leaves her as soon as her fortune is spent. Yet, although his treatment of these women may have been regarded as unpleasant by some contemporary readers, it was also just an extension of what was the legally and socially acceptable relationship between husbands and wives.

BIBLIOGRAPHICAL NOTES

The publication date of *The Life and Actions of James Dalton* is uncertain. It may be the work advertised in the *Daily Journal* on 15 May 1730 as 'The Letter that James Dalton delivered at Tyburn to Mr. Walker last Thursday, relating to the Informing Constables', although if it is, then apart from some comments in the last paragraph, the biography fails to live up to its advertisement.

Other biographies: *A Genuine Narrative of all the Street Robberies Committed since October last, by James Dalton, And his Accomplices, Who are now in Newgate, to be try'd next Sessions, and against whom, Dalton (call'd their Captain) is admitted on an Evidence. Shewing I. The Manner of their snatching off Women's Pockets; with Directions for the Sex in general how to wear them, so that they cannot be taken by any Robber whatsover. II. The Method they took to rob the Coaches, and the many diverting Scenes they met with while they follow'd those dangerous Enterprizes. III. Some merry Stories of Dalton's biting the Women of the Town, his detecting and exposing the Mollies, and a Song which is sung at the Molly-Clubs: With other very pleasant and remarkable Adventures. To which is added, A key to the Canting Language, occasionally made Use of in this Narrative. Taken from the Mouth of James Dalton*, London, J. Roberts, 1728. This was probably published in early May 1728 (*Mist's Weekly Journal*, 4 May 1728; *The Country Journal, or the Craftsman*, 4 May 1728). It has nothing on Dalton's early life; instead it goes straight into an attack on *The Life of Martin Bellamy*, alleging that Bellamy was not a member of the Dalton gang. Presumably, this criticism was provoked by the possibility of *The Life of Martin Bellamy* affecting sales. Many of the robberies it mentions are also in *The Life and Actions of James Dalton*, but since the descriptions given are often quite different, it seems unlikely that it was a source.

The Life of Martin Bellamy; with an Account Of all the several Robberies, Burglaries, Forgeries, and other Crimes by him Committed, Also the Method practised by himself, and his Companions, in the Perpetration thereof. Necessary to be perus'd by all Persons, in order to prevent their being Robb'd for the future. Dictated by himself in Newgate, and Publish'd at his Request, for the Benefit of the Publick, London, J. Applebee, [1728]. Bellamy was hanged on 24 March 1728. He may well have tipped off the authorities as to the whereabouts of Dalton in 1728. This biography lists several robberies mentioned in the biographies of Dalton. It alleges that Bellamy was induced into making a confession to a newspaper because he was led to believe that the journalist was actually a government official authorized to offer him immunity from prosecution in exchange for information. The result of making the confession, which then appeared in various newspapers, was that the authorities were under no necessity to make any deal with Bellamy, and he was tried and hanged (*Daily Journal*, 26 February 1728; *Mist's Weekly Journal*, 2 March 1728; *The Gloucester Journal*, 5 March 1728).

The Life and Infamous Actions Of that Perjur'd Villain John Waller, Who made his Exit in the Pillory, at the Seven-Dials, on Tuesday, the 13th Day of this Instant June: London, W. James, 1732. See p. 108 note 52.

NOTES

1 OBSP, 16–20 January 1730.
2 On Wild see *England's Ingratitude: or Jonathan Wild's Complaint*, Dublin, 1725;

generally, see Ordinary of Newgate's *Account*, 24 May 1725; G. Howson, *Thief-taker General: The Rise and Fall of Jonathan Wild*, London, 1970. For an illuminating, if controversial view, of the eighteenth-century criminal justice system and its place within the structures of power: D. Hay, 'Property, authority and the criminal law' in D. Hay, E.P. Thompson and P. Linebaugh (eds), *Albion's Fatal Tree: Crime and Society in Eighteenth-Century England*, Harmondsworth, 1977.

3 J.M. Beattie, *Crime and the Courts 1660–1800*, Oxford, 1986, pp. 500–13.

4 Philo-Patria, *A Letter to Henry Fielding, Esq; Occasioned by his Enquiry into the Causes of the late Increase of Robbers, &c.*, London, [1751?], p. 7. See also *Tyburn's Worthies, or, the Robberies and Enterprizes of John Hawkins, and George Simpson, Lately Executed for Robbing the Bristol-Mail*, London, [1722], p. 15; *An authentick Account of the Life of Paul Wells, Gent, who was Executed at Oxford, Sept. 1, 1749, for Forgery*, London, 2nd edn, 1749, pp. 8–9; Rev. L. Howard, *A True and Impartial Account of the Behaviour, Confession, and Dying Words of the four Malefactors, Who were executed at Kennington-Common, on Friday, Sept. 6, 1751*, London, [1751], p. 11.

5 See, for example, H. Fielding, *An Enquiry into the causes of The Late Increase of Robbers, &c.*, London, 1751.

4

THE

LIFE AND ACTIONS

OF

JAMES DALTON,

(The noted Street-Robber.)

containing

All the Robberies and other Villanies committed by him, both alone and
in Company, from his Infancy down to
his Assault on Dr. *Mead.*

WITH

A particular Account of his Running away with the Ship when he was
first Transported; and likewise of the
Tricks he play'd in the *West-Indies.*

As taken from his own Mouth in his Cell
in *Newgate.*

LONDON;

Printed and sold by R. WALKER, next
Door to the *Elephant* and *Castle*, without
Temple-Bar.

(Price One Shilling.)

TO THE
READER.

THINGS of this Nature being generally pyrated, or false and spurious Ones impos'd upon the Publick, I thought it proper to let the World know, that this is the true and exact Account of my Life, which I have done to the utmost of my Memory: And notwithstanding several Persons, since my Condemnation, have been with me, endeavouring to obtain it from me, [p. iv] I solemnly declare that I have deliver'd it to none, nor any part of it, except to Mr. ROBERT WALKER, and for which I have received full Satisfaction.

From my Cell in New-
gate, May 1, 1730.
    Witness my Hand,
        James Dalton.

[p. 5]

THE
LIFE AND ACTIONS
OF
JAMES DALTON.

I was born in *Cow-Cross*, in the Parish of St. *Sepulchres*, in the Year 1700. My Parents were Persons in very indifferent Circumstances, and suffered under very great Misfortunes (whether equal to their Deserts I am not a Judge) that are not proper for me to mention.

Before their own Misfortunes, they put me to School to Mr. *Cumberland* in *Cow-Lane*, and I being very unruly, my Master turn'd me out of the School; and then they put me to Mr. *Groves* in St. *John's-Lane*, where I behaved myself very decent for a considerable time. After I left Mr. *Groves*, I [p. 6] went to School to Mr. *Bingley* in *Fleet-Lane*, and remained in all at School about six Years.

While I was at Mr. *Bingley*'s, I broke open the Maid's Box, and took out some Money; and it being dark I could not discern whether it was Gold, Silver, or Half-pence; but this Fact was soon found out, for I went immediately up to School, and sent one of my School-Fellows down to my Mistress (who kept a Chandler's Shop) for a Rowl[1] and Butter, and not minding the Money, gave him a Guinea and a Shilling instead of two Half-pence.

When I came to the Age of Eleven I got acquainted with several Butchers Apprentices, who carried me into the Company of Prostitutes; and one Day in particular I and two more of my Companions made an Agreement with three Whores to go to an Inn in the Evening and lie all Night, to which they consented, and some body at the Inn knowing us, went and acquainted my Parents and my Companions Masters of our being in Bed with three Women, who came immediately and charged a Constable with us, in order to send us all to *New-Prison*, but I had the good Fortune to make my Escape in our Journey thither.

My own Father having at this Time been executed some while, my Mother married a Butcher, and I went to live with my Father-in-Law to learn his Trade. [p. 7] They took a House in *Red Lyon Ally* in *Cow-Cross*, and kept a common Slaughter-House; and one Mr. *Bonnil* rented a Room in the House, and he keeping his Money in a Scrutore² in his own Room, I found means to procure a Key that fitted the Lock, and went Partners with him about a Year before any Discovery was made. He mistrusted his Wife, and was minded (as he often said) to have murder'd her, imagining that she kept Company with other Men, and that she stole the Money to support her Extravagances; but upon his Wife's assuring him to the contrary, and adding, at the same time, that she had a Mistrust of me, he resolved to lay a Trap to catch me in, which had its desired Effect, for he and I being in a Skittle-Ground at Play, I lost all my Money, and going to my old Bank I found Thirty Shillings, and it being put altogether I only took the upper Shilling, which was a Queen *Anne*'s, and which Mr. *Bonnil* had put their on purpose and marked it; then I going into the Skittle-Ground, laid a Bet with Mr. *Bonnil*, which I lost; and when I went to pay him, he discover'd the Shilling, and went home to satisfy himself; finding it to be his, he came back into the Skittle-Ground and seized me; but my Mother made him Satisfaction, and so that Affair ended.

Some Time after, this piece of Roguery reaching the Ears of my Father in Law, he and I parted; and an old Acquaintance of mine, that first carried me into the [p. 8] Company of Lewd Women, persuaded me to go and live with him at his Mother's, which I did; and his Mother desiring me one Day to go of an Errand for her to Mr. *Scott*'s a Butcher, near *Smithfield* Bars, I went accordingly, and there stole a Silver-Spoon. I was not in the least suspected, and I often urged to Mr. *Scott* that it must be some of his own Servants, which caused him to have a Suspition of one of his Men, who they used to call *Tata*. The Fellow was taxed with it when I was present, and I was very pressing on him to make a Confession, but he persisting in his Innocence, the Affair was dropt, and no discovery was ever made.

Some short Time after this I went and lived with one Mr. *Carter*, a Hog-Merchant, where I remained several Months; but the Work being too hard for me, my Mind being fixed for a lazy Life, I came to my Mother, who took me and concealed me from my Father-in-Law; but some of the Neighbours informing him that I was in the House, he came one Morning into the Room where I lay before I was out of Bed, and bid me depart both his House and his Sight, and then went down Stairs into the Kitchen; upon which I dressed myself, and going down Stairs, I found his Bed Room Door open, and knowing the Drawer in which he kept his Money, I broke it open, and took out five Guineas and five Gold Rings, and so marched off, then falling in Company with two ill [p. 9] Women, I soon spent all the Money and made away with the Rings: After this I betook myself to live by my Wits; I first went into *Fleetstreet* to pick Pockets, but that not furnishing me with a sufficient Supply for myself and my two Wives, I went on the *Sneak*,³ and then I went and Lodged at one *Oakey*'s, who was accounted a famous Thief; and he being apprehended for a Robbery, and sent to Goal, I used to turn out and made Collections to support us all three, and lay every Night with his Wife.

Soon after this I ingratiated myself into the Company of one Mrs. *Blauke*, that kept an Ale-House in *Golden-Lane*, at whose House *Samuel Fulsome*, and *William Field*,[4] (formerly Evidence against the famous *Jack Sheppard*, and *Blueskin*,[5] who were both executed) resorted. Mrs. *Blauke* had five Daughters, four of which I was too familiar with. *Fulsome*, *Field* and I soon after our acquaintance discovered our Inclinations one to another, and went out with an Intent to steal; and *Field*, being the most expert Thief, he went into a Stocking Shop in the *Old-Baily*, and the People being backwards, brought out a large Parcel of Stockings, which he afterwards sold, and kept most of the Money himself.

The next Night, as *Field*, *Fulsome* and I were going cross *West Smithfield*, an old Man was crying *Shrewsbury-Puddings*; we [p. 10] went up to him and knocked him down, then led his Horse to the end of *Long-Lane*, where we took the Puddings out of the Basket and throwed them away, Pans and all, and sent the Horse to the Green-Yard; but the Man soon found out *Field*, and obtained a Warrant against him; so that the Money he got by the Stockings the Night before was expended in satisfying the old Pudding Man.

After this we took to robing the *Cloisters*; and being all three in Company, one Night stole twelve Dozen of Handkerchiefs, which we afterwards sold to one *Ann Britton*,[6] that kept a House in *Lewkener's-Lane*, near *Drury-Lane*.[7] Mrs. *Britton* pretended to have a great Respect for me, and by persuasion I quitted my old Lodging, and took up a new one in her House; and then *Field* took an Opportunity of quarrelling with *Fulsome* and I, whereupon we parted.

Fulsome and I meeting one Night, soon after our Quarrel with *Field*, we agreed to pay our Visits to the Inhabitants in the *Cloisters*, with whom we dealt for several large Parcels of Goods. One Night in particular I happened to see a Maid-Servant coming out of one of the Houses with a Pot in her Hands, and as soon as she had quitted the Door, I lifted up the Latch and went in, and the first thing I laid my Hands on, was a Piece of Yard-wide Stuff,[8] which I handed to *Fulsome*, and he made off with it; then [p. 11] I loaded myself with several Pieces of divers sorts of Silk, and made my Escape before the Maid returned. The Booty that I brought away with me, which I afterwards sold for 15 *l.* I concealed from my Companion; but had both the Honesty and Conscience to partake of the Booty that he carried off.

With this Money I purchased me a Suit of Clothes, and got acquainted with a Person that procured Husbands for unfortunate young Women. He told me that he had one at that Time, that was a Gentleman's Daughter who lived in very good Repute, and that being big with Child, her Friends would not admit her into their Presence without the Sight of a Certificate; and that if I would only take the Trouble to go to Church and marry her, he would give me two Guineas for my Trouble; and upon my agreeing with his Desire, he sent for the Gentlewoman, and we went to St. *Clement*'s Church in the *Strand*, and were there married, my Acquaintance the Procuror performing the Part of the Father: After this we adjourned to the Tavern, where I was very handsomely entertained; and the Wine getting Influence over my Brains, I insisted on lying all Night with my Wife: A great many Arguments were made use of to persuade me to the contrary, but to no purpose; upon which a Quarrel ensued, and the Landlord coming to know the Reason of the Disturbance, I related the whole Affair to him; he immediately quitted the Room, and sent [p. 12] to the Church to know the Truth, which he was soon inform'd of; wherefore he took my part; and one of his Servants called a Coach, and my Wife and I went to the *Bell-Inn* in *West-Smithfield*, where we lay together all Night. One Thing made me somewhat uneasy when I awoke the next Morning sober, and that was, I had the Foul Disease, which I knew must in all Likelihood be communicated to her, therefore I arose and left her to pay for our Night's Lodging.

A few Days after this, I met with *Fulsome*, who informed me that *Field* was apprehended for a Robbery, and committed to *Newgate*, and had made an Information against us; whereupon we took private Lodgings, and seldom came out in the Day time; but in an Evening, as soon as it was dark, we used to go out, in order to rob any body we met in the Streets; and one Night in particular we met with a Captain of the Foot-Guards in the Broad Way of St. *Giles's*; I went up to him and bid him deliver his Watch, Money, Rings, &c. but he making Resistance, my Companion *Fulsome* came up and knock'd him down, then I rifled him, taking from him seven Guineas and some Silver, a Leaden Shilling, his Watch, Pocket Book (in which were several Bank-Notes) Sword, Hat and Wigg, and then left him. The Pocket-Book and Notes we burnt for fear of being discovered.[9] The Watch and seven Guineas I concealed from my Companion, but the Silver, Hat, Wigg and Sword, we shared between us.

[p. 13]My Fellowman *Fulsome* being informed that several Persons were in pursuit of him, concealed himself from me, and went and worked privately at his own Trade, which was a Shoemaker; and then I got acquainted with one *Thomas Lambert*, who agreed to go a Snatching of Pockets in the Streets with me; and accordingly at Night we went into *Holbourn*, and he fixed his Eye upon a Woman, we followed her into *Warwick-Court*, where we pushed her down, and I pretending to lift her up again, stole away her Pocket, in which was a Gold Chain and some Silver; and the same Evening coming down *Holbourn* Hill we met another Woman whom I pushed against, in the Interim Snatched her Pocket off, which we never looked into till we went home to my Lodgings, and there I found a Gold Watch, Chain and Tweezer-Case and twenty three Guineas. We sold the Gold Watch, and Tweezer-Case, for twenty one Pounds; and going home to *Lambert's* to make our selves merry, his Wife told me that she had a Wife in her Eye for me, and sent for her immediately; when she came I looked very much at her, and the more I looked the more I liked; so we were married, *Lambert*, performing both the Ceremoney, and the Part of the Father, and we all lived together.

The next Day after this, one *Benjamin Speedman*[10] came to see *Lambert* and dined with us, he being then just returned from [p. 14] Transportation, and he talked mightily of his former Exploits; we took him with us at Night, and going into *Kingstreet* in *Westminster*, where I found means to get the Key out of the Pin of the Window after the Shop was shut up, in the Night-time I enter'd it, and stole a great Parcel of Stockings and Gloves, which we carried to *Hannah Britton*, and sold them for 8*l.*

The next Day we went to *Monmouth-Street*, and bought *Speedman* some Second Hand Cloaths, and in the Evening went out as usual to seek after Business; and *Speedman* espying a large Cag[11] of Anchovies that a Porter had brought out of an Oyl-Shop, and set it down at the Door while he went in again to fetch his Knot, I run away with it, and carried it to *Hannah Britton*'s, and my Companions both followed me. Then we loaded our Pistols which were but two, and went the same Night into *Covent-Garden*, where we attacked a Gentleman, and rifled him of his Watch, and about 30 *s.* in Money. *Speedman* having a great fancy to the Gentleman's great Coat, would of all things have it by Violence, but I recommended to him to pray the Gentleman to lend him the Coat, and that he would return it the first Time he met him that Way again, upon which modest Application the Gentleman surrendered the Coat. The aforesaid Cag of Anchovies, *Hannah Britton* desired us to make her a Present of, which we did; and when we returned home after robbing the [p. 15] above mentioned Gentleman we had some of them for Supper; which she had the vile Concience to make us pay a Penny a Piece for.

The following Evening we went into *Bloomsbury*, with an Intent to break open a Pawn-Broker's Shop, which *Speedman* had pitched upon in the Day Time; but a Gentleman and his Servant with a Portmantue behind him, passing by in the Interim, we left the Pawnbroker's and attacked them, and took away the Portmantue. We immediately carried it to *Hannah Britton*'s and there opened it, and found in it three dozen of fine Shirts with *Flanders* Lace, two suits of Cloaths, three Tye-Wigs, a pair of Gold Buckles, and divers other Goods, altogether computed worth 100 *l.* We sold the whole Cargo, except two fine Shirts, that we reserved for each of us, to Mrs. *Britton* for 19. *l.* and the next Day, my Fellowman *Speedman* would be married, so *Lambert* was Parson, and I Father and Clark. There were two Ladies of the Town invited to the Wedding, besides *Lambert*'s Wife and mine; and Night being come, and we all both Drunk and Noisy, the Watch came and seized us, and confined us in the *Round-House*[12] for that Night; and the next morning we were carried before the late Justice *Ellis*, who committed the Women to *Tothill-Fields Bridewell*, and discharged my Companions and I. We were very Industrious in our Business of thieving during the short Confinement our Fair-Ones [p. 16] laboured under; and at length, having got a considerable sum of Money, we procured sham Bail, and so got them released.

We spent several Days in sporting and revelling for Joy of having our Wives again; but Money beginning to be a little low with us, my Companions, *Lambert*, *Speedman* and myself went towards *Gray's-Inn*, where we met a Woman with a great Bundle under her Arm, which we supposed to be some Councellor's Linnen, wherefore we stopped her and took it from her, and carried it to *Hannah Britton*'s, and there opened it and found it to be nothing but course Towels. Then we went the same Night into *Lincon's-Inn Fieles*, and there attacked three Men and robbed them of 20 *s*.

We retunred to *Hannah Britton*'s after we had committed this last mentioned Robbery; and she said, that she would advise us to take up a new Class of the thieving Trade, and that was to turn Housebreakers, which we agreed to; and she having provided us with Utensils for that Purpose, we made our first Experiment upon a Stocking Shop in St. *Martins-Lane*, from whence we took a Bag full of Stockings, a Silver Tea-Pot and all the Tea Equipage, with all the Money that was in the Till, and then returned to *Hannah Britton*'s and sold the Stockings to her for one part in five of the Value.

A short Time after this Robbery, our Companion *Lambert* was apprehended and [p. 17] committed to *New-Prison*, and made an Information against *Speedman*, myself, and *Hannah Britton*: She was seized and committed to *Newgate*, and afterwards try'd at the *Old Baily*, and convicted upon *Lambert*'s Evidence, and was sentenc'd to be whipt at the Cart's Tail from *Holborn-Bars* to St. *Giles's Pound*, which Sentence she underwent accordingly. *Speedman* and I made off to *Bristol*; and it being the Time of that Fair, we employ'd ourselves in picking of Pockets; but *Speedman* being drunk one Night, I went and broke into a Shop in the Fair, and stole thence two Gold Rings, and a pair of Silver Buckles, but was taken by the Watch with the Things upon me, for which I was committed to *Newgate* in *Bristol*, where I remained till the next Assizes; and my Prosecutor being a *Londoner* that went down to keep the Fair, he did not appear against me, and so I was discharged.[13]

Speedman came the first five Days of my Confinement to see me; but then growing weary, he declined me and came up to *London*, where he was taken up upon *Lambert*'s Information, and was transported for the second Time.

When I came out of *Bristol* Jail, I immediately fell to my old Trade of snatching of Pockets; and having got a little Money by me, I thought it the best Way to come for *London*; and coming thro' *Brentford* on a Market Day, I cut a Woman's Pocket, and took from her near 18*l*. and then meeting [p. 18] with one *John Mallard*, I sent 10 *l*. to *London* by him, and then bought me a Great Coat and a Pair of Silver Buckles, and made the best of my Way for *London*. As I was coming over *Turnham-Green* I was stopt by two Soldiers, who demanded my Money; I soon began to expostulate the Case with them, telling them, that I was a Member of their Society, and talk'd all the Cant Language I was Master of, but all to no purpose, for they took my Great Coat, Buckles and Money, and then beat me very unmercifully: One of them was for tying me Neck and Heels, and throwing me into a Ditch; but the other not agreeing with him, they went and left me, and I proceeded to *London*, where getting the 10 *l*. that I had sent before by *Mallard*, I equipt myself again.

I had not been in *London* many Days before I met with *John Pendell*[14] and *Fulsome*, who inform'd me that *William Field* was at Liberty again, and so there was nothing to be feared from that Quarter, whereupon we all three agreed to go the next Day to our Business; our first Expedition was to go to *Wetstone* in *Middlesex*, where we arriv'd; and I espying a Parcel of Linnen in a Window, I told my Companions of it, and we soon found means to get it into our own Possession; and then made the best of our Way for *London*; but before we had got half over *Finchly-Common*, a Hue and Cry was sent after us, so we were obliged to leave our Booty behind us.

[p. 19]The Night following *Fulsome*, *Pendall* and I, broke open a Shoemaker's Shop in *Cow-Lane*, and took away all the Shoes both made and unmade; and then carried them to a new Lock that we had found out in *Golden-Lane*, where we had a better Price than what we used to have of *Hannah Britton*.

I frequented this House in *Golden-Lane* for a long while, and one Day as I was at Dinner with the Master and Mistress thereof, two Persons nam'd *Cammill* and *Reeves* came in, and sat down to Dinner with us: As soon as Dinner was over, we discoursed upon our Ways of Living; and I finding which way their Pulses beat, discovered my Inclinations of going on the Highway in the Evening, telling them that I had two Friends (meaning *Pendell* and *Fulsome*) that I expected to meet in the Afternoon, and I believed they would agree with us; but they not coming, what Accident detain'd them I could not devise, we three went by ourselves towards *Windmill-Hill*, near *Moorfields*, and meeting with no body we thought worthy of robbing, we concluded to break open a House, upon which they lifted me over a Wall into the Yard; and the People being forwards, I went round the Yard to the Back-Door, and broke in; and getting into a Room where there was a Bed and Bedding, I made two Load of them from the Room to the Wall, where I got them over to my Companions, who stood ready to receive them, and then we made off un[p. 20]discovered. *Cammill* dealing in Household Goods, *Reeves* and I agreed he should have the whole upon paying us 20 *s.* a Man which he did.

A Short Time after this last Robbery, I went into *Lewkener's-Lane*, to enquire after my old Landlady *Hannah Britton*; and in my return home to *Golden-Lane*, I fixed my Eyes upon a Toy-Shop in *Holbourn* near *Turnstile*, with which I acquainted my Companions *Cammill* and *Reeves*, and at Night we went and broke it open, and rifled the Shop of Goods and Money to the Value of 800*l.* as was soon afterwards inserted in the News-Papers, tho' we did not make above 250*l.* of the Plate, and their was not above 20*l.* in Money.

We lived for about three Months upon the Fruits of this last Exploit without once going out to seek after more, and then it being almost spent, we began to think of getting a fresh Supply, whereupon we resolved to rob in the Fields, and made it our Business to ply at *Lamb's Conduit* for several Nights successively, where among sundry other Robberies, we committed one on two Men coming from *Pancrass*, and another on three Men coming from *Tottenham-Court*. We never shared any of our Booties during the Time we ply'd at *Lamb's-Conduit* till we finished, *Cammill* keeping all at his own Lodgings, and when we had done we shared about 18*l.* and two Watches a Piece; and being one Night a Gaming [p. 21] together at a House in *Chick-Lane*, we quarrelled, and made a great Disturbance, whereupon the Watch and Beadles came and surrounded the House, and I being drunk, pulled out a Pistol and swore I would shoot the Beadle, for which I was carry'd before a Magistrate, and for want of Security was sent to *Woodstreet-Compter*,[15] and remained there 20 Weeks.

As soon as I was discharged from out of the *Compter* I went to Mrs. *Britton*'s House, where I met again with *Pendell* and a Foot Soldier, that lodged with his Wife at *Britton*'s. *Pendell* and I lived very well at that Time only by picking of Pockets; and the Soldier's Pay not being sufficient to support his kind Wife's Ambition, she told him he had better go along with us; so the poor Fellow discover'd the Scene to me that he pass'd between him and his Wife, and said, if we would accept of him for a Companion, he would stop any body; whereupon we agreed to take him with us, and we went out with intent to rob the first Man we met conveniently: We had no Arms with us, except the Soldier's Sword, which he carried under his Coat; and when at the Bottom of *Gray's-Inn Lane* we saw a Man before us, I bid the Soldier draw his Sword, and go up to him and stop him, but his Heart then fail'd him; and the Man suspecting us, took to his Heels and soon got out of our Sight; whereupon I went up to the Soldier, and call'd him a faint-hearted Son of a Wh – –, and took the Sword from him; and then I [p. 22] swore I had a great Mind to cut his Ears off, but he begg'd very hard, and promis'd faithfully to stop the next Man he met. Then we cross'd the Fields and went into *Islington* Road, where we saw a Man crossing the Way with a Candle and Lanthorn in his Hand; the Soldier went up to him and bid him stand and deliver, and then drew the Sword out from under his Coat, and swore he would cut his Throat if he made any Noise; then *Pendell* and I came up and put out the Candle, and we robb'd him of his Coat, which was trim'd with Plate Buttons, and 2*d*. in Money, being all he had. Afterwards we crossed the Fields to *Kentish Town*, where we stopt the *Hampstead* Stage-Coach with four Passengers in it, being one Man and three Women, from the Man we receiv'd about 40 *s*. in Money, and from the Women three Gold Rings, a Gold Chain, and some Money; then it growing late, we came to Town directly.

In a few Days after this I was apprehended on Suspicion of robbing the Man abovementioned in *Islington* Road of his Coat and 2 *d*. and was committed to *Newgate*: This News reaching the Ears of my Companions, the Soldier went quite off, but *Pendell* sent his Friends to me not to be discouraged, who told me if I would not turn Evidence against him, but on the contrary take a Tryal at the *Old-Baily* for the said Robbery, they would procure several People to swear that I was dying in my Bed the very Time the Robbery was committed. I agreed to what [p. 23] they said; and just before my Tryal came on at the *Old-Baily*, I had a Note sent to me with a great many People's Names whom I call'd upon in my Defence. The Prosecutor swore positively to me, but I had such a great Number of Witnesses to appear for me, one of whom personated a Physician, another an Apothecary, and a third a Nurse, besides several others who gave me the Character of an honest, industrious Lad, I was acquitted.

Soon after I was discharged out of *Newgate*, as I was going cross *West-Smithfield*, I met with one *Charles Hinchman*[16] (who was afterwards executed at *Tyburn* for returning from Transportation) whom I asked to go with me to buy a pair of Shoes at a Shoe-Maker's at *Smithfield-Bars*: When we went into the Shop the Master was eating of some Spoon-Meat, which he brought into the Shop, and while he was trying the Shoes on me, *Hinchman* took the spoon, which was silver, and put it into his Pocket: I paid for my Shoes, and came away; but the Man soon miss'd the Spoon and followed us, and took *Hinchman* with it in his Pocket, but I made my Escape; so my Companion was carried before a Justice of Peace on *Clerkenwell-Green*, and committed to *Newgate*; but the Prosecutor not appearing at the Sessions against him, he was discharged.

Pendell and I going one Day into *Lincoln's Inn-Fields* to see the Cocks throwed at, [p. 24] we met *Fulsome*, who had been Gaming, and having lost all his Money, invited us to go along with him and partake of a *Chance* he knew of; and tho' it was Noon Day we agreed to go with him, which was to one Mr. *Whitnills*, an Ass Man at *Windmill-Hill*, where we went, and the *Chance* proved to be a parcel of wet Linnen hanging to dry in the Garden. I got over the Pails, and handed to my Consorts as much as loaded them, then filling my Pockets and Breeches with small Linnen, got over the Pails again without any Discovery; but we were soon pursued and taken, and carried before Justice *Benson* in *Shoreditch*, where *Fulsome* was admitted an Evidence against us, and upon his Oath we were Committed to *Newgate*, and he to *New-Prison*, and at the next Sessions at the *Old-Baily* I was found guilty to the value of 39 *s.* and ordered for Transportation, several of Mr. *Whitnill*'s Goods being found on me, but *Pendell* was acquitted.[17]

A short Time after my Conviction, a Draught of Transports were ordered to be sent from *Newgate* to his Majesty's Plantations in *America*, and I was one of them: There were about 36 Men and 20 Women put on Board the Ship *Honour*, Captain *Langley* Commander, for the above Purpose;[18] and one Day when we were at Sea, a Gale of Wind arose that blew very hard, and carried away our Main-Top-Mast, upon which the chief Mate came to the Hatch where we Prisoners were kept, and said if [p. 25] any of us were Sailors we should come upon Deck and lend a Hand, and that he would take our Irons off; accordingly about twelve of us came up and kept the Ship clear that Night, and the next Morning we had calm Weather. The First Mate took a great Fancy to me, and made me Steward of the Prisoners. One *Hescot*, a Prisoner, who had about fifty Pound of Bisket, two Caggs of *Geneva*,[19] a Cheese and some Butter on board, went up one Day upon Deck for the Air, and in the mean while we ransacked all his Stores; but upon his Return, he finding out what had been done, went and made Complaint to the Captain, who threaten'd to whip us all round to find out the right Man, whereupon sixteen of us agreed to secure the whole Ship's Crew (being but twelve in Number, Captain and Boy included) before the *Whipping Gale blew harder*, which we accomplished.

The next Day after we had got Possession of the Ship and Cargo, we made an Agreement to go to *Cape Finister* in *Spain*; and then made a Law amongst us sixteen commanding Men, that every one that was drunk upon his Watch, so as his Arms could be taken from him, or was caught in the Hold with the Women Prisoners, should receive twelve Lashes. We allow'd the Women the Benefit of the Air, and promis'd them that they should go ashore with us. One *William Holyday*, who was Evidence against *Cheshire* and *Williams*, that were executed for robbing the *Bristol* Mail, was one [p. 26] of the Prisoners that would not consent to the taking of the Ship; but as soon as taken was very desirous of Liberty; and we being full well acquainted that he had Money, oblig'd him to give us 10 *l.* for which we gave him a Joint Receipt, and then he had the same Benefit as we. In about fourteen Days after our taking the Ship, we arrived within two Leagues of *Cape Finister*, where we hoisted out our Long-Boat; and having supply'd ourselves with the most material Moveables that the Captain and Mate had, with their Watches and Money, the whole amounting to about 100 *l.* we laid the Ship to, and made the Sailors hawl the Long-Boat a broad-side the Ship, ordering four of them to get into her and receive our Things; then we went and drank with the Captain and Mate, and set them at Liberty, but lock'd down the nineteen Men that would not consent to the taking of the Ship, as also all the Women, and then went into the Boat to go ashore, where in a few Hours we arrived, and the Sailors rowed off to the Ship again.

We travelled over the Mountains for two Days, and then met with a *Spaniard*, who directed us to a Village where we got Victuals, Drink and Lodging; and the next Day after we went over the River, two in a Boat, to *Vigo*, where we fell to drinking in an *Irishman*'s House. Our Captain was come into *Vigo* River with the Ship, and having Intelligence of us, came ashore, and made Complaint to the Governor; upon which the Pitch Pots were immediately ordered to [p. 27] be lighted (it being their way of Notice on any Emergency that happens) and the House we were in was soon surrounded with a Company of Soldiers, who took us and confined us for that Night in the Main-Guard Room. Next Morning we were all examined before the Governor, and we being inform'd the Laws of that Country were such, that if we own'd any thing of robbing the Captain, as he alledged, and indeed was but right, then we must have deliver'd them; and if we deny'd it, all was well; for if you confess nothing, there is no Advantage to be taken: The Captain said the Watch and several other Things were his, and that we had robbed him of them; but we deny'd his whole Charge, and the Governor order'd us to keep the Watch, &c.

Captain *Langley* made great Interest to the Governor to order us to go on board again, but to no purpose, the Laws of the Kingdom not admitting it; but on the contrary, the Governor recommended to us to enter ourselves for Soldiers, which we promis'd him to do, till the Ship was sailed out of the River, and then flew from our former Promise; whereupon he gave us a Pass writ in *Spanish*, which mentioned us to be all Thieves, as we understood by an *Irishman* that could talk the *Spanish* Language, which Pass we burnt.

We travell'd thro' *Spain*, and went to a Place call'd *Port Oport* in *Portugal*, where eight of my Companions ship'd themselves [p. 28] on board an *English* Ship, and myself and the other eight on board a *Dutch* Man of War, both bound to *Amsterdam*, at which Place we arrived very safe, and had a very good Voyage; and there I committed a great Number of Robberies in Conjunction with one *Martin Gray*,[20] who was afterwards executed at *Tyburn* for returning from Transportation.

We continued at *Amsterdam* some Months, and then came for *England*,[21] where I had not been long before I met with one *Goddard* and one *Ciscell*, with whom I went out on the *Sneak*,[22] and committed several Robberies, but our Companion *Goddard* was soon taken from us, for being apprehended for Burglary, he was try'd at the *Old-Baily*, and found Guilty, and was afterwards executed at *Tyburn*.

A short time after this, *Ciscell* and I going down *Fish-Street*, we espy'd a Porter with a large Box on his Shoulders, whom we follow'd; and the Fellow pitching his Load at the lower end of the said Street, I bid *Ciscell* watch him; in the mean while I went into an Alehouse and call'd for Pen and Ink, and writing a Letter, I put a Brass Ring in it and gave it to *Ciscell*, who went to him and desired him to carry that Letter to the Place directed, telling him, that there was a Diamond Ring in it. The Porter went with the Letter, and left his Box to my Companion and I to take care off, which we soon moved to *Ciscell's* Premises, and there open'd [p. 29] it, and found in it some foul Linnen, and about nine Yards of fine Lace. The same Night *Ciscell* and I robb'd a Midship-Man of a Man of War of 16 *l*. in *Thames-Street*.

My Companion *Ciscell* and I continued our Course for a long Time, till at length I had saved about 10 *l*. with which Money I married and cloathed one *Mary Tomlin*, a Barrow-Woman. I had not been married long before I went out of a Night to rob, which caused Words between us, and had I took her advice, I might have been a good Man at this Time; but Justice followed me soon after; for a Woman, whom I had left my Wife to live with, went and acquainted Merchant *Forward* that I was returned from Transportain, who came with Assistance and took me, and carried me to *Newgate* without any Commitment, only by vertue of the Transportation Act.[23] There I remained for a long Time; but at last I was try'd with several of my Companions who assisted in taking the Ship; we were all found Guilty, and received Sentence of Death; under which Sentence I lay six Weeks, and was then reprieved, and order'd for Transportation for fourteen Years.

Some few Months after my above Sentence, I was transported with about eighty others from *Newgate*; and when we arrived at *Virginia*[24] I was sold to one Mr. *Fardle*, an *Irishman*; who not agreeing with my Temper, I run away from him; but he soon took me again. There was no way of help[p. 30]ing myself, so I was contented, and continued with him some time, and then thought of an Expedient to quit myself of his Service, which I effected by running away with a Long-Boat that lay in the River with Masts and Sails in her.

When I got on the other side the River; I bore several Holes in the Long Boat with an Augur, and sunk her. Then I went and stole a Horse, upon which I travelled about the Country several Days, till I arrived at a Place call'd *Portomock River*,[25] where I continued about three Weeks, and then enter'd myself on board a Ship bound for *Bristol*, and had 10 *l*. paid me for my Service in this Voyage.

As soon as I was arriv'd at *Bristol* I went to my old trade, not daring to come to *London*, with one *Abraham Smith*; but at length were both taken in a Linnen-Draper's Shop, which we had broke open and robb'd of a large

Quantity of Linnen, and carried before a Magistrate, who committed us to *Newgate*, where we continued till the next Assizes, when we were both try'd; but the Burglary not being plainly proved, we were both acquitted of that, and found guilty only of the Felony, and ordered for Transportation; in a short time after we were put on board a Ship for that Purpose. We arrived safe in the River where my old Master liv'd; and the Pilot that came on board us to carry us up the River, remembering my Face, went and told my Master *Fardle* of me, who came [p. 31] on board next Day to see me, but would not buy me.

In a few Days after our Arrival I was sold for 14 *l.* but my Mind not being fixed to stay, I made an Agreement with two more to run away from our Masters, which we did: When we had got clear of the inhabited Country, we were oblig'd to live very hard, having no Provision with us. We took Fire-Arms with us and kill'd Deer, and liv'd mostly upon that and the Moss of Trees. At length we met a Horse without either Bridle or Saddle, which we laid hold of; and having made a Bridle of our Garters, we got all three upon him: Coming to a River that we were oblig'd to cross, the Current run so strong that we could not pass it for three Days, whereupon we kill'd our Horse the second Day, and lived upon that. When we had passed the River we made our Way for *North Carolina*, where we no sooner arrived, but were discover'd, and sent back again to our Masters.

I began after this to be very obstinate; and when my Master bid me to go to work, I told him Work was intended for Horses and not for Christians; adding, that if I had a Mind to work, I had no Occasion to have left *England*; and sometimes pretending my self to be drunk, pulled out my Knife and asked him how long I was to be his Servant, which put him into such Consternations, that he never asked me afterwards to go to work. One Day as I was walking in *Jerre*[p. 32]*man Town* I met a *Scotchman*, who falling into Discourse with me, told me he had got a Pass to travel the Country. I told him I would raise some Money to carry us both to *England*; and when we came out of the Town I robbed him of the Pass, and then went home to my Master's and stole a Suit of his Son's Clothes and a Horse, and rid away towards *Anapolis* River,[26] where I had my Pass renew'd; and having cross'd the River, went directly for *New York*, where I entered myself on board a Sloop for a Voyage to the *West Indies*, and we returned to *New York* in about eighteen Months, where I was discovered again, and sent back to my old Master by Water; but he finding me not to be ruled, took my Obligation for 10 *l.* and discharged me.

After this, I hired myself to a Pilot for 20 *l. per Annum*, with whom I remained for five Years: I got acquainted, being always trading in the River, with one Col. *Brown*'s Daughter, whose Fortune was 1500 Acres of Land and 200 *l.* in Money. We lived together as Man and Wife for a long while, till the Money and Acres were all spent: In some short time after this I married a Carpenter's Daughter at *Mobgick-Bay*,[27] with whom I lived for some time, and by her had one Son, if living, named *James Dalton*, but left her before Death parted us.

Being grown very poor again, and meeting with one *John Wellbone* who was a Transport, we agreed to steal two Negroes, which [p. 33] which we did, and carried them on board a *Bermudas* Sloop, where we sold them for 18 *l.* tho' worth 40 *l.* on Suspicion of which Fact, we were seized and committed to Goal, where we remained till next general Court-Day, and then we were try'd; and the Evidence that was produced against us not being able to prove the Fact, we were only sentenced to be sold for five Years to pay the expence of the Goal: We were sold accordingly, and I had five Masters in three Weeks Time; but the last proving to be a Namesake of mine, one Mr. *Dalton*, he used me very well, and soon made me his Overseer; and I going one Day to see *John Wellbone*, we agreed to run away, which we did; and that very Night I robbed the Collector of *Hampton*[28] of 73 Pistoles. We took a Baker along with us who had three Guns, which we put into a long Boat that we had stole; then went up to the Store-House and stole a Hogshed of Rum, which, with other Provision, we put into the Boat, and so steared away towards *New-York*, where we arrived in three Days. We sold our Boat for 23 *l.* and then *Wellbone* came for *London*, and was hang'd in five Months after: I fell sick; and when I recovered, went again to *Virginia*, and the Baker remained at *New-York*.

Soon after my Arrival at *Virginia* I enter'd myself on board the *Madera Galley*, Captain *Cobb* Commander, for *London*; and when we arrived in the *Downs*[29] I was press'd and put on board the *Hampshire* Man of War, [p. 34] commanded by the Lord *Muskerry*,[30] and went to the late Siege of *Gibraltar*, where we remained until Sir *Charles Wager* came, who commanded us to go and bring home the *Turkey* Fleet from *Constantinople*, which we did; and soon after our Arrival, I was paid my Wages, which supported my Extravagance for some time; but my Stock being quite exhausted, I thought of a new Way of Living, and then began to rob in the Street.

Just at this time I got acquainted with one *Benjamin Branch*, and we went a snatching of Pockets; then we were join'd by *Will Field*, who also went a snatching of Pockets with us. We stole a Woman's Pocket in *Holbourn* in which was a great Parcel of Natural Hair, which we had afterwards made into Wiggs; and *Field* and I quarrelling about the Wiggs, we parted; then *Branch* and I went by ourselves for some time.[31]

After this, *Branch* and I, with another Person then in Company (whose Name I forbear to mention, because he is since reformed and now lives very honest) went to St. *Clement's Church Yard*, and tied up a Shop Door belonging to a *Dutchman*, that he might not get out to alarm the Neighbourhood, and then we broke in at the Window and robb'd him of his whole Stock, consisting of Chints, Callicoes and Handkerchiefs; and then we made off undiscovered.

[p. 35]*Christopher Rawlins* was the next Person that *Branch* and I associated with, and we in Company with each other snatch'd, in the Space of three Months, above 500 Pockets; and one Night in particular as we were coming down *Holbourn-Hill*, near St. *Andrew's* Church, I snatch'd a Woman's Pocket off, who feeling me, cry'd out; and a Tallow-Chandler standing at his Door, laid hold of *Branch*, and *Rawlins* and I running to make our Escape, we were seized and brought to the Tallow-Chandler's, where *Branch* was; we pretended not to know each other, and I observing

Branch with a Knife in his Hand, and attempting to cut the Tallow-Chandler's Throat, I discovered him, wherefore it was judged that we were not concerned, and so we went about our Business; but *Branch* was committed to *Newgate*, and afterwards executed at *Tyburn* for the said Robbery.[32]

Rawlins and I[33] went the next Night to a Milliner's Shop in *Covent-Garden*, and robb'd it of Cambrick to a large Value, and 9 *l.* in Money. It was about Eight o'Clock in the Evening, I went in and held a Pistol to the Woman while he stole the Cambrick. The Success of this Robbery was employ'd to make up *Branch*'s Affair with his Prosecutor, but to no purpose.

Rawlins and I walking along *Fleetstreet* saw about twelve Pick-Pockets in a Brandy-Shop, and a young Woman going in for some Brandy with a Handkerchief in her [p. 36] Hand; she laid it down, and I went in and stole it away, and went clear off with it, and one of the Fellows in the Shop was charged with taking it, and sent to Jail: When we unty'd the Handkerchief we found in it six fine Holland Shirts, fringed and ruffled, and six Lace Stocks.

Rawlins and I, with a third Person, went into *Wapping* and broke open a Silversmith's Shop; but we were surpriz'd before we had quite completed our Design, and were oblig'd to make off with only two Tankards. We went down to the Water-side, and took away a Boat for to cross the *Thames*, but were stopt by a Tide-Surveyor in a Boat with two Watermen, they suspecting us to be running of Goods so that we were oblig'd to shew them what we had; as soon as we had so done, I pull'd out a Pistol and demanded the Surveyor's Money, *&c.* my Companions seeing what I was upon did the same, and we robb'd him of about 15 *l.* in Money, a Watch, a Cagg of Rum, and his Debitation, which last we burnt.

Rawlins and I now agreed to go to downright stopping of Coaches; and the first we stopt was in *Castle-Yard, Holbourn*, in which was one Mr. *Keene*, an Attorney, from whom we took his Watch and some Money, and so went off.[34] The next Coach we stopt was in *Holbourn*, over-against the End of *Hatton-Garden*, being join'd then by one *Hulks*, in which Coach also was a single Gentleman, from whom we took four Guineas, a Silver-[p. 37]hilted Sword, a Silver Watch, and a Silver Locket, and then made off.[35]

The third Coach that we stopt was in St. *Paul's Churchyard*, in which was one Mr. *King* an Attorney, and one *Worster* an Informing Constable; from Mr. *King* we took about 18 *l.* and from *Worster* three Guineas and some Silver, and then made off. Going up the *Old Baily* we met a Coach with one Mr. *Williams* belonging to *Drury-Lane* Theatre, and a Gentlewoman in it: We made a Demand of their Money, Watches, and Rings; he deliver'd me some Silver, and said that was all he had; and then telling us who he was, and where he was going, we returned him his Money again.[36]

A few Nights after this, my Companions *Rawlins* and *Hulks*, neglecting to meet me, I met with *William Holden*,[37] *William Russel*, alias *Fine Bones*, and *Robert Crouch*, alias *Bob the Butcher*, in *Fleetstreet*. We presently agreed to go and seek after Business that Night; and a Woman passing by us, we follow'd her into *Lincoln's-Inn-Fields*, where I knock'd her down, and one of my Companions run away with the Bundle; which we went and open'd directly, and found in it a Parcel of Women's Clothes, a Looking-Glass, a Drab Great Coat, and some Moidores ty'd up in a Piece of Cloth. We shar'd our Booty, and *Bob the Butcher* bought our Shares of the Great Coat, and had it made fit for him; and to hinder its being known by the right Owner, had a new Set of But[p. 38]tons and a new Velvet Cape put to it. *Bob the Butcher* meeting with one *Bartholomew Nichols*, alias *Susannah Haws*, alias *Fish Moll*, acquainted him of this Robbery, and he appeared as an Evidence against him at his Tryal at the *Old Baily*.[38]

Russel, alias *Finebones*, *Holden* and I, one Evening going along *Clerkenwell-Green*, saw two Pieces of Stuff lay in a Stuff-Shop Window, and only one Woman in the Shop; I proposed to them to steal it, but *Holden* would not agree, thinking it a dangerous Enterprize, and so left us; but *Russel* and I was resolved to have it; and to effect our Design, *Russel* went into the Shop, and took hold of the Stuff, and I stood at the Door, and seeing the Woman coming from behind the Compter, stept in and pushed her down, and lock'd the Door upon her, and in the mean time *Russel* went off with the Stuff.

One Night *John Featherby*[39] (since executed at *Tyburn* for a Street-Robbery) and I coming down *Snow-hill*, snatched off two Womens Pockets, in the first of which was some Silver and Half-pence, and two Brass Thimbles; and in the other a Purse with 34 Guineas and some Silver. Afterwards going thro' *Newgate-Market* we stole a Turkey, and had it dress'd for our Supper.

A few Nights after, coming along St. *Paul's Church Yard*, I happen'd to see a Coach, wherein was one Mr. *Williams*, then Under-Sheriff, which I stopt and demanded his Mo[p. 39]ney, Watch and Rings, which he deliver'd. There was a Gentlewoman in the Coach big with Child, whom I desired not to be frighten'd; but she gave me some Money, and then I made off.[40]

Some short time after this, *John Hulks, Christopher Rawlins, Isaac Ashby*, alias *Black Isaac*, and I, robb'd a Coach between St. *Sepulchre's* Church and *Newgate*. The Gentleman in it was very honourable, for as soon as we order'd the Coachman to stop, he said, *Come, Gentlemen, I know what you want, so take my Money*, which was six Guineas; but we not believing that to be his all, went into the Coach and searched him and took his Watch, but found no more Money. Then going down *Holbourn* we stopt a Gentleman's Coach, and robbed the Gentleman that was in it of 23 Guineas. As soon as we went to make off with our Booty, he cry'd out, *Thieves*; upon which four Watchmen came up to us with their Staves, and bid us stand; whereupon we pull'd out each Man a Brace of Pistols, and so drove the Watchmen along *Holbourn* (making them first lay down their Lanthorns and Staves) into *Bloomsbury* Watch-house, where we locked the Constable and Watchmen all in together, and then left them.

Rawlins and I coming along the *Strand* one Night, met a Chair with two Footmen before it, and lighted Flambeaux in their Hands. I went up to the Footmen and made them put their Lights out, and ordered the [p. 40] Chairmen not to unstrap upon Pain of Death; in the mean while *Rawlins* opened the Chair Door, and robb'd him of Seventy Guineas in a Purse, a

Gold Watch, a Ring, and a Shell Snuff-Box, which Box the Gentleman desir'd we would return, it being a Piece of Antiquity, which we did, and then took our Leave of him.

A few Nights after, being in Company with *Black Isaac*, and a third Person, we stop'd a Coach, in *Lombard-Street*, upon which the Gentleman in it drew his Sword and made a gallant Defence; and a Country cart happening to come by, my Companions being somewhat afraid, run to the other side of the Way; but I was resolved to have his Money, and told him if he denied me, I would shoot him immediatly; he made answer, I might shoot and be damn'd; then I presented my Pistol at his Head, and he hearing it cock by the Noise of the Trigger, bid me stop, saying, here is what you come for, and take it, it is all the Money I have; and there being a Watch-Man within twenty Yards of us, and several others about the Street, I did not care to stay to search for his Watch; so made off; but took his Sword with me; which proved to be a Mourning one.[41]

The Night following as *Hulks, Black Isaac, Rawlins* and I were sitting at *Holbourn-Bridge*, I perceived a Gentleman coming, which proved to be one Mr. *Downs* a Lawyer, with a Link-Boy before him, and [p. 41] his Sword drawn in his Hand, for fear he should be robbed; I crossed the way, and having the mourning Sword with me, I told him I would fight a Duel with him; upon which he stood upon his Defence; then I drew out a Pistol, swearing I would fight with Sword and Pistol; he then found I came to rob him, and so delivered his Sword to me, I having first made the Boy put out his Light; and my Companions robbed him of eighteen Pounds, which they sunk except twelve Shillings, and my Share of that was all that I had of that Booty; but the Gentleman having appeared at their Trial, swore actually he was robbed of 18 *l*.[42]

Some time after this, *Rawlins* and I went out together, and coming through St *Pauls-Church-yard*, we met a Gentleman's Coach; we made up to it, and there happened to be in it Sir *Gilbert Heathcote*, who we robbed of his Watch, two Shillings in Silver, and a Halfpenny; when I was in the *Compter* he came to see me, and I returned him his Watch, for which he gave me two Guineas.[43]

Not long after this Robbery as we were drinking in a Brandy-Shop in St *Pauls-Church-yard*, a Link-man came in, and said he had been lighting the Queen to the Wax-Work in *Fleetstreet*; and that her Majesty in Company with his Grace the Duke of *Grafton*, was just then gone to the China-Shop in *Leaden-Hall Street* we soon got Intelligence of their Cogg Ways,[44] and resolved to have them, and waited some time [p. 42] accordingly; but another Coach coming by which we took for them, we made up to it, and robbed it of twenty seven Guineas, a Watch &c. and there being a Noice and Outcry of Thieves, we missed of the Queen and Duke, otherwise we would have had his *George* as sure he was born.[45]

I had forgot to mention two Robberies in their proper Places, which are somewhat remarkable; the first of which is as follows: *Benjamin Branch* and I about four Months before he was executed, went out one Night with an Intent to rob. We both took Pistols in our Pockets; and going down *Wood-street* saw a Gentleman walking before us with a Cane in his Hand; when he came to the End of *Milk-street*, *Branch* seiz'd him by the Collar with one Hand, and held a Pistol to his Head with the other, and then demanded his Money: The Gentleman refus'd to deliver, upon which *Branch* offer'd to fire, but the Pistol only flashing in the Pan, the Gentleman struck him with his Cane and ran off in a great Surprize: I follow'd him, and coming up to him, ask'd him what was the Matter; upon which he told me; I immediately pull'd out my Pistol, and notwithstanding there was a Watch-man within hearing, swore that tho' the other could not rob him, I would; and that if he stirr'd one Step, or spoke one Word, I would shoot him dead upon the Spot; I then robb'd him of his Watch and a considerable Sum of Money, and made off undiscover'd.

[p. 43]The other Robbery was with *Russel* alias *Finebones*, who went with me one Night about Seven o'Clock into Cheapside, with Intent to snatch off Womens Pockets; but passing along near *Bow-Church*, we saw a Gentlewoman in a Gold-Smith's Shop, purchasing a Gold Watch; and observing the Man of the Shop to put the Mony he took of the Gentle-woman into a Drawer, and the Key of the said Drawer into his Pocket; *Finebones* went in and cheapened a Stock-Buckle, and then I came and desired to speak with the Gentleman, who came to the further end of the Compter, and then I pulled out a Pistol, and swore I would shoot him if he offered to stir or make a Noise; then *Finebones* came and took the Key out of his Pocket, and unlocked the Drawer, and took thereout twenty four Guineas, and then made off.

Soon after this, I married a Woman, by whom if I had been ruled I might have done well; but going on in my old Way, I was presently after taken up, and for the Preservation of my own Life, was obliged to turn Evidence. There was six of my Companions hang'd upon my Information; and I protest that they were every one guilty of their Crimes they suffered for; tho' I declare to the World, that there were Persons, who make it their Business to take up Whores and Thieves, and too often prey upon honest People, came to me and offered me ten Guineas to impeach *Richard* [p. 44] *Nicholls*; by their Persuasion I consented to their Request, and took the Money; but afterwards being terrified with the Thoughts of taking an innocent Man's Life away, I flew from my Word, and refus'd to return them the ten Guineas: But they not being willing to sit down with that Loss, went and made the same Offer to *Thomas Neeves*, who accepted of it, and swore the said *Nichols* into a Robbery, which he committed by himself, as he confessed at *Tyburn*. A Proclamation was issued out, promising a Reward of one hundred and forty Pounds for every Street-Robber that shou'd be convicted: I having convicted six, consequently was entitled to a very handsom Sum; but the *honest* Men before-mention'd found means to trick me out of almost all; for out of eight hundred and forty Pounds, I only received about forty Pounds.[46]

Being now at my Liberty, I was always afraid of being sworn against by some of my former Accomplices Wifes, who had before threaten'd me;[47] and so to get out of their way, I shipped my self on board the *Wellcome*, Captain *Price* Commander, belonging to that *honest* Man *J – B –*, Merchant, I shipped my self at thirty five Shillings *per* month, and went a Voyage to

Virginia, where I remained some time; then I performed my Voyage back again, and arrived in about ten months at *Wapping*, on the ninth of *September*:[48] coming to Town to see my Wife, I was on the tenth surrendred to the Compter; and hearing the Ship [p. 45] was to be paid off, I made Interest with the Keeper, to send two Keepers with me to receive my Wages, which I received except five Pounds, that I was cheated out off under the false Colours of Honesty. I went back to the Compter, and there remain'd till the twenty first Day of *November* following, when I was discharged.

Soon after my Discharge from the Compter, I kept a publick House in *New-Street* in *Shoe Lane*; where indeed a great Number of idle Persons frequently resorted. Mr. *Stubbs* that keeps the *White Lyon* Alehouse in *Shoe-Lane*, often used me very ill upon account of many of his Customers using my House; for he frequently came to me, and threatened me with a Warrant, which he pretended he had procur'd on purpose to take me up, for keeping a disorderly House, which was the Cause that I was obliged to quit it.

After having spent all my Money, and being destitute of Business, I began to think of taking up my old Trade; and accordingly made my first Attack on Dr. *Mead*;[49] for which I was try'd at the *Old Baily*, and being found guilty; was sentenced to pay a Fine of 20 Marks, to suffer three Years imprisonment, and to find Security for seven Years afterwards.[50] When this Sentence was pass'd upon me I behaved myself very impudent in Court, upon which I was ordered to suffer my three Years imprisonment in the Cells; and I believe that if I had not [p. 46] been impudent, and had had the Liberty to send for my Friends, I had not been convicted of this Robbery for which I was condemned, and of which Robbery I protest I am innocent of.

In the height of all our Robberies, we frequently used to go the Playhouse, dressed like Gentlemen; and when Play was done we would have Chairs call'd for us, and sometimes three or four Link Boys before us. One Night in particular, I remember that *Hulks, Black Isaac, Rawlins* and I, were to see the *Beggar's Opera*; and Captain *Macheath*'s Fetters happening to be loose, *Rawlins* call'd out, *Captain, Captain, your Bazzel is undone*. The Play being over, we went to a House in a *Wood-street* that we us'd, in four Chairs, with six Lights before each Chair.[51]

I have now given a full Account of my Life, and mentioned every particular Circumstance from my Childhood to this present Time, to the utmost my Memory. I have nothing more to add but this, I hope as I am now to suffer Death for what I declare I did not commit, every good Christian will forgive me whom I have really wrong; and that the Person that accus'd me (whose Character is sufficiently known) may be stopt in his Prosecutions against those Persons whom he has sent to *Newgate* since my Condemnation.[52]

FINIS

NOTES

1 Roll.
2 An escritoire.

3 'On the Sneak' means to steal through stealth.

4 Mrs Blauke was probably Mrs Blake, the mother of Joseph Blake, *alias* Blueskin (see note 5 below and *The History . . . of John Sheppard* (1724) in this volume). William Field was described in *A Genuine Narrative of all the Street Robberies Committed since October last, by James Dalton*, London, 1730, as 'the most vile Wretch that ever he [Dalton] contracted an Acquaintance with' (p. 30), presumably because he offered to appear for the prosecution against Dalton and Fulsome. He regularly appeared in the courts, both as defendant and witness for the prosecution, and he was associated with Jonathan Wild and John Sheppard, both of whom he outlived (see G. Howson, *The Thief-taker General: The Rise and Fall of Jonathan Wild*, London, 1970; *The History . . . of John Sheppard* (1724), in this volume). He was eventually transported to Maryland in 1729 for shoplifting: OBSP, 16–24 April 1729; P.W. Coldham, *English Convicts in Colonial America*, 2 volumes, New Orleans, 1974–6, vol. I, p. 94.

5 On Jack, or John, Sheppard see *The History . . . of John Sheppard* (1724), reprinted in this volume. Blueskin, *alias* Joseph Blake, was hanged in 1724 for involvement in the theft from Kneebone's shop for which Sheppard was also hanged. Blake's main claim to fame was that he stabbed Jonathan Wild in the Old Bailey: Howson, *Thief-taker General*.

6 Ann, or Hannah, Britton was transported in 1726 to Virginia for receiving goods. It was said at her trial that she had offered the prosecutor five guineas to drop the case and that she had claimed to be worth £1000: Coldham, *English Convicts*, vol. I, p. 34; OBSP, 31 August to 3 September 1726.

7 Lewkener's Lane was also known as Lutenor's Lane or Newtoner's Lane.

8 Stuff is a woollen fabric.

9 This was to prevent discovery in the likely event that the numbers of the bank notes had been recorded.

10 It seems likely that Speedman was also called Benjamin Speed. Speed was described as 'a Boy' when sentenced at the Old Bailey to be whipped for a felony in 1716, and for further felonies he was transported to Charleston in America in 1718 and to Maryland in 1720: OBSP, 22–25 February 1716, 23–26 April 1718, 12–14 October 1720; P.W. Coldham, *The Complete Book of Emigrants in Bondage: 1614–1775*, Baltimore, 1988, p. 751; Coldham, *English Convicts*, vol. I, p. 250.

11 Keg.

12 A round house was a place for temporarily detaining arrested people.

13 The criminal justice system at this time was based on private prosecution, generally brought by the victim; as a result prosecutions would often fall because the prosecutor, having brought the complaint, later failed to turn up at the trial, perhaps because the stolen goods had been recovered or because the inconvenience or cost was too great.

14 John Pendell was probably also known as John Pindar.

15 A compter was a prison, often used for debtors.

16 Charles Hinchman was convicted of picking a pocket to the value of 10d., and sentenced to transportation in 1719. Hinchman and Dalton may have first met at this time for both were put on board the *Honor* destined for America in May 1720 and both were involved in a mutiny and escape during the voyage. In 1721 he, along with Dalton and several others, was apprehended by Jonathan Wild, condemned for returning from transportation and hanged: OBSP, 4–7 October 1719, 1–4 March 1721; Coldham, *The Complete Book of Emigrants in Bondage*, p. 391; Howson, *Thief-taker General*, p. 310.

17 According to the OBSP report of the trial, Dalton and Pindar were both convicted and sentenced to transportation in March 1720 for stealing clothes to

the value of 39/- from Joseph Whitfield and Elizabeth Rigby on 18 January 1720, the goods being found on them. Pindar was transported to the York river on the *Honor* in May 1720, and, unlike Dalton and Hinchman (see note 16), he does not appear to have escaped on route. Contrary to the version given here, Howson claims that it was Field who impeached Dalton on this occasion. See: OBSP, 2–4 March 1719/20; Howson, *Thief-taker General*, p. 139; Coldham, *English Convicts*, vol. I, p. 211.

18 The *Honor*, with Richard Langley as captain, sailed for Virginia in May 1720. It seems to have been Langley's only trip as a transporter of convicts, and, as the text says, it was interrupted by a mutiny at Vigo: Coldham, *The Complete Book of Emigrants in Bondage*, pp. 915 and 207. On transportation to North America see A.E. Smith, *Colonists in Bondage: White Servitude and Convict Labour in America, 1607–1776*, Chapel Hill, 1947; A.R. Ekrich, *Bound for America: The Transportation of British Convicts to the Colonies, 1718–75*, Oxford, 1987.

19 Geneva was slang for gin.

20 Martin Gray was condemned for returning from transportation before his term had expired. He had been with Dalton on the *Honor* and had also escaped at Vigo: OBSP 1–4 March 1720/1; Coldham, *The Complete Book of Emigrants in Bondage*, p. 329.

21 Dalton presumably returned to England sometime in late 1720 or early 1721, since he was apprehended, by Wild, in 1721 on a charge of returning from transportation, condemned in March, pardoned, and transported again in August 1721: Howson, *Thief-taker General*, p. 139; OBSP, 1–4 March 1721.

22 See note 3.

23 Jonathan Forward, a London merchant, had the government contract for transporting convicts from 1718 to 1739 at the rate of £3 per head: J.M. Beattie, *Crime and the Courts in England 1660–1800*, Oxford, 1986, p. 504. The Transportation Act of 1718 made returning from transportation before the prescribed term had expired a capital offence.

24 Dalton went on the *Prince Royal* under Thomas Boyd in August 1721: Coldham, *The Complete Book of Emigrants in Bondage*, p. 207.

25 Potomac river.

26 Virginia.

27 Mobjack Bay, Virginia.

28 Hampton, Virginia.

29 The Downs are part of the sea off the east coast of Kent.

30 Robert MacCarthy, Lord Muskerry (died 1769), was at this time commander of the *Hampshire*, a fourth-rate ship. MacCarthy left the Navy in 1741 to join the Jacobite cause: *Dictionary of National Biography*.

31 *A Genuine Narrative . . . James Dalton*, p. 13, has a similar incident, but says the crime was committed by Dalton and Rawlins after Branch had been arrested.

32 It was reported that Branch was arrested for this offence on 2 February 1728: *The Weekly Journal, or the British Gazeteer*, 3 February 1728. The victim was Jane Marshall, and Branch was later condemned. At the trial it was said that he had two others with him who escaped, and that in the incident a Mr Trowell, who apprehended him, was wounded in the head: OBSP, 28 February to 5 March 1728. *A Genuine Narrative . . . James Dalton*, pp. 7–8, gives a shorter and rather different version according to which Branch pushed the woman down and Rawlins snatched her pocket; a passer-by then took hold of Branch, so Dalton attacked the man and Branch lunged at him with a knife, cutting both him and Dalton; Branch was then taken.

33 According to *A Genuine Narrative . . . James Dalton*, after Branch's arrest Dalton and Rawlins 'very seldom went upon these Exploits, only now and then

to keep *Rawlins*'s Hand in' (p. 12) because it brought insufficient money 'to maintain them like Gentlemen', or to support their desire to keep women 'who run them to greater Extravagancies'. So Dalton and Rawlins turned to coach robberies (pp. 15–16).

34 Probably the same robbery as one reported in *Daily Journal*, 9 February 1728, as occurring on 6 February in which a Mr Cane was the victim. According to evidence at the later trial (OBSP, 1–7 May 1728), the robbery of Thomas Cane was committed by Dalton and Rawlins in Castle Yard, Holborn. Dalton was reported to have said at the trial that 'this was the first Coach they robb'd, for *Bellamy* being taken from them, they resolved to leave *Haul Cly*, (snatching of Pockets) and rob Coaches'. See also *The Life of Martin Bellamy*, London, 1728, p. 4.

35 These two robberies resemble two described in *A Genuine Narrative . . . James Dalton*, pp. 17–18, one committed by Dalton, Rawlins and Hulks (see note 37), and the other by Dalton, Hulks and Black Isaac (possibly with others).

36 See *A Genuine Narrative . . . James Dalton*, pp. 25–7; *The Life of Martin Bellamy*, p. 4.

37 Hulks was John Hulks, also known as John Rowden. According to *A Genuine Narrative . . . James Dalton*, Rawlins was against Hulks joining Dalton and himself, 'he being a Black-guard Thief, and having neither Courage nor Conduct, they would fain have dismiss'd him'. Rawlins 'said he was a Coward, and a good-for-nothing Dog, for he had tried him, and found him not worth hanging', only 'after many Intreaties' did they agree to let Hulks join them (pp. 16–17). According to *A Genuine Narrative . . . James Dalton* it was with William Holden that Dalton made his first attempt at street robbery (p. 7), and Dalton, Holden and Branch regularly snatched pockets together, Holden's role being to run off with the pockets which the other two had taken (p. 8).

38 For another version of this robbery see *A Genuine Narrative . . . James Dalton*, pp. 8–9. Russell, Holden and Crouch were convicted of this robbery on Dalton's evidence (he admitted his own involvement) in May 1728. The victim was Martha Hyde, and a witness confirmed the alterations to the coat by Crouch noted in the text: OBSP, 1–7 May 1728. On Hawes see *A Genuine Narrative . . . James Dalton*, pp. 31–43; see also *Mist's Weekly Journal*, 4 May 1728, which says (ironically?) that the 'strict Search . . . for Sodomites' around that time was a result of *A Genuine Narrative . . . James Dalton*.

39 John Featherby was one of four condemned in 1728 at the Old Bailey for robbing John Clark. Featherby was alleged to have tried to shoot Thomas Wood, who went to arrest him. At their trial all four defendants were said to have laughed and to have been 'careless, negligent and confident': OBSP, 16–21 October 1728.

40 Reported by the *Daily Journal*, 27 February 1728, as having taken place at the end of Watling Street, near St Paul's on 24 February 1728. See also OBSP, 1–7 May 1728; *A Genuine Narrative . . . James Dalton*, p. 19.

41 This is probably the robbery mentioned in *A Genuine Narrative . . . James Dalton*, pp. 19–21.

42 See, similarly, OBSP, 1–7 May 1728, which says the robbery took place near Snow Hill, and that the robbers dropped the money taken in the river mud. Also *A Genuine Narrative . . . James Dalton*, pp. 21–2; *The Life of Martin Bellamy*, p. 4.

43 According to the *Daily Post*, 1 March 1728, the robbery, which took place on 28 February 1728, was committed by three people, while the *Daily Journal*, 1 March 1728, says there were 'several Foot Pads' and it was carried out between St Paul's School and Cheapside Conduit. See also *Mist's Weekly Journal*, 12 March 1728; *A Genuine Narrative . . . James Dalton*, p. 22; *The Life of Martin*

Bellamy, p. 5. That Heathcote got his watch back from the pawnbroker is reported in *Daily Post*, 15 March 1728 and *Brice's Weekly Journal*, 22 March 1727–8. At the 1728 trials it emerged that Dalton had helped other victims to recover stolen watches (Williams and Cane): OBSP, 1–7 May 1728. Enabling people to recover their goods might provide prisoners with a source of income, but more important was the consideration that without the support of the prosecutor an application for mercy was less likely to succeed. The 'Compter' was Wood Street Compter, a prison.

44 It is difficult to know what is meant since 'Cogg Ways' means cheating ways.

45 Dalton was reported to have sworn an affidavit for Sir William Billers on 14 March 1728 that the robbery of the Queen had been planned to take place 'about 16 Days ago'. Billers took it to the Secretary of State, Lord Townshend: *Farley's Exeter Journal*, 15 March 1727–8. See also *A Genuine Narrative ... James Dalton*, pp. 29–30. In this context a '*George*' may mean a guinea, or, perhaps, refers to part of the insignia of the Garter, either the lesser or the greater George.

46 The arrests followed the proclamation against street robbers issued on 1 March 1728, which offered, in addition to the statutory reward of £40, £100 for the conviction of those who committed street robberies in London or Westminster. A pardon was also offered to any street robber willing to give evidence against his or her comrades: *Daily Journal*, 2 March 1728; *Daily Post*, 2 March 1728. (On the division of rewards see R. Paley, 'Thief-takers in London in the Age of McDaniel, *c*. 1745–1754' in D. Hay and F. Snyder (eds), *Policing and Prosecution in Britain 1750–1850*, Oxford, 1989, pp. 301–41, at pp. 317–23.) The proclamation was believed to have led to many arrests over the following months (*Mist's Weekly Journal*, 16 March 1728) and to an increase in the numbers condemned and hanged, with nineteen being hanged at Tyburn in May 1728: *Mist's Weekly Journal*, 11 May 1728; *Weekly Journal, or British Gazeteer*, 11 May 1728; *Daily Post*, 20 May 1728, 21 May 1728. *Mist's Weekly Journal*, 12 March 1728, claimed that the proclamation was introduced because of the attack on Heathcote, but other newspapers merely regarded it as the consequence of a general outbreak of robberies.

The actual sequence of events which led to the arrest of the Dalton gang is a little unclear, particularly since OBSP provides a slightly different story from the newspapers. The *Daily Post* reported that on Saturday 2 March 1728, John Rowden, Christopher Rawlins, Isaac Aslin or Ashby or Asklin, alias Black Isaac, and Thomas Chambers were arrested while drinking at Isaac Wyat's brandy shop in Chick Lane: *Daily Post*, 5 March 1728; also 4 March 1728. The *Daily Journal*, 4 March 1728 (also 5 March 1728), adds to this list Dalton, James Woodward and Isaac Wyat, and reports that, although Dalton, Aslin and Rawlins had been impeached by Martin Bellamy, it was Dalton who was to be admitted as evidence against the gang. This led to adverse comment from *Mist's Weekly Journal*, 9 March 1728, which referred to Dalton as 'an Arch Villain, and, whatever Character he follows, glories in laying the Schemes, and leading the Gang'. It was then reported that on 15 March William Field had been arrested following information given by Dalton (*Daily Post*, 16 March 1728) and that on 27 March William Russell, alias Finebones, had also been taken, although in his case the link with Dalton was not made: *Daily Post*, 27 March 1728 (Russell was arrested again in 1730 for picking pockets, *Daily Journal*, 1 January 1730).

According to OBSP, 1–7 May 1728, William Russell, William Holden, Robert Crouch, Christopher Rawlins, Isaac Ashley or Ashby and John Rowden were all tried on the evidence of Dalton: the first three for the robbery of Martha Hyde, the others for the robberies of Francis Williams and Downs, with Rawlins also being tried for the robbery of Thomas Cane. During one of these trials it was said by Thomas Willis, who, with his brother Robert, apprehended them, that Dalton had been found during the search of disorderly houses and that he had directed them to Chick Lane.

The Willis brothers crop up with some frequency in the criminal records of the period. Described as constables, they arrested Wild in 1725 (Howson, *Thief-taker General*, p. 233). It seems quite a coincidence that they should raid the very place in which Dalton was staying, and it is possible that they were following up a lead given to them by Martin Bellamy, who had been arrested in late February and who appears to have worked with the Dalton gang. It may have been that having arrested Dalton, they found him to be a more fruitful source of information on the street robbery gangs than Bellamy, who, from *The Life of Martin Bellamy*, seems to have been primarily a petty offender. On the other hand, in 1730 it was said by three London magistrates that Thomas Willis and a Michael Willis had been 'very serviceable in suppressing disorderly Houses' (OBSP, 28 August 1730, pp. 17–19), so that perhaps their discovery of Dalton was indeed a coincidence. (There seem to have been three men involved in law enforcement called Willis who worked together around this time: Thomas, Michael and Robert; see also OBSP, 10 December 1735, p. 38.)

In the same sessions as Dalton impeached his comrades, Thomas Neeves appeared for the prosecution against Edward Benson, George Gale, Thomas Crowder and James Toon in two robbery trials, and against Richard Nicholls in a shoplifting case: OBSP, 1–7 May 1728.

47 This resentment may have been behind the attack by an unidentified woman who threw a bottle at Dalton when he was brought for trial at the Old Bailey in 1730: *Daily Journal*, 17 January 1730.

48 The year was, presumably, 1729.

49 Richard Mead (1673–1754) was one of the foremost physicians of his day; his patients included royalty, Pope, Newton and Robert Walpole, and the income from his practice has been estimated to have reached, at its peak, £5–6,000 per annum: *Dictionary of National Biography*.

50 Dalton was tried on 18 January 1730, and sentenced two days later. The attempted robbery took place on 1 December 1729 in the evening in Leather Lane; from the report of the trial it seems that Dalton was alone. The report also says that he was fined 40 marks, not 20 as in the text: OBSP, 16–20 January 1730. While in prison he was reported to have wounded another inmate (*Daily Journal*, 21 January 1730).

51 See also *A Genuine Narrative . . . James Dalton*, pp. 24–5.

52 By 'the Person that accus'd me' is meant John Waller. While still in Newgate for attempting to rob Mead, Dalton was charged with robbing Waller. He was convicted in April 1730 and hanged the following month. At the trial Waller said he was 'a *Holland*'s Trader' who had met Dalton at the Adam and Eve public house in Pancras. They had left together and Dalton had then robbed him somewhere between Tottenham Court and Bloomsbury. Waller said that when he heard Dalton was in Newgate he went and identified him, and he swore that the pistol Dalton used was the same as had been used against Mead. Dalton denied the allegation, saying that Waller was 'a man of a vile Character, that he was a common Affidavit Man, and was but lately, before the time charg'd in the Indictment, come out of *Newgate* himself; that though he himself had done many ill Things, and had deserved Death many times, yet not for this Fact, he being Innocent of it; and said, the Prosecutor was as great a Rogue as himself'. Dalton brought three witnesses from Newgate to testify on his behalf, but none was believed and he was hanged on 12 May: OBSP, 8–10 April 1730; *Daily Journal*, 12 May 1730.

Waller was said to have received £80 for his part in the conviction of Dalton. However, suspicions about him surfaced even before Dalton's death: the *Daily Post* reported on 28 April that, aside from Dalton, four people were in Newgate on charges of robbing Waller on different occasions. At the Old Bailey in May 1730 he accused Charles Ditcher and John Wells of robbing him. They were acquitted after it was alleged that Waller had accused various other people besides the defendants. Undaunted, Waller carried on. In August 1730 Isaac Pearce prosecuted Robert Newel for robbery; during the trial Newel not only brought alibi and character witnesses, but also made accusations about Pearce's character, claiming that he had been put up to it by Waller. Newel was acquitted, and the judge, having decided that it was a malicious prosecution brought for the reward, ordered Pearce to prison.

Still Waller carried on. In October 1731 he prosecuted Charles Knowles and Sarah Harper for a robbery on him. In evidence it was alleged that Waller had been in Surrey County Gaol with Harper, and that she had prosecuted him at the Surrey Assizes at Kingston, but he had been acquitted. The judge, who had presided at the Kingston trial, seemed to feel that although there was little to choose between the two, Waller's character was marginally worse, having 'rendered himself Notorious, and he having Sworn Robberies upon several Persons (probably only for the reward) who were acquitted as Innocent, and hang'd *Dalton*: The Court thought no regard was to be given to his Evidence against the Prisoners.'

Waller switched his operations to Hertfordshire Assizes where in May 1732 he unsuccessfully charged with robbery John Edlin and a man called Davies, who had, in the previous February, been acquitted at the Old Bailey of cattle stealing. He then managed to get two people condemned for robbery at Cambridge Assizes, but it was reported that there was some local dissatisfaction with the verdict, and the trial judge, Baron Cummins, ordered an inquiry into Waller's activities. Waller was quickly arrested and convicted at the Old Bailey in May 1732 of falsely charging Edlin, Davies and another with robbery in Hertfordshire. His sentence included being put in the pillory with his head uncovered for two hours on three days. The first occasion was on 13 June 1732 at 11 a.m. Within minutes of being put in the pillory he had been pulled down, beaten with cauliflower stalks and then jumped upon. He died soon afterwards. The coroner said that, 'His Head was beat quite flat, no Features could be seen in his Face'. Two men were condemned for the murder, Richard Griffiths and a man called Edward Dalton, who, it was alleged, acted to revenge the death of his brother, James. It was later said that '*Waller* swore against many, and convicted several, yet no Man suffered Death on his Account but *James Dalton*.' See OBSP, 16–21 October 1728, 13 May 1730, 28 August 1730, 13 October 1731, 23–5 February 1732, 25–9 May 1732, 6–11 September 1732; *The Life and Infamous Actions Of that Perjur'd Villain John Waller, Who made his Exit in the Pillory, at the Seven-Dials, on Tuesday, the 13th Day of this Instant June*, London, W. James, 1732.

III

THE ORDINARY OF NEWGATE'S *ACCOUNT*: MARY YOUNG (1741)

5

INTRODUCTION

Mary Young was born, according to this biography, in about 1704, and was hanged at Tyburn in 1741. The role of women in the criminal biographies of men has already been discussed; in this biography a woman is the main subject. As in *The History Of the remarkable Life of John Sheppard*, the route into crime lies in the youth leaving the disciplined supervision of a working environment: Young was 'reckon'd an extraordinary Workwoman with her Needle' whilst she was under her 'nurse'. Unlike Sheppard who is seduced from his apprenticeship by a woman, it is Young who removes herself from the relationship with her nurse: she has 'an itching Desire to see *London* and Quarrelling with the old Woman who kept her' she left. So, whereas Sheppard's initial downfall is blamed on Lyon, Young's downfall lies in her own desire for independence. It is as an independent woman that, like Lyon, she is powerful. Wishing to go to England from her home in Ireland, Young casts around for some means of financing her trip. She alights on 'a young Fellow' who is 'very sollicitous to persuade her to become his Wife', and she promises to marry him if he will get her to England. The man, who is 'a Servant to a Gentleman of Fortune', robs his master in order to pay for the trip. The text assures us that Young had no thought of crime at this stage, but then neither it seems did Lyon when she met Sheppard, and yet both are depicted as corrupting the men with whom they become involved. The source of that corruption is portrayed as lying not in any intentional action by Young or Lyon, but in the mere fact of their independent state which releases the tendency for corruption inherited by women from Eve.[1]

There is an obvious difference between Lyon and Young. Lyon's involvement in crime at any point in *The History Of the remarkable Life of John Sheppard* is indirect, whereas Young is directly involved. Her crimes are marked by their deviousness and their perversion of the values which were regarded as the foundations of society: the 'natural' incidences of 'femininity', such as the mental and physical weakness of women and their dependence on men. For example, she exploits the chivalry of 'the young Spark' at the meeting house in the Old Jewry by stealing his ring when he

113

assists her. The fact of her having taken advantage of the assistance offered marks her corruption as much as the crimes which she commits. His action was offered within a patriarchal view of the male–female relationship; her exploitation of that relationship is only possible because she stands outside such social values. Indeed, her action is more threatening than other criminal acts by men since it depends on a more fundamentally anti-social position. This broader element is exemplified by the passages on her relationship with the other members of her gang. The gang is presented as a perversion of what were regarded as the highest ideals of the nation-state: a world-turned-upside-down. Young, a woman, is the leader, and under her the gang adopts a structure which resembles the national constitution with its own oath of allegiance, rules, punishments, executive authority, treasury, tithe and language. Its rules are not directed towards the virtuous ends of the nation, as contemporary political philosophers saw them, but to the corrupt purposes of the gang.

This biography was published under the title of the Ordinary of Newgate; this was the office of the clergyman appointed by the City of London to attend to people confined in Newgate Prison.[2] Newgate was, amongst other things, the place where those condemned at the Old Bailey were held prior to their execution at Tyburn or, if convicted of a crime at sea, at Wapping.[3] From the late seventeenth century the various Ordinaries produced an *Account* following each hanging day and there might be as many as eight of those in a year. It has been claimed that the *Accounts* 'enjoyed one of the widest markets that printed prose narratives could obtain in the eighteenth century'.[4] In them were reported the behaviour, biographies and confessions of all those from Newgate who had been hanged. For the most part the *Accounts* published until 1712 were a single-sheet, double-sided and double-columned publication which probably sold for a penny. The Stamp Act of 1711, section 101, changed this. Its differential rates of duty for broadsheets and pamphlets favoured the latter. The Ordinary at that time, Paul Lorrain, petitioned for relief from the duty on the ground that the *Account* was within the terms of section 102, which exempted publications devoted solely to 'Matters of Devotion or Piety'. He was unsuccessful and as a result the *Account* moved to a multi-page format.

By the 1730s each *Account* had effectively been split into two parts. They begin with a summary of the 'condemned sermon', the sermon preached, usually by the Ordinary, to the prisoners in the prison chapel; this is followed by a note on the behaviour of all those who were subsequently hanged and the discussions between them and the Ordinary; next come short biographies; then there is a description of the events of the hanging day; this first part ends with the name of the Ordinary, which is placed rather in the manner of one who is signing off at the end of his involvement; there then follow much longer biographies, which are typically alleged to have been written by the prisoners themselves, and which, in view of the differences between them and the biographies in the first part, seem to support the view that the two parts were by different hands.[5]

The first Ordinary to put his name to a publication of this type was Reverend Samuel Smith, whose *An Account of the Behaviour of the Fourteen Late Popish Malefactors, whilst in Newgate. And Their Discourses with the Ordinary* appeared in 1679. But it was not until May 1684[6] that it became a regular series as a result of the joint efforts of Smith and George Croom, a bookseller who had already been granted a monopoly by the City of London over the publication of the reports of trials held at the Old Bailey (OBSP).[7] The justification for the *Accounts* was declared to be the desire 'to prevent for the Future all false Intelligence concerning the Confessions and Dying Speeches of Malefactors at Tyburn'. It was claimed that the state of penitence, or otherwise, of the prisoners was being misrepresented, and that since it was only the Ordinary who had direct access to the prisoners at all times, then he was the only person qualified to inform the public about such matters.

The *Account* seems to have been a market leader in the field of criminal biography for the next seventy-five years.[8] In order to gain a share of the market, rivals were forced to attack the Ordinary and the accuracy or authenticity of his *Account*, or to allege some superior form of contact with the subject, or to publish their biography before the *Account* appeared, or to produce fake *Accounts*.[9] For their part the Ordinaries sought to forestall competition by publishing their work on the day after the hanging day and by warning prospective readers against imitators.[10] The need for speed probably forced the Ordinaries to write most of the *Account* before the hanging day: as early as 1689 Smith wrote of one condemned person, 'I shall say the less of him, because he hath promised to give me the narrative of his Life at the publick place of suffering.'[11]

The Ordinaries declared that it was their function to bring the offenders to repentance through confession. They were always keen to impress on their readers the amount of effort they had put into this task and the success they had achieved where others, such as the courts, had failed: for instance, in an early *Account* Lorrain noted, 'I at last prevail'd upon them to uncover, and own those Crimes, which they had before so industriously endeavour'd to hide or excuse'.[12] Repentance, the Ordinaries told the prisoners, was a precondition to obtaining the divine mercy which would not only ensure entry into Heaven, but also make death easier to face and, therefore, less painful. What amounted to evidence of repentance was clearly defined. Sorrow on its own was insufficient. Emphasis was placed on the need for a 'particular and full' confession not only of the crime for which the person had been condemned, but also of 'all past Sins', and from this came the religious justification for the inquiry into a person's life history. Moreover, as the Ordinary Roger Wykes told John Simpson in 1700, 'his Repentance could not be sincere, till he had discovered all his Accomplices'.[13] All this led one writer to remark that the Ordinary was 'as diligent in inquiring out the Particulars of their Lives, as tho' he were to send a catalogue of their Sins along with 'em for a Passport'.[14] It is wrong to dismiss the tactics used by the Ordinary as far-fetched and unlikely to succeed, although if any confessions were made to him it is inevitable that they would have been subjected to the Ordinary's own selection, interpretation and restructuring to make them 'clear and fit for perusal' by readers.[15]

Richetti has argued that it is this 'struggle for the criminal's soul' which is the key feature of these publications, and he points to the way in which the Ordinary dwelt on this issue rather than on 'the more secular aspects of the execution and . . . the blasphemy and despair which he doubtless witnessed more often than hopeful resignation'. Richetti concludes that this emphasis shows the appeal which 'the spectacle of sinful man confronting certain death and faced with the terrible uncertainty of divine judgement still possessed for his readers'.[16] It is true that the Ordinaries liked to show the lengths to which they had gone in order to bring the prisoner to repentance, indeed one contemporary writer referred to the Ordinary as the 'Physician of Souls',[17] but Richetti ignores the importance of the more secular aspect of the *Accounts*. As the *Accounts* increased in size it was the secular biographies which were expanded and, as a consequence, took on a more central role. The historian Peter Linebaugh has argued that these biographies can provide rare sources of historical data for the study of the lives of the labouring poor.[18] The approaches of Richetti and Linebaugh to the literature are both valuable, but it is important to recognize that the *Accounts* were formed by the intersection between the religious and the secular. The biography was shaped by the fact of the capital conviction, by the views, including the religious views, of the Ordinary and any other writers or editors who may have been involved, by the cultural tradition within which such crime literature fitted, and, because this was first and foremost a commercial venture, by an estimation of what would make the *Accounts* sell.

Linebaugh has argued that the longer of the two biographies of Young published in the Ordinary of Newgate's *Account* and reprinted here was based on an interview with Young. This is because of the similarity between the biography and the OBSP reports of her trials, and because of the inclusion of various slang terms which do not appear in a selection of contemporary canting dictionaries.[19] Of course, it could just as easily be argued that anyone writing a biography of Young would naturally make use of material published on her, such as the report in the OBSP, because the writer would have been well aware that such materials were readily available to readers. Moreover, the similarity with the OBSP does not guarantee the accuracy of other information included in the biography. Employing slang terms is an obvious way of lending credence to claims that a biography is authentic and might indicate nothing more than a familiarity with the language of the street, rather than an acquaintance with a particular offender; indeed the slang seems to be used in a ponderous and deliberate fashion rather than in the natural way that might have been expected had the manuscript been the work of Young herself. On the other hand, as has been argued in the General Introduction to this book, this does not mean that the long biography was not based on interviews with Young which were then written up for publication by an editor.

BIBLIOGRAPHICAL NOTES

Rev. Mr. Gordon, *The Life and Circumstantial Account of the Extraordinary and Surprising Exploits, Travels, Robberies and Escapes, of the famous Jenny Diver, The most noted Pickpocket of her Time, Who was executed for a Street Robbery, on the 18th of March, 1740. With an Introduction Written by Herself. To which is added A Narrative of the chief Transactions of Harry Cook, And also the Gang to which he belonged. Written by the Rev. Mr. Gordon, Ordinary of Newgate*, London, n.d., pp. 27–37: there is a close resemblance between this and the Ordinary's *Account*.

NOTES

1 See the introduction to *The History Of the remarkable Life of John Sheppard*.
2 P. Linebaugh, 'The Ordinary of Newgate and his *Account*' in J.S. Cockburn (ed.), *Crime in England 1550–1800*, London, 1977, pp. 246–69; P. Linebaugh, 'Tyburn: a study of crime and the labouring poor in London during the first half of the eighteenth century', unpublished Ph.D. thesis, Warwick University, 1975, pp. 166–325; W.J. Sheehan, 'Finding solace in eighteenth-century Newgate' in Cockburn, *Crime in England*, pp. 229–45. The Ordinaries of Newgate during the heyday of the *Account* were Samuel Smith, who was succeeded briefly by John Allen (1698–1700) and Roger Wykes (1700); then came Paul Lorrain (1700–19), Thomas Purney (1719–27), who enjoyed some fame as a moderate poet, and James Guthrie (1727–46), who had also been deputy to the often-absent Purney from 1725 to 1727 and under whom the *Account* reached its peak. After him came Samuel Rossell (1746–7), John Taylor (1747–55), Stephen Roe (1755–64), John Moore (1764–9), John Wood (1769–74) and John Villette (1774–99), who compiled *The Annals of Newgate; or, Malefactors Register*, 4 volumes, London, 1776.
3 The Old Bailey, the popular name for the Justice Hall, was situated next to Newgate Prison. Those tried there included people charged with felonies committed in Middlesex and the City of London. The Court of Admiralty, which tried offences committed at sea, also sat at the Old Bailey. Although Tyburn and Wapping were the normal places of execution until 1783, when the regular place of execution in London shifted to outside Newgate Prison, occasionally those charged with what were regarded as particularly heinous offences, such as murder, might be hanged near the place where the crime had occurred: see, for instance, Ordinary of Newgate's *Account*, 14 August 1741, pp. 3–4. Military executions, by firing squad, took place in Hyde Park, not far from Tyburn: Ordinary of Newgate's *Account*, 19 January 1742/3, pp. 13–14.
4 Linebaugh, 'The Ordinary of Newgate and his *Account*', p. 250. See also the General Introduction in this volume, pp. 4–9.
5 In particularly notorious cases the Ordinaries might produce a special *Account*

which was concerned with one individual, although the practice seems to have all but ceased with Lorrain. For examples by Lorrain, see *The Confession of John Peter Dramatti; a Frenchman, Executed at Tyburn, on Wednesday the 21st of July, 1703, for the Barbarous Murther of Frances his Wife, about Bloody-Bridge near Chelsea*, London, 1703; *The Ordinary of Newgate his Account of the Behaviour and last dying Words of Edward Bird, Gent. Who was Executed at Tyburn on Monday the 23d of February, 1718/9, for the Murder of Samuel Loxton, At the Bagnio in Silver-street, Westminster*, London, 1719.

6 *A True Account of the Prisoners Executed at Tyburn. On Friday the 23d of May, 1684. With their Behaviour in Newgate, since their receiving Sentence at the Old-Bayly and dying Confessions At the place of Execution*, London, 1684. The title changed to, *The Behaviour of the condemned criminals in Newgate ... in* September 1684, and then to *The True Account of the Behaviour and Confessions of the Condemned Criminals in Newgate* in June 1685, a title which was kept throughout the rest of Smith's period in office. The next Ordinary, John Allen, published *A full and true Account of the Behaviour, Confessions, and last Dying Speeches of the Condemn'd Criminals, that were Executed at Tyburn, on Friday the 24th of May, 1700*; his successor, Roger Wykes, published *The Confessions, Behaviour, and Dying Speeches of the Criminals that were executed at Tyburn, on Saturday the 20th of July, 1700*. It was Wykes's successor, Lorrain, who more or less settled the title for the eighteenth century as *The Ordinary of Newgate his Account of the Behaviour, Confessions, and Dying-Speeches, of the Condemn'd Criminals that were Executed at Tyburn*, and it is from this that the generic title for such works, the Ordinary of Newgate's *Account*, derives.

7 See OBSP, 15–16 December 1683, 17–18 January 1684, 15–16 May 1684.

8 Clergymen who attended other prisons occasionally copied the example set by their Newgate brethren, but none of these efforts turned into a regular series. See, for example, the irregular series from Southwark Prison, which served as a prison for some of those condemned at the Surrey Assizes: Rev. W. Wilson, *A Full and Genuine Account of the Lives, Characters, Behaviour, last Dying Words and Confessions, of the Four Malefactors, that were Executed on Friday the 6th day of this Instant April 1739, at Kennington-Common*, London, 1739; *A Genuine Account of the Lives, Characters, Behaviours, Confessions, and Dying Words, of the Malefactors viz. James Day, Ann Hazzard, James Harris, Richard Keble, James Hunt, and Thomas Collins. Who were Executed at Kennington-Common. On Thursday the 25th of August, 1743*, London, [1743]; *The Solemn Declaration of Richard Coleman, Who was Executed at Kennington-Common, in the County of Surrey, on Wednesday, April 12, 1749, for the Murder of Sarah Green, Widow, with the Behaviour, Confession, and Dying Words, of the Four other Malefactors, Who were Executed at the same Time and Place*, London, [1749]; Rev. L. Howard, *A True and Impartial Account of the Behaviour, Confession, and Dying Words of the four Malefactors, Who were executed at Kennington-Common, on Friday, September 6, 1751*, London, [1751].

9 See the General Introduction in this volume, pp. 5–6. For a fascinating view from the other side of the book trade, even though it relates to a publication by the chaplain of Southwark gaol, see *The True and Genuine Account of the Confession (Whilst under Sentence of Death) of Thomas Jones, and James Welch. For the barbarous Rape and Murder of Sarah Green, as Taken from the Mouth of Nicholls (the Evidence against them) and by them attested to be the Truth*, London, [1751]. Lorrain seems to have been particularly plagued by fake *Accounts* amongst which are probably *A True Account of the Behaviour, Confession and last Dying Speeches of the Condemn'd Criminals, that were Executed at Tyburn, on Wednesday the 10th of May, 1704*, London, 1704 (signed

'P.L.' and under the imprint of 'Eliz. Malle' – the publisher of the *Account* at that time was Elizabeth Mallet); *The Ordinary's Account of Life, Birth, Death and Parentage Of John Hall, Richard Low, Stephen Bunch, William Davis, and Joseph Montisano*, London, 1707 (writer named as 'Lorrane'); *The Ordinary of Newgate's Account of the Life, Conversation, Birth and Education of Thomas Ellis, and Mary Goddard*, London, 1708; *The Whole Life and Conversation, Birth, Parentage and Education of Deborah Churchill*, London, 1708 ('Paul Lorain'); *The Whole Life and Conversation, Birth, Parentage and Education of Mr. William Gregg*, London, 1708 ('Paul Lorain'); *The Whole Life and Conversation, Birth, Parentage, and Educations of Thomas Browning, and Jeremiah Clark*, London, 1712 ('Paul Larrain, Ordinaray of Newgate').

10 Ordinary of Newgate's *Account*, 23 May 1701, 2 May 1707; *London Daily Post*, 4 August 1739, 21 December 1739, 22 December 1739; *Post Boy*, 22–4 May 1701. See also OBSP, 13–14 October 1703; Ordinary of Newgate's *Account*, 21 June 1704, 22 Sep. 1704, 25 October 1704, 7 February 1704/5, 4 May 1705, 2 May 1707; J. Guthrie, *A Sermon Preach'd in the Chapel of Newgate, Upon the particular Desire of Robert Hallam, Under Sentence of death, for the Murder of his Wife Jane, Then being Big with Child, Upon Sunday, the 6th of February, 1732*, London, [1732]; *London Daily Post, & General Advertiser*, 1 August 1739, 2 August 1739, 3 August 1739. For an attack by an Ordinary on a specific rival see Ordinary of Newgate's *Account*, 20–2 December 1738, p. 20; *Daily Advertiser*, 20 September 1738.

11 Ordinary of Newgate's *Account*, 23 October 1689, Charles Brooks.

12 Ordinary of Newgate's *Account*, 23 May 1701.

13 Ordinary of Newgate's *Account*, 23 October 1689, 20 July 1700. Also ibid., 17 December 1707, 3 October 1750, p. 102; [F. Hoffman], *Secret Transactions During the Hundred Days Mr. William Gregg Lay in Newgate under Sentence of death for High treason, from the Day of the Sentence, to the Day of his Execution*, London, 1711, p. 7; P. Lorrain, *The Dying Man's Assistant*, London, 1702, pp. 10–11; S. Rossell, *The Prisoner's Director: compiled For the Instruction and Comfort of Persons under Confinement. Whether for Debt, for Capital, or other Crimes; more especially for Those under Sentence of Death*, London, 1752, pp. 122n., 239, 241.

14 *Memoirs Of the Right Villainous John Hall, The Late Famous and Notorious Robber. Penn'd from his own Mouth sometime before his Death*, London, 4th edn, 1714, p. 27.

15 See the General Introduction in this volume, p. 9, and *The Affecting Case of Thomas Daniels*, London, 1761.

16 J.J. Richetti, *Popular Fiction before Richardson: Narrative Patterns 1700–1739*, Oxford, 1969, p. 29.

17 Rossell, *The Prisoner's Director*, pp. 236 and 243.

18 Linebaugh, 'The Ordinary of Newgate and his *Account*'; Linebaugh, 'Tyburn', pp. 166–325; Linebaugh, 'Tyburn riot against the surgeons' in D. Hay, E.P Thompson and P. Linebaugh (eds.), *Albion's Fatal Tree: Crime and Society in Eighteenth-Century England*, Harmondsworth, 1977, pp. 65–117.

19 P. Linebaugh, 'The Ordinary of Newgate and his *Account*', pp. 265–6.

6

THE

ORDINARY *of* NEWGATE,

His ACCOUNT of the

Behaviour, Confession, and Dying Words,

OF THE

MALEFACTORS,

Who were Executed at TYBURN,

On WEDNESDAY the 18th of *March*, 1740.[1]

BEING THE

First EXECUTION in the MAYORALTY

OF THE

Rt. Hon. *HUMPHREY PARSONS*, Esq;

LONDON:

Printed and Sold by JOHN APPLEBEE, in *Bolt-Court*, near

the *Leg-Tavern, Fleet-street*. M,DCC,XL.

(Price SIX-PENCE.)

Mary Young, alias *Jenny Diver*,[2] and *Elizabeth Davis*, alias *Catherine* the Wife of *Henry Huggins*, were indicted for assaulting *Judith Gardener* on the King's Highway, putting her in Fear, and taking from her 12*s*. in Money, the Money of the said *Judith*, in the Parish of St. *Mary Woolchurch, January* 17.

... *Mary Young*, alias *Jenny Diver*, about 36 Years of Age, born in *Ireland*, as I was informed, but she denied it, calling herself an *English* Woman, being unwilling to declare either her Country or Family, desiring to be excused in that Point. She had good Education at School, and was instructed in the Principles of Religion, and the Knowledge of other Things which was required, in order to fit her for doing Business. She lived with her Parents, and did not go to Service, but came up to *London*, where she soon became a good Proficient in the tricking Arts of the Town, as now she hath found to her sad Experience. A few Years ago she passed for a Wife to a Prisoner in *Newgate*, whom she daily attended, and supplied him with Victuals, and likewise gave Charity to the other Prisoners under Sentence, and to some on the Common Side. She was thought to be one of the most artfullest Pick-pockets in the World; she was a constant Street-walker, where she exercised her Skill. About 2 Years, or 2 Years and half, she was Transported, for picking the Pocket of a Gentlewoman in St. *Paul's Church Yard*, at the Feast of the Sons of the Clergy; for which Fact she was tried at the *Old Bailey*, and was ordered to be Transported; but she had not been gone long, before she and her supposed Spouse returned to *London*, where she has been a constant Practitioner ever since. She was then tried by another Name, it being usual for such Persons to change their Names upon every Occasion. On *Saturday* the 17th of *Jan* last, as she was walking along the Streets, between 6 and 7 at Night, she met with *Judith Gardener* by the Corner of the *Mansion-house*, a Man held up *Judith*'s Arm with such Force, that she was like to have lost the Use of it; *Mary* came up before the Woman, and put her Hand into her Pocket, *Judith* being frighted, cryed out she was robbed, and like to be murdered; upon this the Man run away, and a Scuffle ensuing, *Davis* taking the Man's Part, came in for her Share in the Fray, and was taken up and convicted for the same Robbery with *Mary Young*. The Man having made his Escape, *Young* and *Davis* were carried to *Devonshire Square*, and several other Places in the City, in order to carry them before a Justice, but not finding one in the Way, they came back to the *Old Bailey*, where the Court was sitting, they was brought before my Lord Mayor, who was pleased to commit them. It is observable of them, *viz. Mary Young* and *Elizabeth Davis*, that the Robbery was committed, and they sent to *Newgate* on *Saturday* the 17th of *Jan* and on *Monday* the 19th, a Bill of Indictment was found against them, and on *Tuesday* the 20th, they were tried, capitally convicted, and receiv'd Sentence of Death.[3] *Mary Young* behaved well while under Sentence, and was very devout to all outward Appearance, often crying at Prayers, and singing of Psalms. She declared that *Elizabeth Davis* had no Hand in the Robbery which she suffered for, and that she wou'd persuade the World (if possible) that she was not the Woman, that she was represented to be; but had always lived a sober Life, (if you believe her) but she could not deny the robbing of *Judith Gardener*, on the 17th of *Jan.* last, and that she was Transported by the Name of *Jane Web*, in *April* Sessions 1738.[4] She believed in Christ her only Saviour, repented of all her Sins, and was in Peace with all the World.

* * * * * * * *

[Part II, p. 5]
The following is a particular Account of the Transactions of the Life of Mary Young, *alias* Jenny Diver, &c, &c, &c.
AS I am in a few Days to suffer for what I most justly deserved, and am to give an Account to the righteous Judge of all Things for my past wicked Transactions, I thought it a Duty incumbent on men, as I could no other Way make Restitution, to publish an Account of my past mispent miserable Life; I know in doing this, I shall give much Offence to those Persons who have been Partners in my Crimes, and Partakers of ill got Goods; but let them consider 'ere 'tis too late, that the Course they are now pursuing, will one Day or other bring them into my sad State! I know if it was possible to speak with the Tongue of Men and Angels, without they beg of God, and have a sincere Desire to reform my unhappy Exit, as that of many Others before me, will be rather an Encouragement to pursue their wicked Practices, than work in them a Desire of reforming, as I must confess with all the Agonies of Horror, Remorse and anguish of Mind, it was formerly with me! But Oh! that they felt the Racks and Tortures I now do! how would they wish! what would they give! had they reformed by timely Advice. I do sincerely hope that my untimely Exit may be a Warning to all unhappy Persons, and that they would take Example by me, and shun the fatal Rock on which I split. I hope those I have any Ways offended or injured, will forgive my past Transactions, for which I am very sorry, and do heartily repent of; as the following Account contains a sincere and faithful Narrative of my Facts; and the various Methods taken in the Performance of 'em, I hope as I have made a true Discovery, that my Companions will forgive me for so doing; and I beg that God would grant them his Grace and enable them for the future to take to some honest, though ever so mean, an Employ. The Hopes of which has engag'd me to say thus much.

Mary Young, alias *Murphew*, alias *Webb*, alias *Jenny Diver*, (whose *true* Name was *Mary Young*) was so great a Proficient in her Art, that she got the Name amongst her Companions of *Jenny Diver*, alias *Diving Jenny* from her great Dexterity in picking Pockets; she followed this Profession between 14 and 15 Years; was born in the *North* of *Ireland*, but was entirely ignorant of her Family. When she was about 10 Years of Age,[5] she was put to School by an old Woman whom she used to call by the Name of *Nurse*, who bestowed some small Matter of Learning upon her, as Reading, Writing, and Plain-Work, which latter she was dextrous at, being reckon'd an extraordinary Workwoman with her Needle. When she was about 15 Years of Age, having an itching Desire to see *London*, and Quarrelling with the old Woman who kept her, she made Enquiry for any Vessel bound for

123

England, and soon finding one for her Purpose, she made an Agreement with the Captain who was to sail in three Days: Now her next Scheme was, how to leave the old Woman, and to get her Cloaths handsomely away, and Money to bear her Expences in her Passage, and when she came to *England*, to live on, 'till she could get into some Business, for as yet, she had not imbib'd any Principle to wrong or defraud any body, as she herself confess'd.

There was a young Fellow who had paid his Addresses to her in the Quality of a Suitor, for the Space of a Month, now this Person being very sollicitous to persuade her to become his Wife, she told him there was but one Way to make them both happy, and that was to go to *England*, telling him the old Woman her Nurse, would never consent for her to marry him, and if he really loved her, as he pretended, he would soon comply with her Request; the young Fellow being overjoy'd at this Proposal, promised her he would, when she had so done, she told him how she had already made an Agreement with the Captain, who was to sail in about three days, and directed him where he lived, desiring him to get Things in Readiness by that Time, he promised her he would, and accordingly took his Leave; as soon as the appointed Time came, the Morning when they were to sail, the young Fellow who was a Servant to a Gentleman of Fortune, and being willing to bring his new Bride a handsome Sum to support Expences, robb'd his Master of upwards [p. 6] of 80*l*. and his Gold Watch; and both getting secretly Aboard, she for fear of her Nurse, and he for fear of being discovered, the Ship hoisted Sail, and arrived two Days after at the City of *Liverpoole*, in *Lancashire*. As soon as they came Ashore, *Jenny* being Sea-sick, her Spark proposed to stay two or three Days, in order to refresh themselves before they proceeded for *London*; so he, for fear of being known, got a Lodging at a private House in that City; now the Day being come in which they designed to depart, he pack'd up her Cloaths, and his own, and put them in the Hands of the Waggoner in order to be carried to *London*, proposing themselves to follow, and so walk easy Day's Journeys, till such Time they should get safe to Town. As soon as they had so done, they went to a publick House in order to get some Refreshment before they set out; and as soon as they came in, who should be there but a Person who was sent in Quest of him by his Master; the young Spark was extremely surprized, and would have retreated faster than he came in, but it was too late, for the Person seized him, and told him he was his Prisoner, and immediately upon this hurry'd him with a great Mob before the Mayor. As soon as they came there (*Jenny* following him at some Distance, for in the Hurry and Confusion no Body took Notice of her) she heard him confess the Robbery of his Master, but never mention'd one Syllable about her; now just before this Accident, he had given her 10 Guineas, in order to put in a little Purse which she had, the rest of the Money and the Watch being found on him, he was committed to Prison; as soon as *Jenny* heard this, she went aside to a Publick House and wrote him a Letter, expressing a great Concern for this Misfortune, and promised to return his Things that were pack'd up for *London*, and likewise the Money which she had of him when it was in her Power; so done, she made the best of her Way to Town, never as she confessed, being the least dismayed at this Accident.

After the Hurry was a little over, she was as good as her Word; for as soon as she arriv'd at *London* she sent his Things, and some Time after that his Money. He was cast (which was after she had been in *London* some Time) for his Life, but was transported afterwards. As soon as she arrived at *London*, she got acquainted with one A. M --- p,[6] who was her Country-woman, who took a Lodging for her near *Long Acre*, where she proposed to take in Plain Work; but Business not coming in according to Expectation, M --- y[7] takes her aside one Day, and thus expostulates the Case with her, says she, *Jenny* Trading being dead, suppose we was to take a new Method of Life, which at present you are a Stranger to; but what I am acquainted with; *Jenny* being mighty desirous to know what it was, why reply'd the other, if you'll go along with me this Evening, you shall be instructed in this new Art; but I must first swear you to Secrecy, for Fear if you shou'd not like it, you should discover; upon which *Jenny* promised she would obey her Directions in all Particulars, and swearing Secrecy she was admitted into the Society that Evening, which consisted of four Persons, two Men and a Woman with herself; their Business that Evening was to go upon *Cheving the Froe*, (that is, *Cutting off Women's Pockets*;) in order to do this they attended the Theatres after the Play was over; she was appointed (as being a young Novice in the Art) to stand *Miss Slang all upon the Safe*, (that is, *to stand safe at a Distance as if not one of the Gang, in order to receive the Things stollen*.) They got that Night 2 Diamond Girdle Buckles, and a Gold Watch, which they fenced at a Lock for 70*l*. now *Jenny* had but 10*l*. for her Share, by Reason that she did the least Execution, and was in least Danger.

Jenny finding Money coming in pretty fast this Way, applied her Time very diligent in this new Study; and in order that she might be well vers'd in this new Employ, and learn the Cant Language, one of her Companions used to come every Day to instruct her in the Theory of her new Calling, as well as the practical Part; in order to which, she used to set aside two Hours every Day for this Purpose, and soon became a good Scholar, and well versed in the aforesaid Tongue; *Jenny*'s Master coming often to instruct his new Pupil, they contracted such a Respect for each other, that they agreed to live together.

By this Time *Jenny* was grown a compleat Artist, and got great Reputation amongst her Companions. One Day when they were all out together upon Business, at a noted Meeting-house in the *Old Jewry*, where abundance of People were crowding, in order to get in, *Jenny* being very genteely dressed, she observ'd a Gentleman who was a very *Rum Muns*, (that is, *a great Beau*) who had a very handsome *Glim Star*, (that is, *a Ring*) upon his *Feme*, (that is, *Hand*) which she longed to make, so giving the Hint to her Companions to *Bulk the Muns forward*, (that is, *Push*) they pushed him quite in; whereupon the Meeting being pretty full, as soon as he was in, *Jenny* held up her Hand to the young Spark, that he might help her forward, which he perceiving, very complaisantly gave her his Hand, in order to assist her, which she readily accepting of, she griped his Hand very fast, and while she had hold of his Hand, the People who were on the outside striving for Entrance, and *Jenny*'s Companions pushing forward, in the Scuffle she squeez'd his Hand so hard, that he was glad to get it away, and did not perceive her take off his Diamond Ring, which as soon as she had effected, she slip'd behind her Companions, saying at the same Time, it is in vain to get in, I'll come another Time, when there's less Crowd; her Companions convey'd her clean off, before the Gentleman had Time to miss his Ring, who called out to stop the Woman, but 'twas too late, for she had brush'd off with the Booty, this gain'd her great Applause amongst her Companions, who now appointed her an equal Share of every Thing they got.

The next Exploit that *Jenny* went on was, *Slanging the Gentry Mort rumly with a sham Kinchin*, that is, (*Cutting well the Women big with Child*) which was thus perform'd, *Jenny* had got 2 false Arms made, and Hands, by an ingenious Artist, and dressing herself very genteely, like a Citizen's Wife big with Child, with a Pillow artfully fixed under Coats for that Purpose, and her Arms fix'd on, she by the Contrivance of the Pillow hid her real ones under her Petticoat, and the artificial ones came across her Belly; dressed in this Condition, with one of the Gang in the Habit of a Footman, she takes a Chair and goes, (it being on a Sunday Evening) to the Meeting-house already mention'd; now it was so contriv'd by the rest of the Gang, that one should go before as a Scout, and bring Word to the supposed Footman in what Part of the Meeting set the *rummest Froes*; and likewise to *Saweer clearly*, (that is, *to keep a good look out*) that they should have *Vid Loges* (*repeating Watches*) by their Side, that *Jenny*'s Footman might place his Mistress accordingly. Now it was so ordered, that our big-belly'd Lady was plac'd in a Pew between 2 elderly Ladies who had both repeating Watches by their Side; she sat very quietly all the Time of the Service, but at the Conclusion of the last Prayer, the Audience being standing, she took both the Ladies Watches off, unperceiv'd by them, and *tip'd* 'em to one of her Companions, who was ready planted for the Purpose (and who went and tip'd them to *Slang upon the Safe*; and then went back to be ready for Business) Now the Congregation breaking up, every body was in a Hurry to get out, and the Gang surrounding the Ladies in order to make a greater Croud, and help *Jenny* off if she should be *smoak'd*.

The two Ladies had no sooner got out of the Pew to the Door, but they missed their Watches, and made a terrible Outcry, which alarmed that Part of the Audience, who enquiring what was the Matter, was answered that the Ladies had lost their Watches, and being asked again who took them, answered, nobody, without the D – – l and the big-belly'd Woman had, who was now got far enough off. Nay, says one of the Ladies, that's impossible, for she never moved her Hands from her Lap, all the Time of the Service. This Accident gathered a great Mob round the Ladies, some enquiring, others confounded at the Strangeness of the Robbery: In the mean while *Jenny* was slipp'd out to a House hard by, and had alter'd her Dress, and delivered herself of her great Belly, and returned with the utmost Precipitation to her Companions, in order to be assisting in the helping of with more Moveables, who was very busy with the rest of the Crowd, and while they were astonished at the Accident, they took Opportunity to make the Gentleman's *Loges* and *Tales*, (or Men's repeating Watches) and to *Chive* the *Froes* of their *Bungs*, (or cut off the Women's Pockets.)

They were succesful that Day, for no sooner was they got to the *Biding* (or Place where they divide the Booty) but they examined the Contents of their Booties, which was three *Bungs*, with *Lowers* (Purses) in each *Lower* there were ten *Ridges* (or Guineas) and two *Vid Loges*. These, with the Money they had got, and 2 *Tales* (or Swords) amounted to 30 *Ridges* a Piece, after they had *fenced* the *Loges*, &c. which was all carried abroad, and disposed of by R − − − J − − − n,[8] since dead.

[p. 8]After this Robbery, the Gang consulted together, and thought it proper not to steer that Way for some Time, for Fear of being discover'd. *Jenny* got so great a Name by this last Affair, that they all swore to act for the future according to her Directions in every Thing, which she thanked them for, and then made the following Speech.

"It is now 2 Years since I entered into this honourable Society, and I think it is a Duty incumbent upon me to advise for our general Preservation, that the following Articles ought to be made for the Use of our Gang.

I. That no one else be admitted without the Consent of the whole Gang.

II. That no one presume to go upon any thing by him or herself upon Pain of being entirely turn'd off, and left to shift.

III. That if any new Member be propos'd by any of the Gang, that he or she shall be a Month upon Trial, and all that Time shall be instructed at convenient Seasons in the *Cant Tongue*, so that they may speak intelligibly to nobody but the Gang.

IV. That if any of the Gang should happen to be taken upon any one Action, that the rest shall stand by him, or her, and swear any thing in order to get such releas'd; and if convicted, a sufficient Allowance to be given him or her in Prison out of the Common Stock, that they may live in a Gentleman or Gentlewoman-like Manner. These Articles were agreed to and sign'd by 'em all".

Their next Adventure was in St. *James*'s-Park upon a fine Day, when abundance of People of Fashion were walking. In that Place, *Jenny* being well dressed, and her sham great Belly, with one of the Gang in the Habit of a Servant attending her, they took the Opportunity coming out at *Spring Garden* Gate, when a great Concourse of People were crouding, for the sham Lady to make a false Step and Stumble; presently abundance of good-natur'd Gentlemen and Ladies seeing a big-belly'd Woman ready to fall, was very busy striving who should first lend their Assistance, notwithstanding which, the Lady fairly contriv'd to fall down, and when they went to help her up, she made Signs, and gave 'em to understand that she had so hurt herself by the Fright, that she could not presently recover so as to be able to stand upon her Legs; by this Time more People came up to see what was the Matter, and she had so order'd it as to fall just in the Middle of the Passage; and while the Croud was gazing on, and commiserating the Case of the poor supposed distressed Lady, the rest of the Gang were very busy in speaking with their Pockets, Diamond Girdle Buckles, &c. They manag'd their Business so dextrously, that they got by this Adventure, two Diamond Girdle Buckles, a Gold Watch, a Gold Snuff Box and two Purses which contain'd upward of twenty Guineas; the next Day the Buckles, Watch, &c.

were advertized, and a large Reward offer'd for them; which $M---y^9$ proposed to restore for the Reward, when *Jenny* started up and ask'd who would venture Home with them? I, says $M---y,^{10}$ would you? do you not consider the Consequence of returning them? why reply'd the other, there is no Questions to be ask'd, What then, replied *Jenny*, suppose there is not, apprehend you no farther Consequence than that; no, replied the other; why then resumed *Jenny*; my Reason is this; suppose you go Home with them and get the Reward offered; here lies the Case, the Parties injured, will, though they ask you no Question, take particular Notice of your Person, and some time or other when you are out upon Business, you may be *smoak'd*, and then perhaps all may be *blown*; so my Advice is, that whatever Things may be got, though we can *Fence* 'em but for two Thirds of the Value offer'd, yet it is much the safer Way, and less dangerous. This Reason the Gang applauded much, and presently consented to send them to their usual *Fence*, (who was one who used to trip over to *Holland* very often upon the Smuggling Business, and who gave most Money for Goods got in that Manner) and the Gang for the future very seldom made Restitution, but generally dealt with this *Fence*.

Some small Time after this last Adventure, 2 of the Gang fell Sick, and were rendered uncapable of turning out upon Business for some Time; now *Jenny* and her *Quondam Spouse* were obliged to turn out by themselves upon the *Slang mort Lay*, described in the following Adventures. *Jenny* being dressed as a big-belly'd Woman already mention'd, and her Spouse as a Footman in a Livery, used to take the Opportunity of the Master of the House's Absence in a genteel [p. 9] Street, when the Lady's pretended Footman knocking at the Door, ask'd if the Lady of the House was at Home, and being answer'd yes, used to say, my Lady here is taken ill and desires to speak with your Mistress; and so when she had introduc'd herself and Servant, they was not idle upon the Occasion, but generally made what they could that lay in the Way. One Day *Jenny* and her Servant being upon Business of this Nature in *Burr Street*, near *Wapping*, *Jenny*'s Servant knocked at the Door, and a Person coming and enquiring his Business, my Lady, says he there, pointing to *Jenny*, is a little out of Order, and being some Distance from Home, desires to speak with your Mistress; the Servant desired the Lady to Walk in, and said, she would fetch her Mistress presently, who was above Stairs.

So directly in goes *Jenny* grunting and groaning as if she was half dead. Down comes the Mistress, and sends the Maid in a hurry up Stairs for the Chamber-pot; while she went to fetch the Smelling Bottle. While they were gone, *Jenny* took the Opportunity of opening the Drawer, and taking out a fine dress'd suit, worth 60 Guineas, which she presently put in a Place made on purpose on the Inside of her large Hoop, and was got sitting in her Chair by the Time the Lady return'd in a very moving melancholy Posture, pretending to be almost dead. As soon as the Lady came, and her Servant with the Pot, the pretended Footman was ordered into the Kitchen, who had till then attended his Mistress; but out of Decency, was desired to walk down till his Mistress wanted him; while he was in the Kitchen, he took the Opportunity to convey half a dozen Silver Spoons, a Salt, and a

Pepper-Box in his Pocket; and as the Lady and her Maid above Stairs were very busy in applying her Smelling-Bottle to Madam's Nose, she took the Opportunity to convey the Lady's Purse out of her Pocket, when she had so done, pretending to be a little Better, ask'd the Lady's Pardon for the extraordinary Trouble she had given her, and returning many Thanks for her great Care and Kindness, desired her Man might be call'd to get a Coach, which he did in a Trice, and order'd the Coachman to drive to Mr. – – – naming an eminent Merchant near *Tower Street*, at the same Time taking Leave of the Lady, and inviting her to the aforesaid Merchant's; but as soon as the Coachman had drove out of Sight, he was order'd to stop, and Madam *Jenny* pretending she could not ride easy in a Coach: Here *John*, says she, give the Coachman a Shilling, and let eim [him] go about his Business. As soon as this was done, *John* and his Mistress retreated another Way, and went clean off with the Booty; two or three Facts of this Nature put a Stop to their farther Proceedings, the Circumstances which attended the committing of, being put into the public Papers, so that they thought it safest to desist from any more Tricks of this Nature.

Some few Days after, *Jenny*'s Companion's recovering, they pursued their old Adventures with great Success; for in less than 3 Years they acquir'd above 300 Pounds a-piece, besides Expences by these illegal Practices.

About this Time the Gang agreed to go in the Country upon Business there; so they took a Progress down to *Bristol*, in the Time of the Fair, kept there in the Summer Season. Here they thought it necessary to admit a new Member, whom they found at that Place; who was esteemed a good Hand upon *The Twang Adam Cove*; that is (*could draw him in by a fine Tongue, or Way of talking those, whom they had a Design to impose upon*) him they admitted after reading the foremention'd Articles, and swearing him to Secrecy; here it was thought proper to metamorphose one of them into the Habit of a Servant in Livery. The 2 Women pass'd for Gentlewomen, Merchants Wives in *London*, and who had come down to see the Fair, and the 2 Men for Persons who came down as dealers, and in order that they might more safely accomplish their intended Designs, they lodg'd at separate Places, their Reason for so doing was, that if any of the Gang was detected, the others might appear for their Characters, as Acquaintance accidentally meeting there; they had their Lessons so perfect, that each knew one another's meaning almost by a Nod: One Day the whole Gang being in the Fair, they espy'd a West Country Clother, who had just received a Parcel of Money, to the amount of 100 Pounds, which he had given to a Servant, and order'd him to carry it to his Lodgings, and lock it up in his Bureau, and likewise gave him a Key, and bad him return in about an Hour to the Sign of the *Fountain*, a Tavern in the *High Street*. The Whole Gang upon this, follows the Fellow and jostles him in the Croud, but he was so careful of his Bag that they could not get it from him [p. 10] by this Means; so they were obliged to have recourse to the following Stratagem.

One of the Gang steps after him out of the Fair, and giving him a Tap of the Shoulder; Friend, says he, did not you part from your Master just now, and did not he order you to go Home with a Bag of Money. *Yea*, replied the Countryman, *and what then*? oh! says he, your Master has alter'd his

Mind, and is upon the Point of Agreement for some Goods with my Mistress, and desires you will bring it, in order to pay for 'em, at the – – – naming a House where *Jenny* and the rest of the Gang were gone to. *Oh! moighte weell, moighte weell!* says the poor credulous Fellow. *I'se go wi you;* so Cheek by Jole they go along together.

In the mean Time, *I – – –,*[11] who was dressed as the supposed Lady's Servant, amused the Countryman with what a handsome rich Lady his Mistress was, and how gloriously he lived with her; and how free she always used him.

By this Time they drew towards the House where the rest of the Gang was waiting. When they came there, *Jenny*'s supposed Servant introduced the Countryman (who artfully as they pass'd along, got his Master's Name, unknown to the poor ignorant Fellow.) When they entered the Room, who is this honest Man says *Jenny*, Oh! Madam, it is Mr. *S – – –*'s Servant, come according to his Master's Orders. Oh! honest Friend says she, sit down, your Master is just gone a little Way, and will return presently, but you must stay till he comes back; *Yea, Yea, Madam,* says the Countryman, *I shall weat on your Lediship.* Come honest Friend says she, will you drink a Glass of Wine; *No Ise thank you Madam.* Come, Come, don't be bashful, you shall drink, so pouring out a Glass of Wine, he drank it off; come now you must drink another towards your Master's Health. *S'Bleed Madaum,* says the Countryman, *Ise drink that, thof 'twas a whole Mile to the Bottom;* so taking the Glass in his Hand, drank it off; now says *Jenny*, you must drink my Health, the Countryman with the two first Glasses being pretty much spiritted, chatter'd, *ads Waudds, Madam, that Ise do thof it was as deep as the Sea; an I codd* ---- and so off it goes; well done, honest Friend, says *Jenny*.

Now every Glass the poor Countryman drank, was mix'd with a certain Quantity of liquid Laudanum.

As soon as she had done this, Here *John*, says she, take this honest Fellow, and treat him handsomely till his Master comes, and then I'll send for him in again; so the poor Countryman making twenty aukward Scringes and Scrapes, goes out, and was convey'd to a more close Room convenient for the Purpose, along with his new Acquaintance.

When they had been there about half an Hour, and drank three or four Glasses of more Wine, the Countryman began to yawn, and in some small Time after, fell fast asleep. As soon as he perceived this, the Signal was given, and the Gang came in, and took the poor Fellows Bag of Money, paid the Reckoning, and ordered the Servant not to disturb the poor Man, who was weary, but let him have his Nap out. They went away, and going seperately to their Lodgings, they got their Things in Readiness, and then made the best of their Way for *London*, leaving the poor Country Fellow to curse his new Acquaintance.

They made so many Things at this Fair, that when they came to Town, and *Fenced* them, they shared Thirty Pounds a-piece, besides Expences.

By these Means, the Gang supported themselves in the most splendid Manner, sometimes living very profusely, like People of Quality; only they kept up what they term'd a common Stock, to support themselves in Case of any Disaster, which was thus raised. When any Booty was got and sold, a Tenth Part was put by, to relieve the Gang in Time of Need, and the remaining Part, was equally divided amongst them.[12]

The usual Places of *Jenny* and the Gang's Resort in *London*, when there was no extraordinary Crowd in other Places, was the *Change*, the *Bridge*,[13] &c. One Day being upon Business at the last mentioned Place about 5 o'Clock in the Evening, the Gang espy'd a Lady very well dressed, on Foot, walking over, and when she had got about half Way, a sudden Hurry of Carts and Coaches coming over at the same Instant, she stood up at the Door in order to avoid them. One of the Gang, being genteely dressed, steps up at the same Time, and says, *Have a Care, Madam*; and so standing before her, catches hold of both her Arms, that she should not be at Liberty to *Tout* the rest, and holds them up: In the mean Time [p. 10] *Jenny*, and the rest of the Gang, were very busy with her, and they was so dexterous, that before the Coaches got by, they made her Pocket, and walked off with it. As soon as the Hurry was over, the Lady dropp'd the supposed Gentleman a fine Curtsey, and humbly thank'd him for his great Care, and so took her Leave, little dreaming of her Loss; for they found in the Pocket upwards of 30 Guineas, a gold Snuff box worth 6 Guineas, and a Case of silver Instruments.

The next Day being upon Business, the Corner of *Change-Alley*, they got a Pocket-Book, in which was two hundred Pound Bank-Notes, which they sold to their old Friend *J – n*,[14] for 130*l*. ready Cash.

Jenny now took genteel Lodgings not far from *Covent Garden*; and living in a very gay Manner, kept a Servant to wait on her and her supposed Spouse. They lodged in this Place, that they might be the readier to attend the Theatre, and convey their Booties soonest off.

One Night when his Majesty was at the Play-House, the Gang dressed *Jenny* up very gay, like a Person of Quality, and going in a Chair with her Footman before her, she got a Place in the Middle of the front Boxes; but having no Opportunity to do any Thing while the Play was performing, she came out before the Entertainment was over, handed by a young Beau, whom she had pick'd up. She sounding him, found him a Country young Gentleman, lately come from *York*.

The Spark being very much enamour'd with his new Mistress, desired the Honour of conducting her Home to her Lodgings. Laird, Sir, says she, that's impossible, for I am married, and if I should let a strange Gentleman wait upon me Home, what do you think my Spouse would say? Then, Madam, quoth the Youngster, permit me the Pleasure of waiting on you to drink a Glass of Wine. Sir, says she, it is what I don't care to do, but added with a Sigh, if I thought you was a Man of Honour, I durst venture to drink a Glass of Wine, for sure there is no Harm in that, but I am told that there is so few Men of Honour, it is hard trusting. Madam, reply'd the enamoured Spark eagerly, I would sooner kill myself than hurt your Reputation. With this last Expression *Jenny* seemed to be overcome, and went with the Spark to the *Rose*, the Corner of the Theatre, and calling for a Room, he said a hundred fine Things to his new Acquaintance. After *Jenny* had drank a Glass, and sat a Quarter of an Hour, she seemed uneasy, and wanted to be gone; our Spark used many Intreaties for her Stay, but in vain, for she positively insisted upon going (for as yet she had not given the Gang necessary Directions upon this new Affair, so to be sure she could not stay) then the young Spark insisted upon going with her, but she begged he would not trouble himself, yet with much Intreaty on his Side, this last Request was, with some seeming Difficulty, granted.

Then he called the Drawer, and ordered a Hackney Coach to be got ready, and handed the Lady in with much Complisance. *Jenny* order'd the Coachman to drive slowly to her Lodgings, naming the Place where she lived, and as they were going Home, he pressed hard for the Pleasure of seeing her again. She told him, she expected her Husband would be out of Town in two or three Days, and in that Time he might call upon her. By this Time the Coach came to the Door, so *Jenny* requesting the Favour, that the Spark would sit still till she got out, and get himself out at some other Place for fear of her Husband, she would be glad to see him in two or three Days, and in that Time prepare for his Reception.

The young Gallant, so overjoy'd, took his Leave; so *Jenny* got out of the Coach, and going up Stairs, found the Gang come there before, for it seems the Signal was for her to stay till the Play was done, and she coming out before, they had missed her. As soon as she entered the Room they began to upbraid her, for being out of the Way, for it seems by wanting her they lost their Right Hand, for they made but one Gold Snuff-Box that Night; but she soon pacified them, by telling them her Adventure, and what she intended to do, the appointed Evening being come, in which *Jenny*'s Spark was to appear, he came dressed very gay with a gold Watch in his Pocket, a gold hilted Sword by his Side, a Diamond Ring upon his Finger, and a Gold headed Cane dangling in his Hand.

Jenny being ready to receive him, had dressed up two of the gang in rich Liveries, and *M – – –*[15] as her waiting Woman very gay, and the Lodgings being genteel, all Things seemed to look very grand.

[p. 12]The young Spark seeing this Grandeur, seemed quite amazed, and to be sure thought her some Person of Quality, as he afterwards privately told her; by and by up comes a Bottle of Wine, and some rich Sweetmeats, then the Footman was ordered to withdraw. Now Sir, says *Jenny*, you must think I have a great Respect for you, to be so free with you in this manner, I hope you are a Gentleman of more Honour than to tattle of a Lady's Favours. The young Gentleman reply'd, he would sooner cut his Tongue out; after some small Discourse, *Jenny* gave him to understand that she did not expect her Husband till very late that Evening, so the Spark begged hard, that during that Time she would make him happy in her Arms; in short, she so contriv'd Matters that she made him believe none of her Servants knew any Thing of the Affair of his Stay, except her faithful Chambermaid and Confident; so conducting him into her Bedchamber, the young Spark being eager to enjoy his Mistress, soon slipped off his Cloaths and got into Bed, she pulled hers off more slowly, pretending to be very bashful, upon which he jump'd out of Bed in order to assist her, as she was unbuckling her Shoes, she pretending to be modest, catched hold of his Hand, and seeming to admire his Ring, took it off his Finger and put it upon hers; as soon as she had got into Bed, the Signal was given from the supposed Maid, who knock'd at the Door, and told her that her Master was come Home: *Jenny* immediately jumped out of Bed, Lord! says she, what shall I do, I am inevitably ruin'd! Madam, says her Lover, what shall I do? Oh Sir! says she, I have hit it, get into Bed and cover yourself all over Head and Ears, and I'll take your Cloaths and hide 'em, least perchance he should take it into his Head to come into this Room, and in the mean Time I'll go and persuade him that I'm not well, and perhaps I can make him lie by himself to Night, which if I do than I can have the Pleasure of being with you this Evening.

The Spark immediately did as he was ordered, and *Jenny* slipp'd on her Night Gown, &c. and went out of the Room, and lock'd the Door after her, when she came into the Place where the rest of the Gang was, they held a Consultation; the result of which was, immediately to quit the Lodgings and leave poor *Pill Garlick*[16] in the Lurch, which was immediately put in Execution, and the poor unfortunate *Enamoretta* left locked up by himself, who no Doubt cursed his New Acquaintance, which for the future 'tis thought gave him a Caution how he enter'd into Intreagues of this Nature; they examined the Contents of this Booty, which amounted when the Moveables was *Fenced* to 250*l.* Now *Jenny* had the greatest Share of this Booty, because she did the most Execution; her Share coming to upwards of 50*l.*[17]

After this Robbery the Gang retired into the Country, where they carried on their Adventures very successfully for the Space of half a Year, when coming to Town they pursued their old Courses as Occasion offered.

She lay in *Newgate* almost 4 Months, and then was Transported; during the Time of her Confinement she turned *Fence*, and bought such Things as came in her Way, she having a quantity of Money by her, and knowing this Business could no ways affect her, she being Cast already; and when she went away she had as many Goods of one Sort or other, as would almost have loaded a Waggon. When she came on Board she was treated in a quite different Manner from the rest of the Transports, and was put ashore at the first Port they came to in *Virginia*. *Jenny* staid no longer there than to see the Country, for Business in her Way could not be transacted there; so after she had diverted herself as long as she thought proper, she agreed with a Gentleman for her Passage who was bound for *England*, who brought her over. When she came back, she did not chuse immediately to come to Town, but went and took a Progress round the Countries; and after she had sufficiently tired herself, and the Country People with her Exploits, she came to *London*, where she with some others used to resort about *London-Bridge*, the *Royal Exchange*, the Play-Houses, and St. *Paul's*.[18]

In *April* 1738, in the Mayorlty of Sir *John Barnard*, she was try'd by the Name of *Jane Web*, for picking the Pocket of Mrs. *Rowley*, who had been at St. *Paul's* to hear the Rehearsal; one Mr. *Addy* who detected her was offered 50*l.* not to appear against her on her Trial; but he like an honest Man refused it. At the very Time Mr. *Addy* seized her for picking the Pocket of Mrs. *Rowley*, she was going to pick the Pocket of Dr. *Best's* Lady. Another Person who appeared against her on her Trial, said he saw her pick

20 Pockets that Day, and had known her to have been a Pickpocket these five Years; she was found guilty, and was ordered for Transportation, and accordingly was Transported, but returned again, [p. 13] and followed her old Practices, till she was detected for robbing Mrs. *Gardener* near the *Mansion-House*, on the 17th of *Jan.* last, for which Robbery she was capitally convicted, and suffered.

All the while she was under Sentence of Death, she never omitted coming the Chapel, behaving herself very devout, and seemingly very penitent for her past wicked Life. The Day before she died she sent for the Nurse that nursed her Child, (who lives in *Little-Britain*) which is about three Years of Age, and begged that she would now and then see it, and telling her the Child would be taken Care of; desiring her to give it good Advice, and instill good Notions into it, when she came capable to receive her Admonitions; which the Nurse faithfully promised to perform while she lived; on which *Jenny* reply'd, I don't doubt of your Love for my poor Child, and so God bless and protect you; Pray for my poor Soul while I am living, for I have greatly offended my good God.

The Morning she went to Execution she seem'd very composed; but when the Officer came to halter her in the *Press Yard*, she was very much shocked. She was conveyed to the Place of Execution in a Mourning Coach, attended by the Revd. Mr. *Broughton*,[19] who went and prayed to her in the Cart, after some Time allowed her for her Devotions, she went off the Stage, crying to God to have Mercy on her, Christ have Mercy on me, Lord receive my Spirit, Sweet Jesus receive my Spirit, *&c.* After she had hung the usual Time, she was cut down, and convey'd to *Pancrass*, in order to be interr'd in the Church-yard.

She confessed the Fact for which she died for.[20]

NOTES

1 The hanging took place in 1741.
2 The slang term 'diver' for a pickpocket predated Young by at least 150 years. 'Jenny Diver' was a part in John Gay's hugely popular play, *The Beggar's Opera* (1728). Young seems to have been the only person at that time to whom this name was applied; when, as Jane Webb, she was convicted for picking pockets in 1738, one newspaper referred to her as 'Jane Webb alias Jenny Diver': *London Daily Post, and General Advertiser*, 12 April 1738, 19 April 1738.
3 OBSP, 20 January 1741. According to another account Young and Davis both pleaded at the trial that they were pregnant ('pleaded their bellies'), which, if successful, would at least put the execution off and, in all probability, would lead to a reduction of the sentence to transportation. But the 'jury of matrons' – women impanelled to examine those who made such pleas – found them both 'Not Quick with Child', and they were condemned: *Daily Post*, 21 January 1741; *London Daily Post, and General Advertiser*, 21 January 1740–1. However, Elizabeth Davis, also known as 'Catherine the Wife of Henry Huggins', had her sentence reduced to transportation for seven years; she was transported to Virginia in January 1739: *London Evening Post*, 10–12 March 1741; P.W. Coldham, *The Complete Book of Emigrants in Bondage: 1614–1775*, Baltimore, 1988, p. 212; *Daily Gazetteer*, 21 January 1741.

4 OBSP, 12–15 April 1738, trial of Jane Webb. The woman robbed was a Mrs Rowley. According to her, she was held by two men while Webb stole from her. Mr Astley, who appears to have been a law officer of some kind, said of Webb, 'I have known her for a Pick-pocket these 5 Years, and saw her pick 20 Pockets that Day. She is so well known, that I could have brought a Dozen People to have prov'd this'. Mr Addy, another prosecution witness, alleged that friends of Webb had tried to bribe him. Six people appeared for the defence to give evidence of Webb's good character: Mary Cherry, Ann Carter, Francis Fletcher, Mary Robes, John Taylor and Thomas Welch. One newspaper reported that after her arrest and as she was being taken to Newgate 'she attempted to stab the Person who apprehended her'. The same newspaper commented that 'This Webb is reckoned one of the Tip-top Hands at Picking of Pockets, and well known at Newgate by the Name of Mrs. *Murphy*; she belongs to a large Gang of Pickpockets that attend the Play-houses, &c. who declare if it costs *Two Hundred Pounds she shan't go abroad*': London Daily Post, and General Advertiser, 12 April 1738, 19 April 1738; Weekly Miscellany, 21 April 1738; The Country Journal: or, the Craftsman, 22 April 1738; Coldham, The Complete Book of Emigrants, p. 849. There is some confusion here over the person called Murphew or Murphy; Rev. Mr. Gordon, The Life and Circumstantial Account of the Extraordinary and Surprising Exploits, Travels, Robberies and Escapes, of the famous Jenny Diver, The most noted Pickpocket of her Time, Who was executed for a Street robbery, on the 18th of March, 1740. With an Introduction Written by Herself. To which is added A Narrative of the chief Transactions of Harry Cook, And also the Gang to which he belonged. Written by the Rev. Mr. Gordon, Ordinary of Newgate, London, n.d., has Ann Murphew, a common corruption of Murphy, as the person who introduced Young to crime, but according to newspapers (above) and the Gentleman's Magazine, March 1741, vol. ii, pp. 161–2, Young called herself Murphy. See also note 6 and *passim*.
5 That is, about 1714, assuming she died at the age of 36 years.
6 According to Gordon, The Life and Circumstantial Account of . . . Jenny Diver, p. 7, this is Ann Murphew. According to Coldham, The Complete Book of Emigrants, an Ann Murphy was sentenced to be transported in April 1746, although there is no record of her being sent abroad.
7 Gordon, The Life and Circumstantial Account of . . . Jenny Diver, p. 7, has 'Murphew'.
8 Roger Johnson: ibid., p. 10.
9 Murphew: ibid., p. 12.
10 Murphew: ibid., p. 12.
11 Johnson: ibid., p. 15.
12 Henry Fielding wrote, in 1751, of the existence of a similarly organized gang: H. Fielding, An Enquiry into the Causes of the Late Increase of Robbers and Related Writings, ed. M.R. Zirker, Oxford, 1988, p. 76.
13 London Bridge: Gordon, The Life and Circumstantial Account of . . . Jenny Diver, p. 17.
14 Johnson: ibid., p. 17.
15 Murphew: ibid., p. 19.
16 'Pill Garlick' was normally a term of sympathy applied to oneself, along the lines of 'poor me'; here it is used in the slightly less sympathetic way of 'poor fool'. It carries the implication of someone who has been left out, as here the 'Spark' is unaware what is going on.
17 '70l.': Gordon, The Life and Circumstantial Account of . . . Jenny Diver, p. 21.
18 The Gordon biography breaks here (at p. 21) and continues at p. 39: ibid.

19 Thomas Broughton (1712–77), a methodist who became, in 1743, secretary of
the Society for Promoting Christian Knowledge. He wrote *Serious Advice and
Warning to Servants. More especially those of the Nobility and Gentry*, London,
1746 (6th edn, 1800) about Matthew Henderson, who was hanged for the murder
of Lady Dalrymple.

20 Including Young, twenty people were ordered to be hanged on 18 March, which,
even for those bloody times, was a large number. It was announced beforehand
that foot and horse soldiers from General Wood's regiment would guard the
procession from Newgate to Tyburn. Such precautions were not usual. There
may have been a fear that Young's gang would rescue her (see *Gentleman's
Magazine*, in this note), but there was also a rumour circulating about a week
before that an armed attempt was to be made to rescue some Irish prisoners. This
alleged plot was discovered by another condemned prisoner, Richard Quail, and,
according to the Ordinary, both Young and Davis confirmed Quail's account.
The truth of this story is left uncertain by the fact that Quail, who might have
expected some sort of reward, was hanged along with the others: *Daily Post*, 12
March 1741, 14 March 1741, 16 March 1741, 19 March 1741; *London Daily Post,
and General Advertiser*, 19 March 1740–1; *Daily Gazetteer*, 18 March 1741, 21
March 1741; *London Evening Post*, 12–14 March 1741; Ordinary of Newgate's
Account, 18 March 1740–1, Part I, p. 17, Part II, p. 20.
     Although the soldiers were almost certainly there to prevent a rescue, they may
have had another, incidental function, to protect the prisoners, or some of them,
from the crowd: the Ordinary, having described the escort of soldiers, continued:
'In this Manner were they convey'd through a vast Multitude of People to
Tyburn, some of whom, notwithstanding the Guard of Soldiers, were very rude
and noisy, hallooing, throwing Brickbats, Mud, &c. at the unhappy Prisoners,
as they passed' (Ordinary of Newgate's *Account*, 18 March 1740–1, Part II, p.
17). However, such behaviour may have been directed, not at the prisoners, but
at the soldiers, or at the other members of the crowd: B. Mandeville, *An Enquiry
into the Causes of the Frequent Executions at Tyburn*, London, 1725. The
Gentleman's Magazine, March 1741, vol. ii, pp. 161–2, reported the hanging day:
'*Mary Young* went to *Tyburn* in a Mourning Coach, veil'd, and strongly guarded,
there being a Design form'd to rescue her. . . . She appeared gaily dressed even
to the last, yet deeply affected with her approaching Fate. Her Concern was so
sensibly expressed, when she took Leave of her little Child, a few Days before
her Execution, that (a weekly Writer says) it drew Tears into the Eyes of the
Turnkey. *So far does Affliction with a genteel Behaviour and Dress move
Compassion beyond what is shewn to the Generality of Objects seen there; at
least it was another sort of Compassion. We are more nearly concerned for Persons
under these terrible Circumstances when they are at last sensible of their Crimes
and wish they had acted a more rational and honest Part. Whereas there is some
Difficulty in pitying those abandoned Wretches, who do not pity themselves; tho'
it might be juster to say, that we cannot sympathize with them – we must pity
them.*

IV

THE DISCOVERIES OF JOHN POULTER (1753–4)

7

INTRODUCTION

A newspaper report of John Poulter's arrest in 1753 for robbery also noted that he had 'made a Discovery of a Gang of Rogues to save himself', and it seems that *The Discoveries* was, in some form, that confession.[1] Although he was not hanged until February 1754, versions of this confession appeared in the *Bath Journal* over two issues in April 1753 and also in broadsheet form. The much more elaborate pamphlet, *The Discoveries of John Poulter*, reprinted here, first appeared sometime in 1753.[2] *The Discoveries* represents the most extreme example of that genre of 'autobiographies' which resemble, and were, perhaps, derived from, confessions made by offenders in an effort to escape death by becoming a witness for the Crown against their old comrades.[3] Doubtless, their function dictated their form; hence the apparent care taken in *The Discoveries* over dates, places and people. Furthermore, unlike the majority of criminal biographies of this period, Poulter's early life, that is, before 1749, is summed up in a brief paragraph which is only tacked on as a supplement to the main substance of the work. So, there is no speculation about the reasons behind Poulter's choice of crime as a career, with the exception of some discussion of his being drawn back into crime after having gone to Ireland.

John Poulter was born, according to *The Discoveries*, in 1715 and hanged at Ivelchester (Ilchester) in March 1754. He had been condemned at the Somerset Assizes held at Wells in August 1753 after pleading guilty to involvement in the robbery, in February 1753, of Dr Hancock, a well-known physician, and his daughter on Claverton Down, just outside Bath. During the eighteenth century a guilty plea in a trial for a capital offence, while not unknown, was fairly unusual.[4] It seems, generally, to have been discouraged on the ground that since not all of the large number who were capitally convicted could be hanged, a selection process was necessary,[5] and this required a report made by the judge on the basis of, amongst other things, the evidence presented at the trial; indeed, when asked for his comments on Poulter, the trial judge, Baron Smythe, wrote, 'on His arraignment, [he] pleaded Guilty: therefore, as No Evidence was given, I cannot inform your Lord[ship] of any Circumstances of the Robbery.' So, why did Poulter plead guilty? In his petition to the King for a pardon, Poulter wrote that he did so because he knew he was guilty and was 'unwilling to trouble the Court'. More likely, he was duped by the authorities, as *The Discoveries* suggests, into believing that he would be admitted as a witness for the prosecution against his comrades, and, perhaps, the guilty plea was part of that deal. Certainly, the title-pages of some early editions of *The Discoveries* have Poulter as having been admitted as 'King's Evidence', and in his petition to the King he referred to his being admitted 'an Evidence' against his comrades, 'agreable to the Promise made by the Justice before whom he made his Information'.[6]

After the trial he was immediately respited by Smythe until 1 November. This was not an uncommon procedure in capital cases where the judge believed there to be a good chance that a petition to the King would succeed in securing some lesser punishment. In his report to the Earl of Holderness, the Secretary of State, on 28 September, Smythe said he was in favour of a full pardon or a pardon conditional on transportation; he said the former should be used if some of Poulter's comrades were taken and Poulter's evidence was needed (a convicted felon could not testify, so a full pardon would have been necessary), or if none was taken then Poulter should be transported. Presumably as a result of this, Poulter was respited until 1 January 1754 and instructions were sent to Bath for the authorities there 'to employ a proper Person to examine the said Poulter touching all such Discoveries as he may be able to make', and to report back to the Secretary of State. It was, perhaps, this that led to the endorsement by Richard 'Beau' Nash, by the High Sheriff of Somerset and by various other dignitaries of Poulter's petition for mercy to the King on 16 October. Along with the petition Nash also sent a letter to the Duke of Newcastle in which, writing on behalf 'of the Gentlemen of [Bath] Corporation and others', he stated that 'every one here wishes he may not be Executed'. The petition and accompanying letter may not, however, have been the consequence of Holderness's request for a report on Poulter, since Nash adds a postscript asking for the matter to be dealt with urgently because 'the Man is reprieved only to the 1st of next Month' – that is, 1 November, so he was unaware that Poulter had already been respited until 1 January. Another letter, sent at the same time, suggests a different explanation, namely, that the matter having been 'put into Mr. Nashes hands . . . he had forgot it.' In any event, on 8 December the High Sheriff of Somerset was told that, 'Some farther favourable Circumstances having been humbly represented to the King', the respite was extended until 1 March 1754.

Then, on 14th December, the matter was referred to the Attorney-General and the Solicitor-General for their view as to whether Poulter 'will, probably, become a material & sufficient Evidence, towards detecting & convicting the several Delinquents therein mentioned, & whether He is an Object deserving His Majesty's gracious & free pardon for that Purpose'.

Presumably their answer was not favourable because on 19 February a letter was prepared instructing the High Sheriff of Somerset that the hanging was to be carried out. Before that letter could be sent, news of Poulter's escape on 16 February and recapture arrived at the Secretary of State's office. A new letter was sent revoking the respite until 1 March and bringing forward the date for the hanging to 25 February. The High Sheriff was commanded, 'that you do cause the proper Steps to be taken, that no Endeavours whatever, that may be used, by himself, or his Accomplices, shall frustrate the same'.[7] Perhaps he was the victim of people anxious to prevent him from adding to his confessions, although this seems unlikely since he had been in custody for almost a year. More probably, the authorities felt that in spite of his confessions his usefulness as an informer was limited, and, indeed, it is difficult to discover anyone who was convicted as a result of his evidence – something which may cast a degree of doubt over *The Discoveries*. At a time when even useful informers were viewed with contempt, so much worse was the position of a useless one. After his recapture, the *Bath Journal* sympathized with his reasons for escaping, but added, 'his Proceedings have been really very wrong, with Regard to his Impeachments, &c. – PROVIDENCE will never suffer such a Villain to escape Justice!'[8]

The success of this biography was doubtless related partly to its revelations of organized crime and partly to the period during which it was published. It appeared in the midst of a lengthy panic over crime that began as far back as 1748 with the ending of the War of the Austrian Succession. This led to the rapid demobilization of large numbers of soldiers and sailors, and with this came the belief that crime was on the increase: as one London writer put it, 'this P - - - e [Peace] has stocked the Town so full of gay young Fellows'. In 1748 and for the next year or so, during the most active period of demobilization, the newspapers were filled with reports of robberies allegedly committed by sailors and soldiers; sailors demolished bawdy houses in The Strand and in Goodman's Fields in 1749, terrifying the authorities; and at Tyburn more than half of the forty-four people hanged in 1749 were described as sailors, including fourteen out of the sixteen hanged on one day in October 1749. Although the link between the panic and sailors and soldiers gradually diminished, the panic itself remained.

In October 1750 a bored Horace Walpole, himself the victim of a robbery, wrote to a friend, that, 'Robbery is the only thing that goes on with any vivacity.' Pamphleteers, such as Henry Fielding, the novelist and Bow Street magistrate, were urging the authorities to take action, and following a speech on the subject by George II, the House of Commons set up a committee of inquiry in 1751. But the following year Walpole clearly felt that things were no better, writing that, 'One is forced to travel even at noon as if one was going to battle.' In May 1753 a correspondent in the *London Evening Post* commented that, 'it is a Certainty that the Gaols of this Kingdom were never so crouded as at present', and on 21 February 1754 – the day before the instructions were sent to bring the date for Poulter's execution forward – the Archbishop of Canterbury delivered to the Duke of Newcastle a letter from the Bishops expressing their continued worries over the crime problem.[9]

It was against this background that *The Discoveries* was first published. Contemporary readers must have regarded it as confirming their worst fears. The pamphlet tells of the existence of gangs of professional criminals moving about the south of England with relative ease and speed, and supported by a network of public houses ('flash houses') where they are made welcome, plan robberies and dispose of their goods. They haunt the markets and fairs which were so important to commerical life at that time. According to *The Discoveries*, they operated, generally, out of a limited number of bases which were, nevertheless, spread over a wide geographical area. They used flash houses spread throughout the southern half of England: John Roberts's in Bath (The Pack Horse Inn), William Trinder's in Faringdon, Stephen and Mary Gea's (The Bell) in Chapel Plaster, Box, Wiltshire, and Edward and Margaret Lines's (The Rock Tavern) near Stourbridge, Staffordshire. These were not the only outlets for their booty; indeed where it was disposed of by the gangs seems, according to *The Discoveries*, to have depended on what it was. Cheap items, such as ordinary clothes, were often sold to the owners of the flash houses, female partners of gang members, or to receivers in provincial towns such as Salisbury and Stockbridge. More expensive items containing precious metals were typically passed on to John Ford, a silversmith at Bath; however, he only dealt with relatively small amounts, and anything really valuable went to London. So, for instance, out of the large haul of goods from a portmanteau stolen in Blandford on 30 June 1752 (*The Discoveries* has the date as 2 July): a pair of sheets and a fly petticoat were sold to John Roberts, and a silk petticoat and a lace cap were bought by Mary Gea; various small metallic items were converted into a small ingot of gold by John Ford; and the more valuable goods, a gold watch and some jewels, were sold in London. It must have seemed to contemporary readers that crime was both organized and easy.

The existence of a network of receivers also appeared to confirm the contemporary maxim – repeated in the biography – that without receivers there could be no thieves. Many held the view that the criminal justice system failed to deal sufficiently harshly with receivers when they were caught, and this too seemed confirmed by the Poulter case. His evidence was reported to have led to the arrest, presumably on charges of receiving, of John Ford, Mary Dawson, Frances Allen, Stephen and Mary Gea, and John Roberts.[10] Roberts died after being taken ill on the way from Shepton Mallet Prison to Exeter, where he was to have been tried.[11] Dawson and Allen were discharged for want of prosecution, as was Ford,[12] who apparently attended Poulter's hanging. The fates of Stephen and Mary Gea are unclear.

For the trading classes the book probably had a special appeal – or terror, which often amounts to the same thing – in its revelations about the frauds, committed with apparently little risk, at fairs and on merchants. More generally, the ease with which vulnerable but valuable property, such as horses, could be stolen and then disposed of must have disturbed all property owners. Referring to 'the late encrease of public Robberies' and, in particular, to the evidence of *The Discoveries of John Poulter*, one writer commented in 1754 from Bath, where Poulter had been centred: 'should these Practices continue much longer, our social Intercourse of Business or Diversion will be render'd more and more hazardous every Year: For indeed, if Credit is to be given to a Pamphlet lately published, (and I have Reason to believe much is to be given to it) what an extensive Scene of Combinations in Villainy, have we before our Eyes?'[13]

This is not to say that people felt themselves to be completely helpless. In London, thief-takers were very active, and at Bow Street from 1748 the magistrates, Henry and John Fielding, set about putting some system into thief-taking. Nor were the authorities in the provinces entirely impotent. The spread of newspapers opened up the possibility of crime advertising. John Styles has recently argued that this technique enjoyed some measure of success,[14] and *The Discoveries* seems to support the view that people at least believed crime advertising to be of value. As the notes to the text show (p. 173–7), a large number of the offences mentioned in *The Discoveries* were advertised in the newspapers, and the text itself indicates how the gang were, generally, careful to move stolen horses – a common subject for the advertisements – a long way before disposing of them.

The Discoveries was not the first criminal biography to make references to geographical location, times and people, but it went into far more detail than others had done. Many of the crimes mentioned can be traced in newspaper reports or advertisements, but, of course, this does not mean Poulter actually committed them. Indeed, the detail in *The Discoveries* might seem to suggest that Poulter was not the source. It seems odd that he would be able to recall, with, so far as can be judged, reasonable accuracy, such a large number of incidents. One possibility is that he was prompted by those who questioned him. Poulter's concern to be admitted as a witness for the Crown might well have made him anxious to assist, but it may also have made him careful to ensure that his evidence was correct and that the accusations he was making would hold up in court. He does omit to mention his criminal life before 1749, which included being sentenced to transportation at the Old Bailey in 1746; perhaps his hope was that no one else would recall it, since he had returned before the expiration of his fourteen-year term, a capital offence, or, maybe, it was omitted with the connivance of the authorities so as not to detract from the confessions.[15]

It is possible that Poulter was able to recall with such detail because he kept a diary in the hope, if he were caught, that he might be able to escape death by turning evidence for the Crown. Since it seems to have been important that such people were both forthright in their confessions and successful in obtaining convictions, then the keeping of careful records might have been regarded as important by some criminals. In 1723 Humphrey Anger, a highway robber, told the court at the Old Bailey that he kept a journal, in which,

> he had entred down a particular Account of all the Robberies he had committed: Being ask'd by the Court what was his Design for keeping a Journal, whether it was upon the Perusal of his Robberies, he might the more particularly repent of them? he reply'd, no, but it was for his own Safety, that he might be the more exact when he should have the Opportunity to save himself, by becoming an Evidence.[16]

So, as one historian has suggested, there were 'some very good reasons for keeping such journals'.[17] The fact that none has been discovered is, perhaps, not surprising in view of the nature of these documents.[18] On the other hand, if they were in general use it might have been expected that some would have survived, and also it is curious that the judges in Anger's case seem to have been unfamiliar with the practice of keeping such journals. Nevertheless, the possibility remains that Poulter was one of the exceptional ones who was able to write, had the foresight to expect to be captured and had the intention that if captured he would impeach his comrades in order to save himself.

For the historian *The Discoveries* provides some important lessons in the use of criminal biographies. The detail with which Poulter describes his activities can lull the reader into believing that, even though this is by no means a life-history, it is, nevertheless, a full and reliable account of a criminal gang. However, as Ruth Paley points out, 'Unless . . . one is aware of John Poulter's motives for avoiding London [his having returned from transportation before the expiration of his sentence] and for concealing an important part of his life-history, it is very easy to conclude, falsely, that there was a thriving provincial network that functioned independent of the metropolis.'[19] *The Discoveries* makes no mention of how the Poulter gang identified the extensive network of safe houses and receivers which they used. Paley argues that the gang was, in fact, one of a number which were collectively known as the 'Royal Family' or simply 'the Family'. The nucleus of its membership had been sailors in the 'Royal Family' squadron of privateers which was disbanded in 1748. She believes that the 'Royal Family' took over an existing network of safe houses, and she shows that, in the parasitic manner of the criminal justice system, there were links between some of the London thief-takers and the 'Royal Family'. So, even if we accept that what *The Discoveries* tells us is accurate, the picture is distorted by what is omitted.

INTRODUCTION

BIBLIOGRAPHICAL NOTE

The publishing history of *The Discoveries of John Poulter* is rather obscure. It seems to have reached its seventh edition by the end of 1753 and its seventeenth in 1779. The title-pages and texts of these editions vary, although in substance and in expression they are very similar and all appear to come from a common root, the variations being due to a desire to edit down the size of the work. Broadsheets appeared which broadly confirm certain of the events described more fully in *The Discoveries*:

The further Information, Examination, and Confession of John Poulter, otherwise Baxter [no place of publication or date].

Devon, (To wit) The voluntary Information, Examination, and Confession, of John Poulter, otherwise Baxter [no place of publication or date].

Note: the text printed here includes the addition in square brackets of names of people and places where these can be identified with a reasonable degree of certainty. As will be seen, the part of this biography which provide descriptions of methods of committing the various crimes and swindles referred to in the main body of the text and also the cant dictionary, which was regarded by Partridge as an important source for his various slang and underworld dictionaries, have, unfortunately, had to be omitted because of the constraints of space.

NOTES

1 *London Evening Post*, 31 March to 3 April 1753.
2 PRO, SP 36/123, Part 2, ff. 11–12; *Bath Journal*, 2 April 1753, 9 April 1753; see bibliographical note above for the broadsheets.
3 For an instance in which the competition between different members of a gang to give evidence for the Crown led to the publication of competing 'confessional biographies' see R. Wilson, *A Full and Impartial Account Of all the Robberies Committed by John Hawkins, George Sympson, (lately Executed for Robbing the Bristol Mails) and their Companions*, London, [1722]; J. Hawkins, *A Full, True and Impartial Account Of all the Robberies Committed in City, Town, and Country, For several Years past By William Hawkins, In Company with Wilson, Wright, Butler Fox, and others not yet Taken*, London, 1722.
4 J.M. Beattie, *Crime and the Courts in England, 1660–1800*, Oxford, 1986, pp. 336 and 446–7.
5 D. Hay, 'Property, authority and the criminal law' in D. Hay, E.P. Thompson and P. Linebaugh (eds), *Albion's Fatal Tree: Crime and Society in Eighteenth-Century England*, Harmondsworth, 1977; P. King, 'Decision-makers and decision-making in the English criminal law', *The Historical Journal*, 1984, vol. 27(1), pp. 25–58.
6 PRO, SP 36/123, Part 2, ff. 11–12, ff. 43–4.
7 PRO, ASSI 23/6, Somerset Assizes, 28 August 1753; SP 44/85, fo. 362; SP 36/123, Part 2, ff. 11–12; SP 44/85, fo. 364; SP 36/123, Part 2, ff. 43–4, 62, 63; SP 44/85, fo. 366; *Bath Journal*, 17 December 1753; PRO, SP 44/85, ff. 370, 376–7.
8 *Bath Journal*, 25 February 1754.
9 D.A. Baugh, *British Naval Administration in the Age of Walpole*, Princeton, 1965, p. 205; *M - - - - C L - - - - N's Cabinet broke open*, London, [1750], p. 8; *Whitehall Evening Post*, 14 June 1748, 2 July 1748; *Penny London Post*, 17 October 1748; *Whitehall Evening Post*, 7 October 1749; P. Linebaugh, 'Tyburn riot against the surgeons' in D. Hay *et al.* (eds), *Albion's Fatal Tree*, pp. 65–117; P. Linebaugh, 'Tyburn: a study of crime and the labouring poor in London

during the first half of the eighteenth century', unpublished Ph.D. thesis, Warwick University, 1975, p. 658; W.S. Lewis (ed.), *Horace Walpole's Correspondence with Sir Horace Mann*, vol. IV, London, 1960, pp. 199, and 312; H. Fielding, *An Enquiry into the causes of the Late Increase of Robbers, &c.*, London, 1751; 'Brittanicus', *A Letter To the Honourable House of Commons, relating to The present Situation of Affairs*, London, 1750; *Serious Thoughts In Regard to the Publick Disorders, with Several Proposals for Remedying the Same*, London, [1751]; 'Civis', *A Method Proposed to prevent the many Robberies and Villainies Committed in and about the City of London*, London, 1752; C. Jones, *Some Methods Proposed Towards putting a Stop to the Flagrant Crimes of Murder, Robbery, and Perjury*, London, 1752; *Whitehall Evening Post*, 17 January 1749, 21 January 1749, 26 January 1749, 18 February 1749; F.W. Torrington (ed.), *House of Lords Sessional Papers*, New York, sessions 1747–8 to 1753, pp. 334 and 388; *Journals of the House of Commons*, xxvi, pp. 27, 39, 155 and 158; *London Evening Post*, 10–12 May 1753; PRO, SP 36/125, Part 2, fo. 117.

10 *Bath Journal*, 23 April 1753.

11 *London Evening Post*, 17–19 April 1753; *Bath Journal*, 16 April 1753.

12 *Bath Journal*, 3 September 1753, 23 April 1753; PRO, ASSI 23/6, Somerset Assizes, 28 August 1753; ASSI 23/7, Somerset Assizes, 1 April 1754.

13 C.D., *A Letter to a Member of Parliament, Upon the Subject of the present reigning Enormities of Murders and Robberies*, Bath, 1754.

14 J. Styles, 'Print and policing: crime advertising in eighteenth-century provincial England' in D. Hay and F. Snyder (eds), *Policing and Prosecution in Britain 1750–1850*, Oxford, 1989, pp. 55–111.

15 He had been convicted of receiving stolen property while he was the Keeper of the Gatehouse Prison in London and was listed as transported to 'America': OBSP, 5–9 December 1746; P.W. Coldham, *English Convicts in Colonial America*, 2 volumes, New Orleans, 1974–76, vol. I, p. 214. As Paley suggests, his tendency to avoid London was presumably motivated by his fear of being apprehended by London thief-takers: R. Paley, 'Thief-takers in London in the age of the McDaniel Gang, c. 1745–1754' in Hay and Snyder, (eds.), *Policing and Prosecution in Britain*, pp. 301–41, at p. 309n. An indictment was brought against him by a thief-taker called Thomas Ind in July 1753 at Middlesex Sessions for returning from transportation.

16 Ironically, Anger was tried, and condemned, on the evidence of Dyer, a comrade who impeached him: OBSP, 28–30 August 1723. See also PRO, SP 36, vol. II, ff. 39–40.

17 P. Linebaugh, 'The Ordinary and his *Account*' in J.S. Cockburn (ed.), *Crime in England 1550–1800*, London, 1977, pp. 246–69, at pp. 264–5.

18 The National Library of Wales has a document apparently written by a smuggler, but this seems to have been composed in prison, not during the time when the events it describes were taking place, and declares itself to be the manuscript of an autobiography, rather than, like Anger's, a journal kept in case of arrest: *The Birth, Life, Education and Transactions of Captn. William Owen the noted Smuggler Who was executed for the murder of James Lilly at Carmarthen on Saturday the 2nd Day of May 1747. Written by his own hand when under Confinement, and delivered to Mr. Daniel Jones of Carmarthen aforesaid in the presence of Mr. John Davies, the Clergyman which attended him, a few Days before his execution*, NLW Ms. 21834B. For an unusual example from nineteenth-century France see M. Foucault (ed.), *I, Pierre Riviere, having slaughtered my mother, my sister, and my brother . . . : A Case of Parricide in the 19th Century*, Harmondsworth, 1978.

19 Paley, 'Thief-takers in London', p. 338.

8

THE
DISCOVERIES
OF

John Poulter, alias *Baxter*;

Who was apprehended for robbing Dr. HANCOCK, of *Salisbury*, on *Clarken Down*, near *Bath*; and thereupon discovered a most numerous Gang of Villains, many of which have been already taken.

BEING

A full Account of all the *Robberies* he has committed, and the *surprizing Tricks* and *Frauds* he has practised for the Space of five Years last past, in different Parts of *England*.

Written wholly by HIMSELF.

To which is added, as a Caution to prevent any unwary Persons *from being imposed on and defrauded,*

An exact Account of the Manner in which GAMBLERS and other SHARPERS impose upon People at Fairs and other Places; wherein their whole Tricks, Behaviour and Language, is so laid open, that any one who reads it, may certainly know them at any Time, and so be upon their Guard against being cheated by them. With some *Precautions* to secure Houses from being broke open, very useful for all Families: And likewise some Cautions to Tradesmen, and others who travel, to prevent their being robbed. With Directions how to prevent Horses from being stolen out of Grounds and Commons.

THE NINTH EDITION, With ADDITIONS.

Printed for *R. Goadby*, in Sherborne; and sold by *W. Owen*, Bookseller, at Temple-Bar, London.

MDCCLIV

The DISCOVERIES of
John Poulter alias *Baxter*.

I Have followed Gambling and Defrauding these five Years last past, and lived on the Spoil of other Men's Substance. About the Middle of *February*, 1749, I and *John Brown*, alias *Dawson*,[1] *Mary Brown*,* and *Mary Davis*, met all accidentally at *Litchfield*, on a Fair Day, and after some Ceremony we all agreed to go and drink a Glass of Wine; accordingly we went to Mr. *William Brooks's*, at the *George Inn*, in the said Town, and were shewn up Stairs; we had not been there long, before *Mary Brown* espied a large Chest, and said, here is a Chance the Lid being loose, and her Hand but small, she pull'd out of the said Chest one yellow Silk flower'd Damask Gown, one green Silk ditto, one brown Silk ditto, and one black flower'd Silk Capuchin,[2] which *Mary Brown* carried out of the said House in her Apron, to the Place were our Horses were: We all made the best of our Way to the B – D – g [Bull Dog], near *Westchester*, where we divided the above Goods among us four. I believe the Goods were worth about sixteen Pounds; the Landlord and Landlady of the B – D – [Bull Dog] very well knew us to be Thieves, and that we lived by nothing else, and also know almost all the Thieves that travel, and harbour them.

But what is very remarkable, at the same Time I sent for a Taylor to take Measure of me for a black Plush Waistcoat, and in his measuring of me a Pistol went off in my Waistcoat Pocket, and the Bullet went under his Arm, and through the Cieling, without doing any Hurt, which very much surprized the Taylor; *Brown* standing by me, I said, what are you always playing your Tricks putting Crackers in my Pocket: But the Taylor was not to be so deceived, for he took home my Plush and Lining with him, and went to *Westchester* to the Mayor, and told him he thought [p. 4] we were all Highwaymen. The Mayor ordered him not to let me have any Thing, until he had sent to search the B – D – g [Bull Dog], and bring us before him; but we did not stay for his Coming, for I made the best of my Way for *Holy Head*, through *Wales*, and directly went for *Dublin*, where I took a House in *Porter's Row* the lower End of *Aston's Kay*; I gave thirteen Pounds a Year, and had good Custom, and drew five Barrels of Ale one

---

* Mary Brown has been tried six Times within four Years and Half: First was at the Apollo Inn Westmoreland, with her first Husband Peter Brown, and several others, but she was acquitted and her Husband executed; it was in the latter End of 1748. Next at Ruthen in Denbyshire, with John Brown, for picking Pockets. Next at Shrewsbury, by herself, for ditto. Next at Cambridge, with Jane Baily, on Suspicion of ditto. Next at Litchfield in Staffordshire, in 1752, for picking Farmer Booth's Pocket of sixteen Pounds in the said Town of Litchfield, with Benjamin Shotton and Eleanor Cummins; the two last convicted, and she acquitted: She was tried by the Name of Mary Robertson. Next she was tried at Exon, at the Lammas Assizes 1752, with Mary Baxter, for picking a Farmer's Pocket at Great Torrington; but she was acquitted, and Mary Baxter convicted: She was tried by the Name of Margaret Dawson, but now she goeth by her own name, Mary Brown.

Week with another, and lived in good Credit, till a very unhappy Affair happened in *London*, and so it proved to me. General *Sinclair* had his Pocket pick'd of his Gold Watch at *Leicester* House, by *William Harper* and *Thomas Tobin*, and they were both taken and committed to the Gatehouse, *Westminster*; and that Day *Harper* was rescued by a Gang of about twenty-four *Irishmen*, in the Middle of the Day, and they wounded one of the Keepers, but *Tobin* did not escape.[3] A Proclamation was issued out with a great Reward for taking them, when most of them flew to *Ireland*, to my great Grief. One Day, as I was standing at my Door, I was seen by one *James Field*, one of the Gang who knew me very well; he came in and called for Liquor very plentifully, and the next Day he brought with him the Gang to my House; I desired them not to come to my House, for I would not harbour them, for if I did I should lose all my Custom, for I told them I could live without them in Credit, and without Fear; but they would not be denied, and my House was always full of Thief Catchers and Constables, which caused me to lose my Custom. Not long after, most of the Gang were taken, by one who followed them from *London*, to which Place they were soon transmitted; but it ruin'd me for I was forced to go away by Night, and left my Cellar full of Ale for my Brewer to take. I went to *Cork* and staid there about three Weeks, but could not take a House to my Liking, so embarked for *Waterford* with all my Household Goods, and staid there about sixteen Weeks. I found I could not live there, for Trade was dead and I but a Stranger. My Brewer sent for me to *Dublin*, which Place I went to again, and in a short Time took a House at the Shades of *Clontarf*, about two Miles from *Dublin*, close to the Seaside, and bought a Smack or Sloop for Fishing, and Hoylightening Ships, which I followed very hard, and sold Liquors at Home: By these Means I cleared three Pounds a Week, lived in good Credit, and got the Good will of every Body. I hardly ever missed a Tide but was at Sea, and found the Pleasure and Benefit between ill got Money, and that got honestly; for the ill-got I always wasted, and my Spirits were never at Rest Night nor Day; but when I lived by my Labour, I eat, drank, and slept at Ease, and was not afraid of any Body.

[p. 5]The latter End of the Year 1751, *Thomas Tobin* and his Wife (two of the most noted Pickpockets in *England*) came to *Dublin*, and found out where I lived, and came to my House; I begged of them never to bring any Person with them, which they promised me they would not, but in a short Time half the Thieves and Thief Catchers in *Ireland* resorted to my House, and laid a Scheme for my Ruin, and so it proved. Gentlemen often came from *Dublin*, and payed me for going into the Channel with them a plovering and fishing, and going aboard of Ships in the Bay; but once among the rest, some of these Chaps came to hire my Smack, to go into the Bay, which I let them have to my Sorrow, for before they came from *Dublin* they told the Custom-house Boat what their Intent was to do that they might come and seize my Smack. When we were out in the Bay, trying for some Fish, the Custom-house Boat came and boarded me, and said they were sure I had prohibited Goods, for I had Smugglers on board. I bid them search and welcome, which they did to my Sorrow, for they found six Pounds of Tea, and twelve Yards of Callicoe and Muslin, which were secreted in my Cabin by one of the Villains that came on board to go a pleasuring. The Officers seized the Goods, and my Boat was condemned. I cannot deny but afterwards I met one of the Persons, and beat him very much; but I had no Rest in *Ireland* afterwards, for I was always troubled with Actions, tho' very false ones, which obliged me to come to *England* again, in *November* 1751.

The latter End of *November*, 1751, I being at Bath at *J – R – ts*'s [John Roberts's],[4] he came to me one Night, and to *Richard Branning*, and told us both in about a Fortnight's Time he could help us to about five or six hundred Pounds if we were both willing. I said, How, *John*? He answered, on the Scamp, and the Cull does not come above seven Straches of; that is, *on the Highway, and the Man does not come above seven Miles off*. I said, how do you know, *John*? He told me the Gentleman came every setting Day[5] from *Trowbridge* to *Bath*, to change Bills for Money, for he is a Gentleman Clothier, and his Money is to pay his Men; he has never missed a setting Day for Years, and I have threatened him several Times before now, but could never get any of the Family to do it; *Little Dick* would have done it last Year, but his Partner, when the Day came, got drunk, and so it passed off; but now is your Time to make us all, for it is a great Deal of Blunt, and worth venturing your Scraggs for; that is, *it is a great Deal of Money worth venturing your Necks for*. I then told him I had no Pistols; and he said you must go to *T – r*'s [Trinder's] at *F – n* [Faringdon, Oxfordshire], and send him to *Oxford* to buy them, and keep your Horses there until two Days before the Time; the setting Day is *Tuesday* the tenth of *December*. Accordingly we agreed, and set out for *F – n* [Faringdon] to *T – r*'s [Trinder's], and I sent [p. 6] him to *Oxford*, to buy me a Brace of Pistols and a Hanger, which he bought, and we stayed there till the 8th of *December*, and told *T – r* [Trinder] what we were going to do, and that he must set up all *Tuesday* Night, and have two Horses ready to carry us sixty Miles further, and we told him we would be there on *Wednesday* Morning by four o'Clock. It was all agreed, and we set out for *G – *'s [Gea's][6] at *Ch – p – l Pl – r* [Chapel Plaster, Box], but we did not trust him with our Design. I went to *R – ts*'s [Roberts's] on the Ninth, to agree what Time we should come on the Tenth, and for him to show us the Way over the Water at *Clarken Down* [Claverton Down, Bath] Mills, which he did. We agreed to give him fourscore Pounds out of our Booty. *R – ts* [Roberts] said that he would be the last Man that would pay his Excise in at the Bar, and then said he, I shall be able to give you an Account what Money the Gentleman receives, and where he puts it, and if you come into the Inn I will show him and his Man to you, that you may not be mistaken when they come on the Down. Accordingly I did as he said, and about four o'Clock *R – ts* [Roberts] met me and told me that the Gentleman had changed his Bills, and had received upwards of five hundred Pounds, and he then shewed me the Gentleman and his Servant. My Horse was left at *Mount Pleasant*, and I did not show myself there; but just as the Gentleman was going he was persuaded not to go that Night, for it was just dark, and a Robbery was committed but on *Saturday* before at *Stocks Bridge*, in his Road home on a Farmer, and he was used very ill after being robbed by some Footpads,[7] which made the Gentleman stay in *Bath* till the Morning. If he had went home that Night he would have lost all if it had been a thousand Pound, for we had made a Place in the Wood, just before he came to the *Flower-de-luce*, to take him and his Servant into and tie them, but Fortune was not on *R – ts*'s [Roberts's] Side that Time. We both went to *F – n* [Faringdon] that Night according to our Promise, and found the Horses ready and our Landlord up, but he was disappointed. – – I advise all People that have got a Charge of Money or Bills not to travel after Sunset.

In *March* 1752, I, *John Brown* alias *Dawson*, *John Allen*, alias *Robert Jones*, alias *Robert Graham*,[8] and *Thomas Tobin*, went a Journey into the North Part of *England*, and coming through *Hallifax*, in *Yorkshire*, we overtook a Minister; and we rode with him till we came to the first Inn, where we defrauded him of twenty-two Pounds at Pricking in the Belt;[9] he said it was as much as his Gown was worth to have it known, and accompanied the Loss of his Money with this Ejaculation, *Alas! what have I been at?* to which I answered, *The Sailor*[10] *has done by you Sir, as you would have done by him, so I wish you good Night.* We came that Night to *Stockport*, in *Cheshire*, and lay at an Inn in that Town that Night. The next Morning *Tobin* left [p. 7] our Company, and went for *Westchester* on the File:* We stayed on purpose to rob a Pack Horse, accordingly we all went to one *J – n R – ts*'s [John Roberts], an old Acquaintance of my Accomplices, but not of mine. We call'd for Liquor plentifully, and ask'd him when the *Manchester* Carrier came by, He said, To-night, and they travel best Part of the Night; but if you stay till they come by, I will shew the best Pack, but have you no Sacks; and turning to *Brown* said, you had three the last Pack you got. We said, *J – n* [John] you must let us have three of yours, and we will pay you for them: Accordingly he gave us three old Sacks, and we promis'd him Half a Guinea for his Trouble; at Night the Horse came by, and he shew'd us all, one particular Pack, and said that's your Mark, and your best Place is beyond the Village, to take him into one of the Fields, and he will not be miss'd for an Hour or two after, so that you may get far enough by the Morning. And accordingly we went after and stole one of the Horses, but not the right, for he was the hindermost next to the Man: The Horse, as soon as the others past began to wicker, so that we were obliged to gag him. We got upwards of one thousand Yards of Callimanco, unscower'd, and rode about thirty Miles that Night before we baited, when we reach'd within four Miles of *Whitchurch* in *Shropshire*, and lay at a *Flash†* House. The next Day we arrived at the Rock Tavern,[11] near *S – r B – e* [Stourbridge] in *Staffordshire*, kept by one *E – and M – L – s* [Edward and Margaret Lines], the greatest Place of Rendezvous in *England* for Thieves, and that Night put our Goods into a Grave in their Barn, where they lay three Days, we then fetch'd them up to the House, and cut all the Marks off both Ends of the Pieces. We sold *E – d* and

---

* A Cant Word for Cheating.
† A House that harbours Thieves.

M – t L – s [Edward and Margaret Lines], three or four Pieces for three Pence *per* Yard, we gave them one Piece for their Trouble;[12] and divided the Rest into three Parts. I sent mine to *Bath* to *J – n R – ts's* [John Roberts's], where it lay for some Time, till he got me a Dyer to dye it: and the Remainder was left at the Rock Tavern with our Landlord and Landlady, who never paid any Thing for it to this Day. Some Time after, I sold twenty eight Yards of mine to *Mary Brown*, alias *Dawson*, after it was dyed; but when she had it made up, she told me she would not pay me for it, for I had better Luck than her Husband and *Allen* had with theirs; they all well knowing the Callimanco to be stolen, and from whence; and, if we or any Body else was to carry the King's Crown to the Rock Tavern, they would to my Knowledge, secrete it.

Soon after, I and *Thomas Tobin* went to *Grantham*, in *Lincolnshire*, and met with one *Walter Cauhone*; and there we defrauded an old Farmer of fifteen Guineas, at the old Nobb, call'd Pricking [p. 8] in the Belt. From thence *Tobin* and I went to *Nottingham*, where we met with several of our Accomplices; but Luck running bad that Day, *Tobin*, *Hurst*, and I went on the Sneak, and stole a silver Tankard without a Lid, from the Black-Moor's Head, and paying *Hurst* for his Part, we went for the Rock Tavern again; but Money being short there, we carried it to *B – grove* [Bromsgrove], in *Worcestershire*, to *G – e L – ll* [George Linsdale], a Shopkeeper there, and *Tobin* sold it to him; but I cannot say he knew it to be stolen, for I was not present, but I have seen *G – e L – ll* [George Linsdale] buy stolen Goods of several Persons, he well knowing the same to be stolen.[13]

Tobin and I went directly for *York*, and on our Journey into *Yorkshire*, we dined at an Inn, and there stole a large silver Spoon; but where the House is I cannot recollect. We arrived at *York*, and went to see an old Friend and his pretended Wife, and the next Day went to a Fair, and defrauded a young Gentleman of seven Pounds at the Belt; and came back the next Day to York, being the Day before the Judges came into Town. The next Day *Tobin* and I went on the Sneak to the Black Swan Inn in *Coney Street York*, and stole from thence a Silver Tankard, and a large Sugar Caster and carried them to *Christopher Fet – one* [Fetherstone],[14] and his pretended Wife Sarah Ca – n [Cagan], to keep them for us till we went out of Town, and told them from whence they came. The same Day I, *Tobin, Fet – one* [Fetherstone], *Sarah Ca – n* [Cagan], went to the same House on purpose to steal some more Plate, but the People had lock'd the Rest up, to our Disappointment. The next Day *Tobin* and I went for our Plate, which *Sarah Ca – n* brought us; and we gave her a large Silver Spoon for her Trouble, which we had stolen, but where I cannot recollect. Then we went directly to *London*, where I sold the Tankard and Caster to a Silver Smith near *Smithfield Bars*, in St. *John-Street*, but he did not ask me any Questions how I came by them.

I went just after to *J – n R – ts's* [John Roberts's] at Bath, to meet the rest of my Accomplices at our old House, where I was sure to hear News, and a Welcome into *Bath*. The latter End of *April* there was twelve of us together, all Gamblers and Pickpockets, to our Landlord's Knowledge. We all went into the West for *Sampford Peveral* [Sampford Peverell], and made three Setts; two Setts got ten Pounds a Piece, from two Farmers that had just sold their Cattle, at the unlawful Game of Pricking in the Belt. The Farmer I was concerned with, swooned away for the Loss of his Money; we made a Pretence to fetch some Water to bring him to himself, but went clear off, not regarding whether he lived or died. Two Setts went to *Great Torrington* [Torrington]; and one Sett, just as they had got into the Fair picked up a Flat, and got twenty Pounds of him, which so Alarmed the Town, that the rest came away for *Exon* [Exeter]: So all dis[p. 9]persed but *John Brown* and I, and we defrauded a Man in *Exon* of five Pounds.

We then went to *Crewkerne*, where we heard at the Green Dragon that our Accomplices were gone forward: The next Day we rode out of Town, but promised to come back the same Night, which we did: But just before we came into Town, we heard that two Sharpers were taken up at *S – l C – l*'s, and that their Horses were there: So we called, and the Horses were delivered to us, to take them away for Fear they should be stopt; for they were both stolen, one by *William C – s*, and the other by *William S – w*, both then Custody at *Crewkerne*, for defrauding a Man at *Chard* of five Pounds; and one of them stole a Great Coat at *Chard*, and they were both cast for Transportation at *Bridgewater* for the same.[15]

Brown and I took the two Horses to *Bath*, to *John R – s* [Roberts], and told him what had happened, and that he must sell the Gelding, and Mare: We told him where they were stole from, and he said it was far enough off, and asked us what we would have for the Gelding; we told him four Pounds; he said that if we would take a Thirty six Shilling Piece he would run all Hazards; so we agreed for him: And he told us if any Body asked what he cost, we must say four Pounds, for he would sell him to a Farmer that he bought his Straw of, that never went five Miles from home.

I left *Brown* at *R – ts*'s [Roberts's] with the grey Mare, whilst I, *William Elger*, and *John Allen*, alias *Robert Jones*, alias *Robert Graham*, went to the Rock Tavern, to see his Wife and Child, that was at Nurse there: from thence we went into the North of *England* to Fairs, Horse Races, and Cock Matches, on the Sharping Lay, and won between thirty and forty Pounds at Cards, alias *Broads*. From thence we went to *Newcastle upon Tine*, where we got about three Pounds from a Butter Man at the Belt, or *Nobb*. From thence we went into the South again; and picked up in our Way Money enough to bear our Expences to *Bath* for the Benefit of the Waters, to the great Joy of our Landlord. We stayed off and on at *Bath* about six Weeks, and passed for Smugglers:[16] We used to give seven Shillings a Pound for Tea and sell it again for four Shillings and Six-pence, on purpose to make People believe we were Smugglers. We went to a Fair now and then in that Time, and if we could not get any Money at the *Nobb*, we would buy a Horse or two, and give our Notes for the Money, telling the Dealer we lived at a Town where we did not. This is called *Masoning*.

July the 2d, 1752, I and *William Elger*, *John Brown*, alias *Dawson*, *John Allen*, alias *Robert Jones*, alias *Robert Graham*, and *Thomas Walker*, went to *Blandford* Races,[17] where we met *Charles Handy*: We went to the Cocking in the Morning, and to the [p. 10] Races in the Afternoon; some went on to the Turn to the Booths, and others to laying Wagers on the Course: A flattish Gentleman laying seven Pounds with one of us, they both asking who should hold Stakes, one of us sitting on Horseback just by on Purpose, says, put it in that Man's Hand, pointing to one of us that was well dressed; the Money being so delivered, the Man winning, he that held the Stakes rode off the Course. After the Races we all meet at *Blandford*, and agreed to go on the Sneak for any Thing we could get. In the Dusk of the Evening, we went to the Crown Inn, and stole, out of the fore Parlour, a large Portmanteau Trunk, and carried it into the Fields to skin it, that is, to search it, when we found in it the following Things, *viz.* Eighteen Guineas, a Jacobus, and several other Pieces of Gold and Silver Coin, a Gold Repeating Watch, with all the Trinkets thereunto belonging, a Pair of Gold Shoe Buckles, a Gold Coral and Bells, a Gold Girdle Buckle, and Necklaces set in with green Stones, a great Quantity of Jewels, a fly white Petticoat, a great Quantity of young Girls wearing Apparel, and one pair of Sheets.[18] *Thomas Walker* and I carried the Gold Watch and Jewels to *London*, and *Walker* sold them to a Person unknown to me, because I was not with him; but he said, he told the Man he sold them to, that he got them at Sea, in a Prize. He brought me Twenty-seven Pounds for the Watch and Jewels. We then came back to *Popham Lane*, to the Sign of the Wheatsheaf, where our Accomplices were waiting for us; we there divided the Money equally between us, and came to *Bath*, where I sold the Pair of Sheets to *J – n R – ts* [John Roberts] for two Shillings, and the fly Petticoat worked with a Needle for a Guinea, tho' it was worth four: he secreted the rest for me in a Closet. Just after I sold a red Silk quilted Petticoat to *M – y G – a* [Mary Gea], for her Daughter, for Half a Guinea: At the same Time she begged a lace Cap, with Wire about the Border; and I told her she must not let her Daughter wear it, for it was stole from a Portmanteau at *Blandford* and that it was advertised at the same time in *Bath*: She said I need not fear, for it should be altered, she well knowing the same to be stolen and from whence.

I sold the Bells, Seal, Shoe Buckles, and Girdle Buckles, all of Gold, to *J – n F – d* [John Ford],[19] a Silversmith in *Bath*, and he melted them down before my Face, into an Ingot of Gold, not quite an Ounce. I told him from whence they came, and he said he did not care if they came from the Ruffen, (that is the *Devil*) I wish we had as much as you and I could put out of Twig, or break in sunder.[20]

We went out of *Bath*, to *Corsham* Fair, about eleven Miles from *Bath*; that is, I, *William Elger, John Brown*, alias *Dawson, John Allen*, alias *Robert Jones*, alias *Robert Graham*, and we stole a silver Tankard from an Inn in *Corsham*:[21] I brought it directly to *J – n* [p. 11] *F – d* [John Ford] at *Bath*, who not being at Home, I told his Wife we had stole a Silver Tankard from *Corsham*, and wanted to melt it down; I then went up Stairs with her, and she fasten'd a Pair of Sheers into a Vice, and began to cut it in Pieces; when her Husband came in, and told us, he had heard of the Tankard, and where it came from, but he would soon put it out of Twig; and said, *Betty* go and make a Fire in the Shop, and bring a large Crucible; which she did, and they melted it down before my Face; and she said, Mr. *Poulter*, at any Time, if you have Gold or Silver, I will melt it down for you if my Husband is not at Home; but you must not take any Notice to my Brother of what passes between my Husband and you: At the same Time she ask'd me for a Shilling for her Trouble, which I gave her. They both knew the same to be stolen, and from whence.

Brown, Elger, and Allen, bought a Horse at the Turnpike near *Corsham*, of a Farmer, for six Pounds, but gave their Note for it; and *St – n G – a* [Stephen Gea] said he knew *Brown* very well to be the same Person he represented himself to be, though he knew at the same Time they were defrauding the poor Farmer.

October the 26th, 1752, I, with *John Brown*, alias *Dawson*, *William Elger*, *John Allen*, alias *Robert Jones*, alias *Robert Graham*, went from *Bath* in order to rob a Pack-Horse: We made the best of our Way to *W – m T – 's* [William Trinder's], at *Farrington*, in *Berkshire*, and after Supper we called plentifully for White Wine Negus; then we ask'd *W – m T – r* [William Trinder] when *Charley*, the *Coventry* Carrier, came to *Morton* in the Marsh [Moreton-in-Marsh]: He answered, on *Monday* or *Tuesday*; and now is your Time, for he takes up all the Ribbons that are left at *Stow* Fair, and carries them to *Bristol* this Journey. To which we replied, How shall we know the right Pack? *W – m T – r* [William Trinder] said, you must observe the Pack that has Boxes in it, that is the right, and is either full of Ribbons, or Things of Value; and, if you succeed, bring them to me, and I will buy them all of you. We then told him we had no Sacks, and he ordered his Ostler to go and buy three new Sacks, for which I paid six Shillings before his Face. The next Morning he wish'd us good Luck, and we set out for *Morton* in the Marsh, where we got that Night, and put up at *W – m N – s's* [William Nipps's]. He was glad to see my Accomplices, but did not know me; after Supper we ask'd him when *Charley* came to *Morton* in the Marsh: He answered, I cannot tell, but I will go to his Brother and enquire. When he came back, he told us To-morrow Morning; but it will be late before he gets to *Park corner*, because he takes up Ribbons at *Stow*, that were left at the Fair. We did not stir out all the Time we were there; for, he said, if we were seen, it would be known who did it, for he well knew our Intent was to take one of *Charley's* Packs; and [p. 12] he assurred us, that at any Time he would go and swear for us, (as he did for *Robert Jones* and others at *Warwick*,) if Occasion required. We set out the next Day for *Park-corner*, which Place we reached just as *Charley* came there; *Brown* then rode before us to detain *Charley* at a Publick-House, under Pretence of carrying a Letter for him, which he wrote and gave him: In the mean Time we went forward, and try'd the Packs as *T – r* [Trinder] had directed us; and catch'd the Horse by the Neck, but he was so shy and startish, that he throw'd me and *Allen* into a Ditch, and got away from us, so that we could not catch him any more. We then took the next, and led him down into a Park about a Mile from the Place, where we could not get out: But it was remarkable, *William Elger* rode a Gelding that he gave eighteen Guineas for, and in conveying along the Pack Horse, rode into a great Hole, and his Gelding and he tumbled over, when the Pack Horse ran back almost to *Park-corner* before we could catch him. We tied the Horse to a Bush, and gag'd him, whilst we put the Goods up in our Sacks, and left them in that Place till we rode almost to *Park-corner* before we could get out, and there we saw *Brown* and *Charley* going together. *Charley* asked us whether we had seen his Horses, and how many there were: We said six, but they were a Mile before him, and then bid him a good Night. We rode round the Park Wall, just against the Place where we left our Goods, and the Horse whicker'd: I was forced to stand upon the Horse's Back to get over the Wall, to throw over the Goods. We then loaded our Horses, and made the best of our Way to *Chapel Plaster*, at which Place we arrived about Five o'Clock in the Morning, and calling up *S – n G –* [Stephen Gea], we stayed there that Day. I ask'd *S – n G – a* [Stephen Gea] to get me a Horse, and something to carry my Goods in; which he did, for he lent us his own Horse that he bought of us some Time before at *Weyhill* Fair, and a Pair of Butcher's Pots, in which we packed up all our Goods except one Piece of Camblet, and twelve Pair of Scarlet Stockings, which *Brown, Allen,* and I, kept for our Women. We divided the Piece (I think it was thirty-nine Yards) into three Parts, and the Stockings into the same. I gave my Part to *M – y G – a* [Mary Gea], to keep for me, and so did they, till I came again. The next Morning we set out for *Farringdon*, where we arrived late at Night, it being fifty Miles from *Chapel Plaster*. We sent *Allen* before to bespeak Supper for us, and open the back Gate, and to put the Ostler out of the Way until we had unloaded our Goods; which was done. After Supper we drank plentifully of Punch and White Wine Negus; and the next Morning we sold *W – m T – r* [William Trinder] all the Caps and Stockings: He got us a Box to pack up the Pieces of Stuff in, and we put it into his Warehouse, with Directions to be left at [p. 13] *W – m T – r*'s [William Trinder's], at *Farrington*, in *Berkshire*, till called for. The next Morning we set out for a Fair at *Newbury* in *Berkshire*, where we defrauded a young Man of his Watch, Horse, and four Guineas in Money, at the *Old Nobb*, or pricking in the Belt. We then went back to *T – r*'s [Trinder's]; and when we came there, he show'd us a Letter he had received from Mr. *Grovenor*, of *Bristol*, for *T – r* [Trinder] to make all the Enquiry he could after such Goods, among all the Shopkeepers about that Country, for he had lost a Pack: At the same Time *T – r* [Trinder] had bought all the Caps and Stockings of us, and had all the Pieces of Stuff in his Warehouse, and that to his Knowledge. His Wife *H – h* [Hannah] came to me, and desired me to ask her Husband to buy all the Stuff, for he could dispose of it all; but he refused, because it was advertised. *H – h T – r* [Hannah Trinder] said she would buy one Piece of Stuff for her own Use, unknown to her Husband: Then she and I went up Stairs, and she pick'd out a very large Piece of brown strong Stuff from all the rest, and gave me eighteen Shillings for the same, they both knowing the same to be stolen, and from whence. If there was not such People as these to encourage Thieves, and receive their Goods, there would be no thieves.[22] We set out the next Morning for *Salisbury*, with the Goods that were left, thinking to sell them to *C – H –* [Charles Handy?]; but he was not at Home: So I carried them to *Stockbrige*, to another Fence of our's, that is, a Receiver of stolen Goods, one *R – t L –* [Robert Lyte], a Publican, that always bought the Watches of us we got at pricking in the Belt, or any other Defraud: I sold him six Pieces and a half, which he pick'd out from all the rest, and he gave me eighteen Shillings a Piece for them, but he would have the half Piece into the Bargain. He ask'd where the said Stuff was stolen from; and I told him: He said he would sell some to one, and some to another, in the Country; but we cut off all the Marks of both Ends of the Pieces, for Fear of a Discovery. He also lent me a Box to pack up five Pieces and a half that was left, to send up to *London* to *William Elger*, who was gone to Town to see his Friends, directed thus, For Mr. *William Elger*, to be left at the *Swan*, on *Holbourn-Bridge, London*, till called for; which the said *L – [Lyte]* did send away, he well knowing the same to be stolen, and from whence; he knowing us all to be Sharpers and Thieves, and that we had no other Way of Living but by defrauding and robbing. We went to *G – a*'s [Gea's], and I sold the Piece of Stuff and four Pair of Scarlet Stockings to *M – y G – a* [Mary Gea]: *Mary Brown*, alias *Dawson*, had another Piece, and four Pair of Stockings: I bought the four Pair of Stockings of *Mary Brown* again. *Frances Allen* had the other Part.[23]

The Beginning of *November*, to the best of my Remembrance, I, and *William Elger, John Brown* and *John Allen*, came from *Wil[p. 14]ton* towards *Bath*, on Purpose to break open a House in *Wade's Passage*, which we looked at several Times before. We stole in our Way from *Wilton*, a large Iron Crow from a Sheepfold on *Salisbury Plain*, on Purpose to wrench open the Door of the said Shop: We left our Horses at *Mount Pleasant*, while we went a milling that Swagg, that is, a breaking open that Shop: We wrenched open the Pad Lock, but could not open the Door, altho' we made a great Purchase with the Iron Crow; we made several Attempts, and in the mean Time the Scout came by, that is, the Watch; but *Brown* took him off, while we were at Work, which is easily done for a Quart of Drink: *Brown* knew the Watchman, but I can't say the Watchman knew him. If all the Doors of Shops and Houses shut as close as that did, it would prevent a great many Robberies in Cities and Towns; for no Doors ought to have any Play, if they have they are easily broke open. We tried two Shops in the Church yard, at their Windows, the one a Toy Shop, and the other a Watchmaker's, but were disappointed by a drunken Man's coming into the Church-yard, and sitting himself down.[24] We had got a Spring Saw to cut the Bolts asunder, that *F – d* [Ford] made for *Brown*; the Iron Crow I threw over the Bridge[25] on the Left Hand Side.*

The latter End of *November*, all of us being at *Bath*, we agreed to go to *Bristol*, to get something towards our Expences; where *John Allen* pick'd up a Countryman near the Mount, that is, the Bridge, and brought him into the *H – R – st*, near the Back, which House we had made Flash before hand; the Countryman had but little Money, which the Sailor knew, and therefore laid him Half a Guinea that he could not borrow ten Pounds in half an Hour; then *Allen* and he went into the *Fish Market*, and he borrowed the Money of a Shopkeeper, and brought it to the said *H – R – st* to us, and received the Wager; but we defrauded him of all the Money in about ten Minutes, at the *Old Nobb*, or Belt. A Countryman came just afterwards to the House to enquire for us, but the Landlady hush'd the Man, and said she knew nothing of him nor us. The Countryman went Home, and told

---

* This was found lately in the River.

in his Neighbourhood that he was robbed by three Fellows on the Road. I have seen him several Times since at *Bath* Market, and have spoke to him, and he told me the same; I contradicted him, and said, I believed he lost it at Gaming: He did not see my Face at *Bristol* when he lost his Money, so did not know me at *Bath*. The Man keeps *Bath* Market, and stands at the upper End of the Market-House, selling Hog's Haslets, and wears his own Hair.

Just after, about the 28th of *November*, we were all at *Bath*, when *Brown* took the Opportunity at Night to go on the Sneak by himself, to one Mr. *Bartlet's*, on the *North Parade*; he went into a Parlour, where he saw a Candle lighted, and stole from thence a Portmanteau Trunk: The Key was in it, and a Bundle on it, he took off the Bundle, and unlocked the Trunk, and seeing it was full of rich Cloaths, he locked it again, but took out the Key; and in the mean Time a Servant came and looked into the Room, and *Brown* hid himself behind the Door, and when the Servant was gone, he took up the Trunk and went into *King's Mead* Fields, and left it there while he came and told us what he had done:[26] I was in Bed, and so was *Allen*, but *Elger* and he went and skin'd the Trunk, and put the Things into a Sack, and *Elger* sent his Horse to S – n G – a's [Stephen Gea's] that Morning. The Horse was taken out of R – ts's [Roberts's] Stable unknown to him or his Ostler until Morning, when R – ts [Roberts] knew it, but the Ostler did not. In the Morning *Elger* and *Mary Brown* went on Foot to *Chapel Plaster*, to look over the Things, and *Allen* went that Night to them: The next Morning we all set out for the *Devizes*, to one J – n A – 's [John Allen's]; *Elger* and *Allen* did not lie at the said House, but *Brown* and I did. I went and bought a Deal Box, into which we put our Things, and nailed it up, and left it under a Bed in a Room, and told J – n A – [John Allen], the Landlord, to take Care of it. He said, if it was Diamonds you know it is safe in my House. Some Time after we saw our Landlord, and *Brown* ask'd him if the Things were safe; he said yes, I have one of the Advertisements at my House, but do not mind that, for nobody will suspect my House; he well knowing we lived by nothing but Robbing and Defrauding the Country.

We went from thence to *Salisbury*, to see a Crop Horse run over that Course, belonging to *Thomas Brooks* of *Coleharbour*, he was Seventeen Years of Age, and ran nineteen Miles within an Hour: We could take nobody in at *Salisbury* at any Trick, so we went that Night to *Wilton*, to consult what to do. *Brooks* lay with us that Night, and the next Day we agreed to go and steal some Horses, and take them into the North, and bring others back into the South; we went that Evening, about all the Grounds within three Miles of *Salisbury*, and could see none worth taking, but a Colt worth about fourteen Pounds, and him we could not catch. We went towards *Salisbury*, and just by a Mill in the Marshes, we caught two Galloways, both with cut Manes, but we thought them not worth taking; we therefore went that Night to *Salisbury*, and the next to *Farrington*, in *Berks*, we made it Night before we got to *Marlborough*, where we stole a black Mare out of a Ground just by,[27] in the Road to *Farrington*, which we reached the same Night; we lay at W – m T – r's [William Trinder's] that

Night and the next Day, and at Night we went into a Field of Mr. *Lock*'s, at the Crown Inn and stole from thence a Bay Gelding,[28] and I rode all [p. 16] that Night with the Mare and Gelding towards *Highamferris*, [Higham Ferrers] for there was a Fair there the next Day; but *Brown*, *Elger*, and *Allen* staid there that Night to prevent our being discovered: They met me at *Highamferris*, but we could not sell our Horses. *T – r* [Trinder] our Landlord, knew the black Mare, and of our stealing the Gelding. We made the best of our Way into *Yorkshire*, and we sold the Gelding to a Baker in *Doncaster*, for four Pounds, but he did not know it was stolen. We then went for *Wakefield* Fair, but when we came there were disappointed, for there was none. *Elger*'s Horse fell sick at *Newark on Trent*, and he borrowed a Horse of the Baker that bought the Bay Gelding; but when we were at *Wakefield*, *Allen* borrowed a Horse to go to *York*, and *Elger* sent his Horse back to *Doncaster*, for we saw in the *London Evening Post*, the bay Gelding advertised,[29] and made the best of our Way to *Bantry* [Bawtry, Yorkshire], but did not come near *Doncaster*: We sold the black Mare there to a man of *Rotherham*, for one Pound one Shilling and Sixpence;[30] she broke out with the Grease. We went the next Day to a Fair in *Lincolnshire*, and picked up a Man on the dropping of a Shilling, and brought him into the House, where *Elger* and *Brown* were set on Purpose. *Elger* passed for a Sailor, and *Brown* for a Dealer; the Man had no Money, but *Elger* laid him a Guinea he could not borrow twenty Guineas in half an Hour; I went the Countryman's Halves, and went with him, and at the first Place he borrowed Ten, and a thirty Pound Bank Note, and in returning he borrowed twelve more; we went back to the Sailor, and showed him the Money, on which he paid him the Guinea, and we went to play at Pricking in the Belt, we made stakes for twenty-two Guineas, and fain would have played for fifty, which the Countryman would not, but said, if he won he would play again; but the Sailor took Care not to let him, he pricked and lost, and was most terribly frightened, but he would prick again for thirty; we were afraid he would make too big a Row when he lost that, that is, a great Noise, however we made Stakes for the sixty, which was the Note and our thirty; he pricked and lost, and then stood as if he was Thunder-struck, for some Time with his Back against the Door: I seemed to be the same; but at last got him out of the Room, under Pretence of borrowing some Money, while the Sailor and *Brown* went to our Horses, which *Allen* had got ready; I gave the Countryman the Slip, and followed after them, not letting any Grass grow under our Feet for thirty Miles before we stopt, and that was at *Bantry*, at a House of our own Sort. There was a great Search made all the Country round for us, but we were at Home. The next Day we made our Way for the City of *Cambridge*, in order to mill some Ken, that is, to break open some House; but we had no Success there, so we agreed to prig some Peads, that is, [p. 17] steal some Horses, and take them away West: *Allen* and I went for *Newmarket*, and *Brown* and *Elger* for *Leighton Buzzard*. I and *Allen* stole a black Gelding and Bay Colt, near *Brinkley* in the *Woodlands*, and brought them to *Hungerford* in *Berks*, and sold them to *William B – ge* [Barbridge], of the same Place: He did not know that they were stolen, but thought that they were got on the Mason, that is, for Paper.[31] *Brown* and *Elger* stole a flat headed Bay Gelding from the Bell Inn in *Leighton Buzzard*, and brought him to *Bath*, and kept him for his own riding.[32] We sold the sorrel Mare that was stole from *Wakefield*, to our Landlord *J – n R – ts* [John Roberts], at *Bath*; he would not buy her till he knew where she was stolen from, but he had no Luck with her, for she fell sick and died in a Fortnight after. Here we divided all the Money we got this Journey.

About the latter End of December, being all at *Bath* together, *J – n R – ts* [John Roberts], our Landlord, came to *Brown*, *Elger*, and *Allen*, and ask'd for me; he told them he could help them to twenty Pounds; just after I came to his House, when he told me the same: I ask'd him how it was to be got; and he replied, on the Scamp, that is, on the Highway; for, says he, there is a Man that puts up at my House, that is going to receive twenty Pounds, but a great deal of it will be in Halfpence, and it is easy to be napt, that is, taken. We then agreed that I should go and rob the Man by myself, and they would be at a small Distance for Fear of Resistance. *R – ts* [Roberts] helped the Man to tie the Sack behind him, that the Money was in, I standing by him at the same Time; the Man went his Way, and we followed him up to the Top of the Hill, I got on a Collier's Horse, with Coal Sacks on the Pack Saddle, I spoke to the Man going up the Hill, and when I got on the Down I let him go on before, and then rode after, overtook, and robbed him; I had a Stick in my Hand, which *R – ts* [Roberts] and my Accomplices gave me, and a Tinder Box instead of a Pistol: I rode the Man's Horse back again to the Foot of the Down, where my Accomplices were waiting for me, and we went directly to *John R – ts's* [Roberts's]. The Money that I robbed the Man of, was one Guinea and some Silver, and thirty-nine Shillings in Halfpence, which we divided between us, and *R – t's* [Roberts] had eight Shillings worth of the Halfpence. The Man came to *R – ts's* [Roberts's] the next Morning, and said he was robb'd, and ask'd what Time the Ostler came home, for he suspected him: We told him he was at a Friend's House all Night; and we all laugh'd to hear the Man say the Person who robbed him put a Pistol to his Cheek, it being nothing but a Tinder Box.[33]

About the 18th of *January*, 1753, I, *Brown*, *Elger*, and *Allen*, agreed to go to *Bristol* on the Sharp, or the Sneak; which we did, [p. 18] but we could not get any Thing on the Sharp that Day: But at Night we went on the Sneak, first into *Queen Square*, and tried several Houses. At last *Elger* jump'd the Glass of a Gentleman's Keen;[34] that is, lifted up the Window of a House at the lower End of the Square, and jump'd into the Parlour, and brought out five Silver Tea Spoons and one Pair of Tea Tongs, with a Delft Server from a Tea Table. We then pull'd down the Window, and went our Way: I think the Tea Spoons were marked with the Spread Eagle. We went directly over the Draw Bridge for *College Green*, and tried all the Doors and Windows there: At last we went into *Orchard-Street*, to one Mr. *Smith*'s, a Watchmaker, as I was since informed. *Brown* got Entrance in at the Door, and went up Stairs into the Bed Chamber, whilst the Family was below, and he staid about twenty Minutes in the House; and in the mean while Mrs *Smith* came to the Door, and *Elger* ask'd her where such a

Gentleman lived; she told him, and went in and shut the Door after her. We all resolv'd if *Brown* was grabb'd, that is, taken, to rescue him; but he soon came out with his Arms full of Men's wearing Apparel, such as follows, *viz.* Three Coats, two Waistcoats, three Pair of Breeches, a great Quantity of Stockings and Neck-cloths, and one Handkerchief. The said Things I carried to *Frances Allen*'s Room that Night for her to secrete for us, and accordingly she did; and I went next Day to Bristol again, to meet my Accomplices: I left with Mrs. *Allen* a Pair of Silver Shoe Buckles of Mr. *Smith*'s.[35] We went at Night on our old Rigg; and went over the Draw-bridge towards *College Green*; *Brown* went into a Peruke-maker's House, and went up Stairs, and had got all the Things in a Table Cloth that was in the Drawers, when he heard a Noise of the Barber and another Man coming home; who suspecting us, (as having heard of Mr. *Smith*'s House being broke open the Night before) followed us, and shut his Door: However, *Brown* got out of a Garret Window, and over the Tops of several Houses, and got behind a Stack of Chimnies for the Space of two Hours: He could not get into any House, but was forced to go back again into the same House, and come softly down Stairs along the Entry: A Boy hearing some Body in the Entry, ran to him with a Knife in his Hand, and call'd him Rogue; upon which *Brown* told the Mistress of the House, that as he was coming over the Draw-Bridge, a Bailiff was in pursuit of him, and that he ran into her House for shelter, and had been on the Stairs a Quarter of an Hour, which the weak Woman believing, bid him stay for Fear the Bailiffs should be about the Door; but he did not care to stay for Fear the Master should come home, and so bad her good Night and went his Way, but we were at *Bath* five Hours before him.

[p. 19]The next Day we divided the Stockings and Neck-cloths between us four, except some Thread Stockings and the Handkerchiefs, which *Mary Brown* and *Frances Allen* would have for themselves: The two Women kept the rest of the Things for us till *Bristol* Fair. Our Landlord *R – ts* [Roberts] had one of the Bills of the Robbery left at his House; and when we came into his House, he said, *Why will you not let me have some of the Cloaths, to make my Son some Cloaths? You never let me have any Thing as you do other Landlords: I think I ought to have a Penny's worth as well as they.*[36]

The 25th of *January*, 1753, we went to *Bristol* Fair on the Sharp; but we had no Luck that Day, so at Night we went to milling of Swaggs, that is, breaking of Shops, or Ware-houses: Accordingly we went to the *Bell Inn*, in *Thomas Street*, and broke open the Ware-house, and with a dark Lanthorn they brought out of the said Ware-house to me, two Pieces of broad Livery Cloth, one brown and the other blue, directed for Mr. *Harford* of *Bath*:[37] I staid in the Street till the other three went into a House in *Temple Street*, just by the Back of the said Inn; where *Elger* went up Stairs, and opened a Box that was not locked, and brought out a Piece of brown Stuff, and Linen for a Gown, and gave it to me; I came to the *Lamb-Inn*, at *Lawford's-Gate* with it, and took Horse directly for *Bath*, and delivered the Goods to *Frances Allen* to secrete for me, and I then went to Bed: About Two o'Clock in the Morning *Brown*, *Allen*, and *Elger*, came to *Bath* with a Pack of Handkerchiefs that they had stolen from the *London* Ware-house in *Peter-street*;[38] and they told me they had lost a good Booty for Want of the Lanthorn that I had in my Pocket. *Elger* went forward with the Pack of Handkerchiefs to *Chapel Plaister*; and *Brown* and *Allen* called for the Cloth, Stuff, and Cloaths, that *Mary Brown* and *Frances Allen* had secreted for me; and they followed *Elger* to *St – n G –* 's [Stephen Gea's] where *G – – –* [Gea] got a Box made on Purpose to nail up the said Goods in. I went the next Morning to them, and put the Things into the Box: We staid there a Day or two, and at last we sold *St – – – – n G – – –* [Stephen Gea] upwards of twenty Dozen of the said Handkerchiefs, and four Yards of the blue Cloth, and to his Wife *Mary* the Piece of Stuff for a Gown, they both well knowing the same to be stolen, and from whence.

The next Day we all set out for the *Rock Tavern* in *Staffordshire*, with our Goods; but it raining, we left *Brown* on the Road with them, and went forward to the said Tavern, it being our old Place of Rendezvous; where we sold a Silk Camblet Coat, two Pair of Breeches, and a Silk Cream-coloured Waistcoat, for one Pound six Shillings, to *Edward* and *Margaret L – –* [Lines], and they helped me to cut off the Gold Lace from an embroidered blue Padusway Waistcoat, and we burnt it before their Faces, and gave them [p. 20] the Remainder of the Waistcoat, and told them from whence it was stolen: We sold the Remainder of the Handkerchiefs, about nineteen Dozen, to *John – –*, and the Mazarene blue Coat for one Pound, he being at *Bristol* the same Time they were stolen, and saw them at *G – –* 's [Gea's] House; but he would have nothing to do with them there, until we carried them to the *Rock Tavern*.

Brown came to us the next Day, and told us he had sold the Cloth for 4s. 6d. per Yard, to Mr. *Thomas B –*, at *Coalharbour*, in *Gl – r* Road; but I cannot take upon me to swear it, because I was not a Witness of it.

The *R – k* [Rock] *Tavern* has been a Place of Rendezvous for these People for thirty Years past, tho' never detected till now; but all the Country knew it, and used to call those who used it, *Thieves* and *Highwaymen*. The Landlord and Landlady have appeared at their Trials several Times; but once especially for *Christopher F – stone* [Fetherstone or Feterstone] at *Northampton*, for a Robbery on the Highway, and got him off by swearing him to be at their House at the Time.

When we came to *Bath*, I sold the Silver we took off the embroidered Waistcoat to *John F – – d* [Ford], which was not quite an Ounce. I told him it was taken off a Waistcoat which was stole from Mr. *Smith* of *Bristol*; but I never got above one Shilling of *F – – d* [Ford] for my Silver to this Day.[39] *Brown* likewise sold the Silver Spoons and Tea Tongs that were stolen from a House in *Queen's Square*, to *John F – – – d* [Ford], for nine Shillings; he well knowing the said Things to be stolen, and from whence.

We all staid in *Bath* to spend our ill got Money until *March*, *R – ts* [Roberts] had got one *Burk* [Thomas Burk][40] at his House, very poor, and just out of *Bristol* Gaol, whom he kept for a Month at Bed and Board. On the 11th Day of *March*, *Brown*, *Elger*, and *Allen*, went to *Abingdon* Fair, and left *Burk* and I at *R – ts*'s [Roberts's]; when the latter came to me, and said, JOHN, *Will you take* Burk *with you, for he owes me Money?* To which I answered, *Not I; I am not going out at all any more*: He said, Abingdon

Fair is To-morrow, and Burk *will show you where you may buss a Couple of Prads, and fence them at* Abingdon *Gaff; that is,* Burk *will show you a Couple of Horses that you may steal, and sell them at* Abingdon *Fair*: Accordingly we did steal two Geldings from a Ground of Mr. *Smith*'s at the *Castle* and *Ball*, one a Black and the other a Bay,[41] and rode all Night, and the next Morning we got to *Abingdon*, where I saw my Accomplices, who had no Luck that Day. I sold the black Gelding to a Countryman near 'Squire *Dashwood*'s in *Oxfordshire*, and we stood in the Fair all the Day with the other; but we could not get our Price for him: At last we sold him to a Flash Dealer, one *Bishop*, of my Acquaintance, for three Pounds thirteen Shillings and Six-pence, and told him where he came from, he at the same Time [p. 21] very well knowing him to be worth seven Pounds;[42] and then we had no Horse between us both, but I chanced to go into the *Ram* or *Lamb Inn*, when the Ostler asked me if I wanted my Horse, I said *Yes*; when he brought me a fine Bay Gelding, bridled and saddled: I ask'd him what he came to, he said *Five pence*; but I gave him Six pence, and rode away, sometimes riding and sometimes walking. We lay that Night at *Lackdale*, and the next Night at *Cheltenham* in *Gloucestershire*. About a Mile from that Town, *Burk* stole a Grey Poney, and we rode that Night to the *Rock Tavern*, our old Place of Rendezvous.

The next day we went within three Miles of *Newport* in *Shropshire*, to another Flash House; and the Day after went to *Nantwich* Fair in *Cheshire*, where we met with two Flash Horse Jockeys, to whom I sold the Bay Gelding: Their Names were *John S-* [Small] and *Joseph S –* [Shoten], both Partners, and who live at *N – p – t* [Newport, Shropshire]: They both ask'd me where the Horse came from, and I told them that I stole him from the *Ram* or *Lamb Inn*, in *Abingdon*: They said they would take Care what Part he went to, and then gave me six Guineas for him, tho' it was worth fourteen.[43]

We did not sell the Poney at *Nantwich*, but that Night we stole* a black Gelding, Saddle and Bridle, from a Publick House Door;[44] and we rode back to our Flash House, three miles from *Newport*, the Sign of the *W – H –*, on the *London* Road.

The next Day we went to our old House, the *Rock Tavern*; but *Burk* sold the Poney to a Stranger on the Road: Then I carried him behind me to the *Rock Tavern*, where we staid that Night there being five more there of our Way of Calling. We went next Morning towards *Birmingham*, and got there just before Night; where we bought two Brace of Pistols, and went that

---

* The only Method that I know to prevent Horses being stolen, is to send to Birmingham for some of their Case-hardened Locks, which are made on Purpose; no Thief or other Person can get the said Lock off the Horse's Fetlock without the Key. They must be lined with Leather to prevent their galling the Heel of the Horse, and not have any Chain to it, for that will fret the Horse if he has any Spirit. If any Thief steals him over Night, in the Morning when they see the Lock on him they will turn him up, for the said Lock cannot be filed off, nor broke; and the Expences of it will be but two Shillings each Lock. It must not be put on too tight, neither too big.

Night and stole a Bay Gelding from a Ground about a Mile and half from thence; and we rode that Night to *Worcester*,[45] and knocked up a Flash Landlord at the *B – Inn*, near the Bridge Foot whose name is *D –*: The next Night to the Cross, to another Flash House, and the next Night to *Bath*, and the next Morning to *St – – n G – –* 's [Stephen Gea's] at *Chapel Plaister*, where I sold the black Gelding we stole at *Nantwich*, to a Dealer in Needles, whose Name is *Darby*, and who came from *Bromsgrove* in *Worcestershire*, for three Guineas, and *St – G –* [Stephen Gea] vouched for the same.

[p.22]That Night I and *Burk* went over *Clarken Down* [Claverton Down],[46] towards *Trowbridge* in *Wiltshire*, but not on any Design of robbing; and going down the Hill at the watering Place, we met a Post Chaise, which *Burk* swore he would go and rob: I denied to go with him, But he still swore he would: I asked him, as we followed the Chaise, if he thought I was mad, to do such a Thing so near *Bath*, and just as I came out of a House I was so well known in: but he again swore he would do it himself, if I would not go with him: Then I thought with myself that if he was taken, I should be in as much Danger as he, for being with him just before; so I consented to go with him. I desired him not to be guilty of any Mischief, or hurt any Person, for that four Men were as easily robbed as one, and that the Sight of a Pistol unawares, is a great Terror to any Man, and without they fire at me, don't fire at them; he told me he would not: Then I rode up to the Chaise, and bid the Boy stand, but I believe he did not hear me, for he kept on. The World may think it is false, but I assure them it is true, as I am not sure whether I am for Life or Death: It being dark before I got up with the Chaise, I did not know whether the Window was up or down, but I ran my Hand through the Glass, and cut my Fingers all across, and I believe in drawing my Hand out of the Window, pulled the Cock of Pistol, for it went off through both Windows unexpectedly; but I thought at first the Fire came from the Chaise, till I put my Hand on the Cock and felt it down; and *Burk* (he being behind the Chaise) also thought the Fire came from the Chaise at me, as he told me afterwards, which was the Occasion of his firing: Then we had no Pistol loaded, for we had but a Brace loaded when we attacked the Chaise, having discharged a Brace just before at a Mark on the Down. The World hath said that I threatened the Child's Life, but I declare I had not such a Thought; for Mr. *Hancock* gave her to me, desiring me not to hurt her, and I took her in my Arms and kissed her, and then set her down: I do not deny but there was very bad opprobrious Language passed at first; but at last, if any Body had come by, they would not have known what we were at. It was reported we got above thirty Pounds from Mr. *Hancock*, but I do assure the World we got no more that [than] one Guinea and a half in Gold, and above six Shillings and Sixpence in Silver, his Gold Watch, and a great Quantity of his Lady's wearing Apparel and Child's Linnen.[47]

After this Robbery we went directly back to *St – G –* 's [Stephen Gea's]; but they were all in Bed, except *M – y G –* [Mary Gea], whom I called down and she let us in and made a Fire, and got us a Tankard of Toddy, then called up her Husband, who came down directly, and we told him and his Wife what we had done; and *Burk* fetched in all the Things we had robbed

Dr. *Hancock* of, in order to shew them, and Mr. *G –* [Gea] took the Gold Watch in his Hand: I then asked *M – y G –* [Mary Gea] to lend me a Wallet (which she did) [p. 23] to pack the Things in, and she folded up the Gowns as well as she could; for she said it would spoil them to rumple them; and she assisted us in putting them into the Wallet: I then ask'd Mr. *G –* [Gea] if he had any Gunpowder to load our Pistols with, who took down a Fowling Piece that lay on the Rack in his Kitchen, drew the Charge, and gave me the Gunpowder; when I asked *M – G –* [Mary Gea] for a Spoon and a Pipe to make two Brace of Balls to load our Pistols with, which she gave me, and they both assisted me in making them, and in loading our Pistols: *Burk* asked *M – y G –* [Mary Gea] if she was not afraid to see us load our Pistols; she said, *No; they are not the first I have seen loaded by Night in this Kitchen:* She then hash'd us some Veal. I bought a Bay Gelding of *S – n G –* [Stephen Gea] for six Pounds, and then we drank four or five Tankards of Toddy, and paid our Reckoning; and *M – G –* [Mary Gea] said, *I would have you get as far as you can by Day light, and send to us, and we will send you Word what News there is at* Bath.[48]

We set out again for *Clarken Down* [Claverton Down], and so by the Glass-House, where *Burk* stole a Bay Gelding with a Pack Saddle. We went that Morning to *Wells* before we baited, and at Night to *Taunton*, and the next day to *Exeter*. *Burk*, as soon as he put up his Horse, went to one *W – C –*'s [William Cooper's], a *H –*, in *Northgate street*,[49] and told him what we had done, and gave him his Pistols to lock up for him, and said Baxter *will come and bring his to you by and by*: he said, *and welcome.* Just after, I went to see *C –*'s [Cooper's] Shop, but *Burk* was not there; when *C –* [Cooper] told me what *Burk* had told him, and said, *I have lock'd up his Pistols; shall I lock up your's?* I said, *No; I will not put mine out of my Pockets:* Then I told him I had been on the Scamp and what I had robb'd the Chaise of; I show'd him the Gold Watch, and told him what rich Cloaths we had got to sell: He wanted me to change Watches with him, the Gold one for a Silver one, which he said was got the same Way up at the Start, that is at *London*, and sent him down as a Present by a Family Man,[50] but that it was christen'd before it came, that is, the Name and Number taken out, and others put in. He had told me if I would bring a Gown to his House, he had a Sister in Law who sold old Cloaths, she should buy it of me, and would say they were his Wife's: Accordingly he went with me to the Inn, and I show'd him the Gown; and I gave him some of the Child's Caps and a Gown, and some other Things, which he carried to his House and kept for me, he well knowing the same to be stolen, and from whence, and that they were got on the Highway. The said *C –* [Cooper], *Brown*, and I, were never apart last *Lammas* Assizes at *Exon* [Exeter]; for *Brown* knew him for twelve Years last past in *London*, and they had been out together on the Sneak: He is an old Family [p. 24] Man and left *London* on that Occasion, and came into the Country.

The 24th and 26th of *March*, one – – and his Wife came to me, and bought a Shirt and a great Coat of Dr. *Hancock*'s Servant's, which we stole from the Chaise: I told him he must take off the Buttons and Lining, which he did accordingly; and when it was ask'd for, he denied it; but afterwards it was found in his Custody. One of the above two Days, he and his Wife also came to the Goal of *Exon*, and fetcht out a Fly Petticoat and Sack; and she put them under her Petticoats, and said, *No body will mind what I carry out of Prison, because I am always bringing Things in and out here, and at any Time we will give you as much as any Body shall, for any Thing that lies in our Way:* They both well knew those Things to be stolen.

At the same Time one – and his Wife came to the said Prison; and he told me he would serve me or Mrs. *Baxter* at any Time,[51] and secrete any Thing for me or her: Accordingly Mrs. *Baxter* gave them a great Quantity of wearing Apparel, which he and she told me they had sent to *Launceston*; and I was forced to hire a Horse for him, which cost me five Shillings, and two Shillings and Six pence for his Trouble to fetch the said Things back again, they having sent away those Things unknown to me or Mrs. *Baxter*, at the same Time both knowing them to be stolen, for I told them they were. And if it were not for such People as those I have mentioned in this Treatise, *Sharping* and *Thieving* would be but a miserable Calling; and, in short, if the World will allow me to be a Judge of the matter, I think it but a dismal Profession at best; for I can speak it by experimental Knowledge, that a Man that follows this Way of Living, can never be at Rest Night nor Day: Such has been my unhappy Condition a great while; for as the wise Man saith, *A wounded Conscience who can bear?*

I forgot to mention that in *Sept.* 1752, I, and *John Brown* alias *Dawson*, *William Elger*, *John Allen*, alias *Robert Jones*, alias *Robert Graham*, went to *Wayhill* [Weyhill] Fair, where we met *Thomas B – s* [Brooks], and *A – m G – g* [Abraham Garing], of *Sh – on* [Sherston]; and we agreed among us to buy two or three hundred Sheep of one Mr. *Medlicott*, of *Sheston* [Sherston], a Neighbour of *B – s* [Brooks] and *G – g's* [Garing's], and never pay for them; but I coming late to the Fair, the Sheep were all sold, and we then agreed to meet at *Appleshaw* Fair, on the same Purpose. We four then went on the sharping Lay, and *Allen* pick'd up a young Contryman, that came out of *Sussex* to buy Sheep, and his Shepherd with him; we defrauded him of fourteen Guineas and his Watch, and drank plentifully of Wine while we were at Work, and when his Money was gone took him out of one Door of the Booth, while the Sailor went out at the other; but the Contryman soon [p. 25] returned again, and finding we were gone, the Reckoning paid, and half a Bottle of Wine left upon the Table, then discovered, tho' too late, that he was bit: he bore it with Patience, and he and his Man sat down and drank the Remainder of the Bottle of Wine before they departed.

The next Day we went to a Booth that was *Flash*, (we always have two or three Booths or Houses in every Fair *Flash*, as we generally spend a great deal of Money every Fair Day.) I picked up an old Man that sold Cheese, by dropping of a Shilling, and took him into the same Booth to spend the Shilling, where the Sailor and Capper[52] was; the Sailor ask'd the old Man to change a Guinea, and finding he had not much Money, laid him a Guinea that neither he nor I could borrow fifteen Guineas in half an Hour: I went the old Man's Halves; but the Sailor said he must not bring any Person with him, but must come by himself: Accordingly he and I went together, and borrow'd the Money of the old Man's Son, and came back and won the

Guinea. The old Man was so rejoiced at his good Luck, that expecting to win all the Sailor's Money, he made a Stake for the whole, and lost it at the first Prick. We both went to borrow more; but when we came back the Sailor and his Companion were gone, as the Landlord told us, so we parted. We then went to our first Booth, where I staid within, and my Companions that were out at Work, brought in the Master of a Sloop, belonging to *Portsmouth*, by finding Half a Crown; we laid him the same Wager, that he did not borrow twenty Guineas in half an Hour; the Sailor had upwards of one hundred Guineas in his Pocket; the Captain went out and borrowed twenty-two Guineas, and made Stakes for the whole, and lost; he cried and stamped very much; but the Landlord came and turned him and us out of the Booth, and said we were all a Parcel of Rogues, that we all came in together, and should all go out together; so we all went out together at one Door, but we returned again at the other Door, and staid and drank very plentifully: We carried forty-five Pounds out of the Fair.

The Beginning of *November*, we, the same four, went to *Appleshaw* Fair, to meet *B – s* [Brooks] and *G – g* [Garing]; accordingly we all met together, and agreed what to do with *Medlicot*: *B – s* [Brooks] and *G – g* [Garing] show'd me *Medlicott*'s Penns, and I bought one hundred and eleven Sheep of him, and desired him to come down to the *Iron-Pear-Tree*, where I would pay him for the Sheep: He asked me what Country I belonged to; *B – s* [Brooks] and *G – g* [Garing] had told me before to say *Brackley*, in *Northamptonshire*, which I did: *B – s* [Brooks], *G – g* [Garing], and my Accomplices, were at the *Iron-Pear-Tree*, waiting for us, and we going into the same Room, *B – s* [Brooks] said, *How do you do, Mr*. Poulter? I answered, *At your Service: What*, [p. 26] says *B – s* [Brooks] and *G – g* [Garing], *here is our old Neighbour* Medlicott; *Have you bought all, Mr*. Poulter? I said, *Yes, Mr*. *G – g* [Garing], *but I am indebted to you fifteen Guineas*: On which I pull'd out my Purse, paid him the Money, and thank'd him: He said, *You are welcome to all the Sheep I have at any Time; I am sorry you did not deal with me now, but I am glad you have dealt with our Neighbour*. I then went out to give them an Opportunity of talking: *Medlicott* ask'd them where I lived; they told him at *Brackley*, that they had dealt with me for many hundred Pounds, and that my Note was worth a thousand Pounds. When I came in, one of my Accomplices came and ask'd if Mr. *Poulter* of *Brackley* was there; I said, *yes:* He said, *If you are the Gentleman I have a Draft on you for sixty Pounds*: I said, *Very well; you must meet me at Night, and I will answer it:* He said, *Very well*, and went his Way. I said to Medlicott, *What doth the Sheep come to?* He replied, *Sixty Pounds and upwards:* I said, *I will pay you at* Andover *Fair:* He said, *You must let me have some Cash, for I have a great Sum to pay away:* I said, *How much will do?* He replied, *Twenty Pounds*: I then said, *Mr*. *G – g* [Garing], *can you lend me so much?* He answered, *Yes, five Times as much, if you want it:* I said, *No; but twenty*. He lent it to me, and I gave him my Note for the Money; but he had fifteen Guineas of my Money before, when I owed him not a Farthing, nor never had any Dealings with him nor *B – s* [Brooks], only under a Colour to blind *Medlicott*. I paid *Medlicott* twenty Pounds, and gave him my Note for forty more, to be paid at *Andover* Fair:

Accordingly, we let run the Sheep, and as *B – s* [Brooks] and *G – g* [Garing] claim'd as great a Right to them as we; we paid them two Parts out of six. We drove the Sheep to *Penzon*,[53] about a Mile from *Wey-Hill*, to one Mr. *L –*'s; and *B – s* [Brooks] sent a Man with twenty Pounds for forty Pounds worth of Sheep, which we let them have, so that they two had as much as we four: But they said they would make it up in the next; and then they sent to me, and said *Medlicott* was to be had again, if I would write him a Letter, for three or four Score more to meet me at *Luggershall* [Ludgershall, Wilts.]; and at the same Time write a Letter to *G – g* [Garing], and desire him to carry the *Letter* to *Medlicott*, and shew him his at the same Time: I did as he desired, and *G – g* [Garing] went with the said Letter to Mr. *Medlicott*. *G – g* [Garing] asked Mr. *Medlicott* if would send me the Sheep; he said, *I can't tell: G – g* [Garing] said, *I will give you Six-pence a Head for the sixty Ewes, and send them to Mr.* Poulter *myself*; but Mr. *Medlicott* refused, and said, *I will send them to Mr.* Poulter, *for they are fit to turn into any Gentleman's Park: G – g* [Garing] said, *I shall send him sixty, if you are willing:* But all this was done to deceive Mr. *Medlicott*, they both having Sheep to come that way to *Andover* Fair, where all the Money was [p. 27] to be paid for the Sheep: Accordingly I sent *John Allen* to meet the Sheep Mr. *Medlicott* was to bring to *Luggershall: Allen* passed for my Man, and said I was gone into Dorsetshire for more; accordingly he met Mr. *Medlicott* with the Sheep: He had a Note from me to Mr. *Medlicott*; who delivered the Sheep, on Sight of the Note, to my Man *Allen*; and sent me back a Note of the Delivery of the same, according to my Order. *Allen* drove the Sheep to me, where I was waiting on Purpose, about a Mile from *Wey-Hill*: We staid there till *B – s* [Brooks] and *G – g* [Garing] came to us, and we sold them the Sheep that came to thirty-nine Pounds for twenty; for they said I should not have had them, had it not been for them, and they ought to have Half; so they got seventy-nine Pounds Worth of Sheep for forty Pounds; And at that Time they said, *Damn* Medlicott, *We have not done with him yet, if you are willing, for he gets Money faster than we do: If you are willing* Poulter, *you shall rob him one Night or other; when he has got a Sum of Money about him, we will stay him at a Fair or Market late, and we will come home with him, so you must rob him and us too; and we will fill our Purses full of Halfpence on Purpose, and say we have lost forty or fifty Pounds: He keeps his Money in his Boots; for the other Night he was drunk, and I undressed him, and pulling off his Boots I found upwards of forty Pounds: This is the Way we may ruin him, if you are willing:* But I would not agree to these Proposals at that Time; if I had believed it would have ruin'd him.

I think such People as these are worse than myself or my Accomplices: This is called in the Cant, *Masoning*; that is, giving your Notes for Money, and never designing to pay it: This Defraud was carried on by two of Mr. *Medlicott*'s near Neighbours; and, as they pretended themselves, his particular Friends, of the same Calling, Sheep Jobbers. *T – B –* [Thomas Brooks] lives at the *S – h*'s [Smith's] Shop on the *Gloucester* Road, between *F – e* and *F–r: A – G – g* [Abraham Garing] lives at *S – n* [Sherston] in *W – e* [Wiltshire], within three Miles of his Grace the Duke of *Beauford*'s at *Badminton*.

I do not think there is one out of ten of those People called Horse Jockeys, but will buy stolen Horses of any Family Man, though at the same Time they know them to be stolen; and they will capp to any masoning Cull for any Horse or Beast of any Sort, and buy them afterwards.

[This takes the text up to the end of p. 27.]
[p. 28]
> The Way that Convicts return from Transportation, and
> the only Way how to prevent their Return.

AFTER they are in any Part of North *America*, the general Way is this, just before they go on Board a Ship, their Friend or Accomplices purchase them their Freedom from the Merchant or Captain that belongs to the said Ship, for about ten Pound Sterling, some gives more and some less; then the Friend of the Convict or Convicts, gets a Note from the Merchant, or Captain, that the Person is free to go unmolested when the Ships arrive between the Capes of *Virginia*, where they please. But I never heard of any Convict that came home again in the same Ship they went over in, for the Merchant or Captain, gives a Bond to the Sheriff of the County where such Convicts go from, to leave them in *America*, and they get a Receipt from the Custom there; but as there are ships coming home every Week, if they can pay their Passage they are refused in no Ship. Some Men will work their Passage back again, and them that cannot free themselves, take an Opportunity of running away from their Master, and lay in the Woods by Day, and travel by Night for *Philadelphia*, *New York* or *Boston*; in which Places no Questions are asked them. This encourages a great many to commit Robberies more than they would, because they say they do not mind Transportation, it being but four or five Months Pleasure, for they can get their Freedom and come home again. I knew one that never went over, but bribed some of the Ship's Crew lying in the Transport Hole, *Bristol*. Her Name was *Elizabeth Connor*, I think it was in 1748, she was convicted at the said City for picking Pockets, and was ordered for Transportation, but is now in *England*, which I gave an Account of to Mr. *Stokes*, an Attorney at Law in *Bristol*.

To prevent any Convict coming back before their limited Time is out, is for the Government to lay a Charge or Fine on such Merchant or Captain not to free them before hand, and for the Colonies in *America* to do as they do in the Islands in the *West Indies*, that no Person or Persons can go on board any homebound Ship, without publishing his or her Name on the public Crosses such a Number of Days before; and for such Person or Persons to bring a Certificate from the Governor, with Proof that he or she is not indented, nor a Convict; that would prevent such a Number of Convicts coming back again before their Time is expired.

[On pp. 29–42 are outlines of the different techniques used by thieves and fraudsters, it is printed, 'To caution all Shopkeepers and Salesmen against Shoplifters of both Sexes, and the best Way to prevent their Villainies is as follows:'; on pp. 42–3 is a cant dictionary.]

[p. 43] *It being necessary that some Account should be given of Mr.* POULTER's *Birth, (which was omitted in the former Part of this Book,) we have thought proper to insert it here, as it was wrote by Himself.*

I Was born at *Newmarket*; in *Cambridgeshire*, the noted Town for Horse Races, in the Year 1715, and in the Year 1728, I went to live with his Grace the Duke of *Somerset*, in the Running Sta[p. 44]bles, which Place I stayed in till the Year 1734, and then went to live with Lord *James Cavendish* untill 1737, and then to Colonel *John Lumley*, the Earl of *Scarborough*'s Brother untill 1739, and have been in *France* three Times with Horses and Hounds; once to his Grace the Duke of *Kingston* another Time to King *Stanislaus* near *Sankelne*, and once with Captain *Rutter*. I afterwards went to *Bristol*, which Place I sailed out of several Voyages to *Africa*, and to all Parts of *America*, and one Voyage out of *Weymouth*, in a Ship commanded by Captain *Tivitoe*, and another Voyage from *London* to *Jamaica*.

A LIST of Persons informed against by John Poulter, *alias* Baxter, *before* Francis Drew, *Esq*; *and others of his Majesty's Justices of the Peace at the City of* Exon; *and before* John Halliday, *Esq*; John Tripp, *Esq*; *Mayor, and* Benjamin Hall, *Esq*; *all of* Taunton.

JOhn Brown, alias Dawson, John Allen, alias Robert Jones, alias Robert Graham, Thomas Tobin, Christopher Feterstone, Sarah Cagan, John Hurst, William Elger, Charles Handy, Thomas Walker, Elizabeth Ford, Mary Gea, John Small, John Dean, William Trinder, and Hannah Trinder, John Bishop, Thomas Burk, Thomas Brooks, and Abraham Garing, these are not taken.

James Ramscroft, in Westchester gaol, Edward Lines and Margaret Lines, in Stafford gaol, John Ford, in Shepton Mallet, bailed out, Stephen Gea, in Salisbury gaol, bailed out, Robert Lyte, in Winchester gaol, bailed out, Joseph Shotton, in Worcester Gaol, William Nipps, in Gloucester Gaol, Mary Brown, and Frances Allen, in Ivelchester-Gaol, John Roberts, in Shepton Mallet, dead, John Allen, of Devizes, bailed, William Cooper, and two Women and one Man in Exon Gaol, bailed out.

A List of Persons returned from Transportation, now in England *before the Expiration of their Time.*
MAry Dawson alias Brown, from Lincoln, in the year 1746, for picking Pockets; Margaret Brown, alias Wilson, alias Long Peg, from Lincoln in the year 1750, for picking Pockets; Rosey Brown from Lincoln, for ditto, in 1751; she took Shipping from London, and has got a Child at Nurse at Bath-Ford, and two at the Bell Inn near Bromsgrove. Elenor* Connor, alias Tobin, transported from Bristol in 1748, for picking Pockets; Eleanor Wilson, alias Sparrow, from Litchfield, in the Year 1750, for Shoplifting; William Evean, alias Sparrow, and Robert Jones, alias John Allen, from Warwick, in the Year 1750, on Suspicion of robbing on the Highway; John Brown, transported in the Year 1743, fourteen Years for House breaking. James White, from York, transported in the Year 1740 for picking of Pockets. William Evean, alias Sparrow, made his Escape from Ivelchester Gaol the latter End of November 1752.[54]

FINIS

---

* She was forcibly rescued out of Liverpool Goal, the 15th of November last [1753], and is since retaken and committed to Newgate in London.

[The following section was not included in the ninth edition: it comes from the eleventh edition.]

[p. 45] AN ACCOUNT OF the Behaviour of *John Poulter* alias *Baxter*, during his Confinement under his Condemnation, the Examinations he went through, the Motives that made him attempt an Escape; and the probable, tho' secret Reasons, of his being at last executed, with his Behaviour at the Place of Execution.

THIS unfortunate Man, after having made very important Discoveries of great Use to the Publick, and for much less than which many a Man has not only receiv'd Pardon for capital Offences, but even Rewards had the Fate, by a Series of unlucky Circumstances and Incidents, to be brought to suffer, after having entertained the most flattering and assured Hopes to the contrary. When he first made his Informations against his Accomplices, which was soon after he was taken up at *Exeter*, for robbing Dr. *Hancock* of *Salisbury*, he desired that they might be kept very secret; and particularly he gave a Charge to the Officer who was sent to *Bath* to apprehend his Accomplices, not to divulge his Errand at his Arrival to any one Person there except the Mayor, because there were several Persons who lived in good Credit in the Eye of the World, who yet had Intelligence with his Gang: But notwithstanding this strict Charge so much Imprudence was committed, that it was universally known all over *Bath* upon what Errand the Officer was come within a Hour after his Arrival; and the very next Morning even the Names of all the Persons, as well as those who harboured in *Bath*, as in other Places, whom *Poulter* had informed against, was printed and publickly sold. This Affair being managed so imprudently (not to say worse of it) his Accomplices had Notice of it every where, and consequently Time to escape, which they took Care, especially the principal ones, to make use of.

Dr. *H – k* hearing of the Informations *Poulter* had made, and having received back some of the Things he had been robb'd of, gave him Hopes that he would be very favourable to him in the Prosecution; however, when the Day of Trial came, the Doctor acted against him with the greatest Inveteracy, and used all his Interest to prevent the Judge from granting him any Respite from Execution; however, one of six Weeks was granted him, and he was ordered back to *Ivelchester* Goal. Here he behaved very so[p. 46]berly and seriously, and as the Corporations of *Bristol, Bath, Exeter* and *Taunton*, besides many private Gentlemen, interested themselves greatly in his Favour; and as the Discoveries he had made to several of his Majesty's Justices, and particularly what he had wrote and published in his Book, were thought to be of very great Importance to the Publick, and further Respites from Time to Time were given him, not only himself, but every one else imagined that a free Pardon would at last be granted, or, at least, that his Life would be saved. A very eminent Attorney of *Sherborne* in *Dorsetshire*, by Order from above, went over to *Ivelchester* several Times to examine him, to whom he declared the same he had published in this Book, without any material Difference or Addition, except only the Mention of one Person, who now lives in good Credit, and, tho' not concerned, knew of the

Proceedings of himself and Gang, and could bear Evidence to corroborate all he had declared; but he desired very earnestly that the Name of this Person might never be mentioned, except it was necessary to call upon him to corroborate his Evidence in a Court of Justice. But during this Time he had the Misfortune to have the ill Will of the Gaol-Keeper, who treated him with great Severity, and even seeming unnecessary Cruelty; for tho' he was in a very ill State of Health, yet he would not let him have, in the severest cold Weather, any Thing to lie on but Straw, tho' he offered to pay more than the accustomed Fees for a Bed. Several Gentlemen of the County who thought the Life of a Person, which was prolonged for the Good of the Publick should not be destroyed by Severity of Usage, wrote to the Gaol-Keeper in his Favour, to allow him a Bed, but no Regard was paid to their Remonstrances, till the Sheriff of the County sent a positive Order that a Bed should be allowed him. Whether these unhappy Differences with the Gaoler might not occasion Representations, little in his Favour, to be made to the M – – m – – r of the Town, who has great Influence at Court, is very doubtful; however this was, when every one expected a Pardon for him it was given out that he would certainly suffer on the first of *March*, and *Poulter* declared, in a Letter he wrote to a Gentleman a little while before his Death, that the Gaol-Keeper was constantly sounding in his Ears that he would certainly be executed the first of *March*: This being repeted so often, first tempted him to try to make his Escape, as from the Gaoler's Representations he thought, that notwithstanding all the Discoveries he had made, and the great Hopes he had received, he should at last suffer; accordingly on *Sunday* the 17th of *February*, observing a fit Opportunity, he made his Escape from the Gaol in Company with a Debtor, by forcing an Iron Bar out of a Window.

[p. 47]He was obliged to travel as far as Glastonbury on Foot, with one of his Irons on, but there found Means to get it off; but his Legs were so galled by them, and he was in so weak a Condition, that he found he was not able to travel with any Manner of Expedition; however, they travelled forwards on Monday Night, (having concealed themselves the greatest Part of the Day in a Hay Rick) intending to have steered their Way to *Pill*, and so have got a Passage over into Wales; but not knowing the Country well, about Eight o'Clock on Tuesday Morning, they came into the Parish of Wookey near Wells, thinking they had been got near *Axbridge*; *Poulter* being quite fatigued to Death, they went into a little Public-house there, where he went to Bed, and lay till about 2 o'Clock in the Afternoon, then got up. While they were proposing to set out again, a Mason who was employed on a Building near by, went in for a Mug of Drink, and knowing *Poulter* he immediately went out and calling several of his fellow Workmen, they took him without any Resistance, and he was again back to Ivelchester Goal, on Wednesday.[55]

As soon as he was brought, a Petition was drawn up by the Gaoler and some other Inhabitants of the Town of *Ivelchester*, and sent by Express to their Member, desiring him to use his utmost Interest that *Poulter* might be ordered for immediate Execution, tho' according to his last Reprieve he had then only nine Days to live. Accordingly, by the Interest that was made, an

Express was sent on Purpose from *London* to *Ivelchester*, to order his Execution within twenty-four Hours after his Arrival at *Ivelchester*. This Resentment, Prejudice, Interest, and other unlucky Causes, perhaps contributed to shorten the Life of a Man, the Preservation of whom would in all Probability have been for the Welfare of the publick, for it is agreed on all Hands, that he was sincere in his Discoveries, that he would strenuously have endeavoured to have taken his Accomplices, and that whilst he was living, his Gang would never have dared to have staid in *England*, because as he well knew their Haunts, &c. it would be impossible for them to have abided any Time here without being taken.

Poulter received the News of his speedy Execution with Surprize, as it was quite unexpected, and so short a Warning,[56] yet he declared he should be very willing to die provided he could first see his Wife, upon which a Messenger was immediately dispatch'd for her to *Bath*.

After receipt of the Dead Warrant he spend the Day in fervent Prayer, receiving the Sacrament, &c. and being solemnly questioned about his *Book of Discoveries*, he declared there was not a Word in it but what was Truth; and being asked about the Report that was spread, concerning the Gaol-Keepers having re[p. 48]ceived a Sum of Money to favour his Escape, he declared it was absolutely false, and that neither of the Keepers were privy to it. He expressed very firm Hopes of receiving Pardon from God, as though his Crimes were many, yet he had never been guilty of Murder, or injured the Person of any one.

When he came to the Place of Execution[57] he behaved very Penitently, but with a decent Resolution. He stood up in the Cart, and declared three Times aloud, that the Report of the Gaol Keepers having been privy to his Escape, was false and without any Foundation. Hearing that *F – d* [Ford] of *Bath*, was among the Spectators, he called out for him to come to him, and then told him that every Thing he had related of him in his Book about being privy to their Robberies, and melting down Plate for them was true; *F – d* denying this with bitter Imprecations, *Poulter* affirmed, that as he was going to appear before his great Judge and hop'd to receive Mercy from him, what he had said was true, he then desired the Spectators to take Warning by his sad End, and to avoid all ill Company, acknowledging he deserv'd to die, but most of his Accomplices much more so.[58]

FINIS.

NOTES

1 According to *Devon, (To wit) The voluntary Information, Examination, and Confession, of John Poulter, otherwise Baxter*, [no place or date of publication], Brown was sentenced to transportation for fourteen years in the early 1740s.

2 A woman's cloak with a hood.

3 According to *The further Information, Examination, and Confession of John Poulter, otherwise Baxter*, [no place or date of publication], Harper was rescued by 'a Gang of Irish People' and Tobin was acquitted.

4 Roberts kept the Pack Horse Inn (*Bath Journal*, 2 April 1753) and the Turk's Head at Bath (*Devon . . . The voluntary Information . . . of John Poulter*). There

were at least two Pack Horse Inns in Bath: one was in the centre, near St Michael's Church, and was the starting point for the carriers to and from Exeter and Tedbury; the other was on Claverton Street and was allegedly a centre of Jacobitism: T. Strange Cotterell, *Historic Map of Bath*, Bath, n.d., p. 7.

5 Presumably, what is meant is settling days, that is, the days appointed for the settling of accounts between debtors and creditors.

6 Gea kept the Bell in Chapel Plaster, Box, Wiltshire: *Bath Journal*, 9 April 1753.

7 *Bath Journal*, 9 December 1751, reported that a Mr Hawkins of West Ashton had been robbed on 30 November in the evening 'between Claverton down and Stoke-Bridge' by two people 'who us'd him in a very barbarous Manner'.

8 According to *Devon . . . The voluntary Information . . . of John Poulter*, Graham was sentenced to transportation for fourteen years at Warwick Assizes in about 1750.

9 Pricking in the belt, or the art of old nobb or mob, is rather inadequately and confusingly described in a later section of this biography; it apparently involved betting on the ability to prick a piece of string, but the most important part of the trick was the way in which the gang tricked an individual into becoming involved.

10 One of the people who takes the main part in the trick is disguised as a foolish and slightly drunken sailor since their profligacy with money was proverbial: as the biography puts it, 'Sailors get their money like horses, and spend it like asses'.

11 The Rock Tavern was between Kinver and Enville, near Stourbridge: *Bath Journal*, 5 April 1753.

12 According to *Devon . . . The voluntary Information . . . of John Poulter*, Poulter, Brown and Allen stole roughly 2,000 yards of cloth from a pack horse about 7 miles from Manchester and a mile from 'Sopforth'; they took it to Margaret 'Lyne' who paid 3d. per yard.

13 George Linsdale often bought stolen goods: *The further Information . . . of John Poulter*.

14 Fetherstone had been tried at Northampton in about 1750 for highway robbery: see generally *The further Information . . . of John Poulter*.

15 William S – w is presumably William Sparrow, who was sentenced to transportation at Bridgewater Assizes in August 1752 (see note 54). The other William is difficult to identify: according to one report the only other person with this forename transported at these Assizes was William Golden, but another lists William Green, William Cowling and William Harley as transported: *Bath Journal*, 17 August 1752; *Felix Farley's Bristol Journal*, 8–15 August 1752.

16 Even though smugglers were hunted by revenue officers, they were not necessarily unpopular with the local ruling elite both because they imported desirable luxury goods and because they brought wealth to the local area: W. Page (ed.), *The Victoria History of Somerset*, London, 1911, vol. ii, p. 325.

17 Blandford races actually started on 30 June: *London Evening Post*, 7–9 July 1752; *Bath Journal*, 13 July 1752.

18 Handy or Hardy was described as 'a little Man, lives in Salisbury, and travels with a Licence as a Pedlar'; Walker or Walter 'is a little Man, about 30 Years of Age, much pitted with the Small-Pox, of a fair Complexion, is frequently at Horse-Races and cock-Matches, and his Mother lives at the Wells, and serves the Waters near Derby': *Devon . . . The voluntary Information . . . of John Poulter*. This robbery, which took place on 30 June, was advertised in the *Bath Journal*, 10 August 1752. The advertisement includes a lengthy list of the items stolen and concludes, 'One of the Persons suppos'd to be guilty of the above Robbery, is a short thick Man, and had on a brown Coat, and goes by the Name of ABRAHAM the JEW.' See also *Bath Journal*, 2 April 1753.

19 Possibly a coincidence, but a 'Mr. John Ford' was listed as one of the subscribers to a fund set up in Bath for the prosecution of thieves: *Bath Journal*, 22 January 1753.
20 See also *Devon ... The voluntary Information ... of John Poulter*.
21 This tankard was advertised as 'LOST' from the George Inn, Corsham, on 24 August, and 'a Handsome REWARD' was offered: *Bath Journal*, 31 August 1752. See also *Devon ... The voluntary Information ... of John Poulter*.
22 This was a familiar theme: see, for instance, H. Fielding, *An Enquiry into the Causes of The Late Increase of Robbers, &c.*, London, 1751.
23 The attack on Charles the carrier took place at Park Corner, about three miles from Cirencester. Some of the goods were sold to Trinder or Trindle who kept the Swan and others to Robert Lyte of Stockbridge, a publican and former smuggler: *Devon ... The voluntary Information ... of John Poulter*.
24 See also *Devon ... The voluntary Information ... of John Poulter*.
25 In December 1753 this crow bar was reported as having been found 'a few Weeks since': *Bath Journal*, 17 December 1753.
26 The theft was advertised as having taken place in the evening of 28 November, and a ten guinea reward was offered: *Bath Journal*, 4 December 1752; *Public Advertiser*, 5 December 1752.
27 This theft was advertised by a Mr Major of Marlborough: *Bath Journal*, 18 December 1752; *Devon ... The voluntary Information ... of John Poulter*.
28 Advertisements about this theft offering a reward of five guineas if the horse was stolen and a guinea if strayed were carried in the *London Evening Post*, 9–12 December 1752, 12–14 December 1752; *Devon ... The voluntary Information ... of John Poulter*.
29 *London Evening Post*, 9–12 December 1752, 12–14 December 1752.
30 The horses were said to have been sold at the Pack Horse, Bawtry, Yorkshire, and to a miller in Doncaster: *Devon ... The voluntary Information ... of John Poulter*.
31 According to *Devon ... The voluntary Information ... of John Poulter*, on the way from Yorkshire to Bath, Poulter and Allen sold the horses to William Barbridge of Hungerford.
32 See also *Devon ... The voluntary Information ... of John Poulter*.
33 ibid.
34 A misprint for ken, the slang term for a house.
35 The theft was reported as having been carried out on 16 January by people who had secreted themselves in the house and, while the family were in the back parlour, had gone upstairs and taken £50 worth of goods, but had missed a gold watch: *London Daily Advertiser*, 23 January 1753; *Public Advertiser*, 23 January 1753. Soon afterwards the Bristol magistrates promised a £50 reward for the conviction of anyone guilty of a capital crime in the city between 1 January and 1 April 1753: *London Daily Advertiser*, 30 January 1753.
36 See also *Devon ... The voluntary Information ... of John Poulter*.
37 The cloth was later sold to Stephen Gea: ibid.
38 The theft of a box with goods worth £33 from 'the London Waggon Warehouse in St. Peter street' was reported as having been committed by three people on 26 January at about midnight: *Felix Farley's Bristol Journal*, 20–7 January 1753.
39 See also *Devon ... The voluntary Information ... of John Poulter*.
40 Burk was described as 'an Irishman, much pitted with the Small-Pox, about Twenty-five Years of Age, with an Irish Brogue'. When, later, he escaped from prison, after the Hancock robbery, he was said to be 'about Five Feet Five Inches high; is by Trade a Taylor, and has a Wife in Prison at Worcester': *Devon ... The voluntary Information ... of John Poulter*.

41 These horses were advertised by William Edwards of the Castle and Ball, Bath, as 'STOLEN or Strayed' from a field in 'Walcot', near Bath, between 11 and 12 March, and a reward of one guinea was offered: *London Evening Post*, 17–20 March 1753.

42 Bishop, a horse dealer, lived near Bath: *Devon . . . The voluntary Information . . . of John Poulter*.

43 ibid.

44 ibid.

45 Poulter and Burk were making their way towards Exeter: ibid.

46 'Claverton-Down is . . . a pleasant Place to take the Air, indeed, the Ascent up the Hill is pretty steep; but when you surmount it, you have a delightful View: Here you overlook the City of *Bath*, and have an agreeable Prospect of the Vale between *Bath* and *Bristol*': *The Bath and Bristol Guide: or, the Tradesman's and Traveller's Pocket-Companion*, Bath, 3rd edn, [1755], p. 27.

47 The robbery was reported in both national and local newspapers: see *London Evening Post*, 24–7 March 1753; *London Daily Advertiser*, 27 March 1753; *Public Advertiser*, 27 March 1753; the fullest report was in the *Bath Journal*, 26 March 1753, indeed it seems likely that this was the report to which *The Discoveries* refers. The *Bath Journal* described the two robbers:

> One was a lusty well-set Man, about five Feet ten Inches high, dress'd in a light-colour'd Great Coat, and a Scar on each Cheek; the other was a thin Man, not quite so tall, and dress'd in a light-colour'd Great Coat. They both rode on a little Brown bay Horse with a short Cut Tail, and often threaten'd to kill the Child to make the Doctor discover if he had any Bills, &c. with him; and curs'd and swore most bitterly during the whole Transaction, which lasted near a Quarter of an Hour. They were both thought to be Smugglers, and to have been about Bath some Time.

From the descriptions we have of Burk, it seems likely that Poulter was the taller one with the scars. See also PRO, SP 36/123, Part 2, ff. 43–4.

48 See also *Devon . . . The voluntary Information . . . of John Poulter*.

49 They stayed at the Falcon Inn, without Northgate: ibid.

50 Although this came to mean a thief, at the time *The Discoveries* was published it was a term for a highly organized gang which operated the network of receivers and safe-houses used by Poulter: see the introduction, p. 144.

51 It was reported that Poulter was arrested with another person (presumably, Burk) at Exeter on 27 March; this other escaped soon after from Exeter Castle, where they had both been held: *Bath Journal*, 2 April 1753; *Public Advertiser*, 3 April 1753; *London Daily Advertiser*, 3 April 1753. As to 'Mrs. Baxter', one witness at his trial in 1746 had said of Elizabeth Bradbury, who was charged with him but acquitted, that she 'goes for his Wife; but several Women have come and claimed him for their Husband besides her': OBSP, 5–9 December 1746.

52 A capper was someone who assisted 'the sailor': see note 9.

53 Presumably, either Penton Grafton or Penton Mewsey.

54 William Knibs was acquitted at Gloucester Assizes in August 1753: *Bath Journal*, 3 September 1753. Roberts died after being taken ill on the road from Shepton Mallet Prison to Exeter, where he was to be tried. According to some reports he had been poisoned, although why is not explained, but the *Bath Journal* attributed his death to 'excessive Grief': *London Evening Post*, 17–19 April 1753; *Bath Journal*, 16 April 1753. Sparrow's escape was advertised as having taken place on 6 November 1752; he was said to be 'a Shropshire Man, of a brown Complexion, short black Hair, well set, about Five Feet Six Inches high, his Nose is pretty long, and stands awry by a Blow. He is about 30 Years old, and a noted Gambler; and 'tis suppos'd, when he made his Escape, he had on a white Fustian Frock': *London Evening Post*, 23–5 November 1752.

Of the others listed here only the following can be traced with any confidence as having been transported: Mary Dawson or Brown, Robert Jones, James White, John Brown and Margaret Brown: P.W. Coldham, *English Convicts in Colonial America*, 2 volumes, New Orleans, 1974–6, vol. I, pp. 5, 75 and 286; P.W. Coldham, *The Complete Book of Emigrants in Bondage, 1614–1775*, Baltimore, 1988, pp. 220, 456 and 888. A woman called Mary Brown was said to be in the Coventry Gang of robbers in 1763, and both Smith and Ann Tobin were also members of that gang. Margaret Clark, or Long Peg (also called Sarah Jones, or Ferguson, or Wilson) was hanged near Coventry in 1763 for returning from transportation. At that time she was aged 'near 60'. John Parry, the gaoler at Ruthin where Clark had been imprisoned in 1756, wrote: 'I can distinguish her from amongst a great multitude of women, her person is very remarkable ... she was a tall straight woman, swarthy complexion, long visage, much pitted with the small pox, together with some other marks or cuts upon several parts of her face'. Margaret Brown (also called Ogden, Peggy Richardson, and Anderson) was hanged at the same time as Clark, who was her aunt, for robbing with the Coventry Gang. On the Coventry Gang generally, see J. Hewitt, *A Journal of the Proceedings of J. Hewitt, Coventry*, London, [1779].

55 Poulter escaped on 16 February 1754 at about 11 p.m. with Charles Newman, a debtor. Both were recaptured on 19 February at the Ring of Bells, Wookey: *Bath Journal*, 25 February 1754.

56 A special messenger had come from the Secretary of State's office with the order: *Bath Journal*, 4 March 1754. See also the introduction to this biography, p. 140–1.

57 The regular place of execution in Ilchester was at Gallows Five Acres on the west side of the Yeovil Road: R.W. Dunning (ed.), *A History of the County of Somerset*, London, 1977, vol. III, p. 186.

58 These last two paragraphs are very close to the report carried in the *Bath Journal*, 4 March 1754, which adds:

He then went and looked into his Coffin, and afterwards gave Directions to tie the Rope shorter, it hanging down too long; then having spent a short Time in private Prayer, he let his Book drop, and calling aloud upon God to have Mercy on his Soul, the Cart was drawn away. It was observed, that he never struggled once after he was turned off, but hung quite motionless from the first Moment.

V

THE LIFE, TRAVELS, EXPLOITS, FRAUDS AND ROBBERIES OF CHARLES SPECKMAN (1763)

9

INTRODUCTION

Charles Speckman was condemned at the Old Bailey under the name of Charles Brown and hanged at Tyburn in November 1763. The editor of this biography said he was 'of genteel appearance, a likely person, thin narrow face, somewhat cloudy brow'd, about five feet nine inches high, of a spare slender make, his demeanour courteous and affable, and his countenance, though pale, carried the vestigia not only of serenity but innocence' (p. 211). Stephen Roe, the Ordinary of Newgate, had rather a different view of him as 'thin, tall, and of a sallow complexion, so close and crafty that he never truly and particularly opened his family name or birth place', adding that he had 'an oily tongue, with an insinuating address'. The reason why Speckman was less than forthright and why Roe was so antagonistic towards him seems to have originated in a quarrel between the two over Speckman's life story which gives some insight into the biographies. Roe complained that instead of 'being open and sincere in his repentance, and the confession of his crimes and scheme of life', Speckman 'referred me to a written narrative of his life and actions, which he had promised on several occasions, to let me see, and now fixed to give me in the afternoon, but he did not: At the same time, he had amused others with the expectation of it, insisting on high terms, which were to provide for his funeral; boasting, as I was informed, that "he would be buried like a Lord"'.[1] Roe gives the impression in his *Account* that Speckman could not be trusted, and indeed he recounts, in a passage which reveals as much about Roe as it does about Speckman, that on another occasion Speckman said he would not give Roe his life story because:

> he had been informed, it would be of some advantage to me to get their confessions, (he mentioned a handsome thing, 25l. each sessions for that service, added to the benefit of the trials or proceedings, which he supposed, with equal truth, to be mine) and his meaning was that, in effect, he envied me these large emoluments, notwithstanding all the labour laid out on him and the convicts, and

some particular kindnesses shown himself, and so by his witholding
his confession he would disappoint me of them.

Roe told Speckman that he misunderstood Roe's purpose since the account
of an unrepentant prisoner 'would probably sell better, as being more suited
to the taste of the world, wherein blasphemy is at a higher price than piety',
and that, therefore, it was Speckman who would be the only loser if he failed
to confess, since it would ruin his chances of divine forgiveness.[2] Relations
between the two worsened, with Roe accusing Speckman of having tried to
incite other prisoners to attack him.[3] The final blow came when, shortly
before his death, Speckman told Roe that he had sold his life story.
Interestingly, Roe did, however, note that Speckman had 'owned he had put
in some things, particularly about horses, that were not true, only to fill up;
the rest he said was pretty right'.[4]

Chandler calls The Life ... of Charles Speckman one of the 'more
entertaining pamphlets'. He argues that it reveals a shift from the purely
picaresque story to the adventure story.[5] But works such as The Life
and Actions of James Dalton, in which Dalton engages in a series of foreign
adventures, show the difficulty with the view that criminal biographies as a
genre progressed in a linear fashion through a series of different styles.
Yet, it may be that The Life ... of Charles Speckman illustrates the
development of a type of biography which, while not new, acquired a
greater prominence in the second half of the eighteenth century without
achieving overwhelming domination. Stripped of its rhetoric and its tales
of travel in North America, Speckman's biography is one of a petty thief
and confidence trickster who did not fit into the mould of the criminal
as seen in the biographies of Sheppard and Dalton. It may be that,
with the expansion and greater sophistication of commercial activities
such as shopping and banking, there was a shift in the biographical
literature around the middle of the century away from the portrayal
of crime as purely a violent, terrifying, confrontational and essentially
working-class activity, to one which is perpetrated by people posing as
members of the gentry and in which the victim's co-operation and consent
are essential. But, just like the street-robber biographies, the stories of
confidence tricksters do not suggest the corruption of the middle classes,
instead they present an image of shopkeepers and merchants as islands
of morality in a sea of corruption; indeed one of the objectives of these
biographies is the instruction of shopkeepers in the protection of their
property. So that, whilst the biographies of Sheppard and Dalton depict
the corruption of the labouring classes, the biographies of confidence
tricksters, like Speckman, taint the gentry. Not that these offenders were
necessarily actually members of the gentry, but the biographies did link
into a critique focused on the moral corruption of the gentry which
runs through eighteenth-century literature.

NOTES

1 Ordinary of Newgate, *Account*, 23 November 1763, p. 10.
2 ibid., p. 11.
3 ibid., p. 12.
4 ibid., p. 16.
5 F.W. Chandler, *The Literature of Roguery*, 2 volumes, Boston, 1907, vol. I, p. 165

10

THE
Life, Travels, Exploits,
Frauds and Robberies,
OF
Charles Speckman, *alias* Brown,
Who was Executed at TYBURN, on *Wednesday* the
23d of *November*, 1763.
By far the most dextrous of his Profession in this
or any other Country.
CONTAINING,
A genuine Recital of more than Five Hundred Thefts, Frauds,
and Felonies, committed by him in *England, Scotland,
Ireland, North America*, and the *West Indies*, during the
Course of Fifteen Years.
WITH
Several Maxims, Hints, and Remarks, by Way of Caution
to the Public, to prevent or detect the Designs of Sharpers
and Thieves from being carried into Execution The whole
NARRATIVE being wonderful and surprizing, and yet in all
Respects strictly true.
Written by HIMSELF,
Whilst under Sentence of Death in *Newgate*.

LONDON:
Printed for J. FULLER, in *Blowbladder-Street*, near
Cheapside. M.DCC.LXIII.
[Price ONE SHILLING.]

I DO hereby empower Mr. John Fuller, *of* New-gate-street, *to Print this only Genuine and True Account of My Life and Transactions for many Years. Containing the most astonishing Variety of Incidents, of any Person ever under the same Misfortunes with myself.*

Press-Yard, Newgate,
   22 Nov. 1763.   Charles Speckman.
Witness,
       Francis Caveac,
       John Anstey.

THE
LIFE
AND
WONDERFUL TRANSACTIONS
OF
Mr. CHARLES SPECKMAN,
alias BROWNE, &c.[1]

THERE is not perhaps in the world a more agreeable study than that of Biography; nor any thing sought after and read with greater avidity, than the lives of unfortunate men, and those who suffer under the hands of the executioner more than any. In this narration will be seen, the early propensity to acts of robbery, preying upon, and living in an absolute state of war with all mankind, the long series of years Mr. Speckman escaped punish[p. 2]ment, in which time he committed more robberies than any person before him brought to publick shame; all of them related by the unhappy man himself, in the following plain and undisguised manner.

I think proper for the benefit of the public, and to make all possible attonement for the injuries I have done to my fellow creatures, in England, Scotland, Ireland, North-America, and the West-Indies, in all which countries I have committed acts of hostility and depredation innumerable; I have no interest at all in this, only to warn the unwary, how they shall in general avoid the falling a prey to thieves and sharpers, and make those who tread in my wretched paths, be sensible and be warned in time to fly evil courses, as too truly will they find verified, that *the wages of sin is death*; besides that of undergoing in their wicked career, what is worse than death, the stings and daggers of a guilty mind: so that let their race be as long as it will, and their illicit practices attended with continual success, yet not one hour of true and solid happiness is the consequence.

About sixteen years ago, to the best of my memory, my father who lived in good reputation in London, where I was born,[2] put me to a boarding-school, and bestowed more money on my education, than on all the rest of my brothers and sisters, (I was the eldest of eighteen) for all which I never made any grateful return, which gives me great affliction, and the most pungent remorse, when added to my present load of trouble. To shew my early inclination to what has brought me to this deserved doom, I well remember, as I was standing by the side of Mr. Andrews, a waterman, in Charles-court in the Strand, my nurse being with me, I took a fancy to pull his watch out of his [p. 3] fob, at the same time laughing in his face; on detecting me, Mr. Andrews said, my dear, you begin betimes; the nurse, however, appeased him, so that no ill consequences followed: I mention this affair, as my friends rebuked me many times, by telling me of this deed, and my early inclination to what would, and indeed has proved my ruin.

I was put to board with a worthy clergyman, by my father, at thirty pounds a year, in order to inure me to what was good, and improve me in learning; but my delight was riding of horses at livery-stables, ran away

187

from school; the wicked disobedient child, soon finds out evil courses. The first injury I plunged myself into, was robbing my parents of a suit of cloaths, and pawning them to go to Sadler's-wells. Now every fraud that my fertile brain could device, I put in practice in my father's name, and got various sums of money, which answered my present purpose very well; however, my father had me catch'd, carried home, and kept me naked in a room several days, till I found an opportunity to get my sister's cloaths, and with them on, I escaped from the house. I have been often brought home from Covent-Garden playhouse, by the orange women, to whom my father gave two shillings each time for their trouble. I was at length taken up by my father, and put into Covent-Garden round-house; but through the hole the prisoners received their victuals at, I escaped, though it was so small, no one could have conceived it possible. I learned more wickedness here in one night, than in all my preceding excursions, and verily believe, it tended greatly to fix me in the determinate resolution of aspiring at every act of wickedness, my unfortunate life has since been so fruitful of; making it my daily study [p. 4] to defraud every one who came in my way, and rob every one I could conquer.

One day I and two other boys, went into a grocer's shop in Drury-lane, for some sugar-candy, the grocer told me, he sold not small quantities, on which asking him, if he was above his business, and perceiving a watch hang up in the parlour, I rolled a halfpenny as by accident into the parlour before me, I got the poor grocer's watch; in coming out, he asked me, how I dared to go there? he was answered by my throwing some powder sugar in his eyes, which was lying on the counter, and got off without any molestation.[3]

Soon after this, coming from Westminster with my two companions, there was a man had a stand by the Horse-guards, to sell all sorts of handkerchiefs, muslin, lawn, stockings, and other things in the pedlery way; I made bold to take him on one side, to talk about what I was to buy of him, which he was told was to a considerable amount; whilst I was thus amusing him, my two comrades[4] made off with the pedlar's whole stock, to the amount of fourteen pounds, and upwards: I however resolved to leave my companions, being determined, for the future, not to keep company with any, but act entirely on my own bottom.

I now set out for Newmarket; and, on my return home, hired a horse, under pretence of going express for a certain lord, well known on the turf, and came full gallop to the Blue Boar inn in Whitechapel, where I instantly ordered twelve stalls for the horses of my lord, which was to be there that night; telling the landlord, I was going to Hyde-park-corner for a running horse, and my haste occasioned me to come from my lord, without a sufficiency of money to defray all expences, and therefore begged him to let me have twelve [p. 5] guineas, to pay the charges of the horse and servant, and let his own servant go with me, to assist in bringing to the Blue Boar the running horse this night; all this he readily complied with; but the inn-keeper's servant I took French leave of in Piccadilly, put my horse up in the usual stable, and then went home to my lodgings.

Shortly afterwards, I took upon me to go about the town in a genteel dress, with a green apron on, as a watch-maker, under pretence of buying pieces of handkerchiefs to send abroad to my friends; I commonly found fault with the thinness of them, holding them up with one hand, and putting a dozen, or a piece, with the other into my apron; generally in these expeditions, after a sufficient quantity was obtained, I went into the country, and what could not immediately be sold, were raffled for. – In practicing one of these tricks upon a good worthy woman, who kept shop in the Borough of Southwark, I was detected putting a piece into my apron; I immediately flattered the honest woman, that I was a weaver in Spitalfields, telling her, my uncle had a journeyman who had stole four pieces, and had sent me with that piece to match the other, upon information my uncle had, that the pieces were sold by his man at this shop; by this means I got clear off, the unsuspecting woman not knowing her own.

In genteel apparel I next went among the silversmiths and jewellers, where my dexterity and success was so great, that I used among them in their respective branches, it is almost incredible what quantities of spoons, rings, buttons, buckles, stones, &c. I stole; the robberies of this kind are so numerous, that I cannot particularize them, but I made bold to borrow something from every silver-smith and jeweller in the bills of mortality,[5] [p. 6] and not only in these attempts had the good fortune to escape, but on many occasions, had the most lavish encomiums passed on me, for the honesty of my looks, and the humanity expressed in the lineaments of the countenance. Alas! how seldom is it, that the outward appearance corresponds with the inward disposition. I am a shocking instance that my face was the most deceitful in the world. Of this kind of fraud and robberies, I believe I have not perpetrated less than two hundred.

I went one day to Mr. Brogden, in Long-lane, West-smithfield, who lent out wearing apparel, of him I hired a suit fit for any little master in London; bought at the same time a satchel to put some books in; thus equipped, I went to Mr. Greg, a watch-maker in St. James's-street; on going into the shop, I perceived there was but one man therein; upon his being told my father had bespoken a watch for me, and I wanted to know if it was ready, he replied, as indeed well he might, that he knew nothing of the matter, but that Mr. Greg his master, being at the coffee-house, he would go to him, and ask the qustion; the minute he was gone, I fixed my eye on a gold watch, chain and seal, with which I marched off with all speed, took a hackney coach in Pall-mall, away to Holbourn, and sold the watch, though it was worth fifty-five, for seven guineas only, to Mary Keen, a woman who understood that business much better than myself. She has been transported four times.

At this time, and with this money, I went down to Reading in Berkshire, where I took great delight in going out with my gun; at length money falling short, I went to a milliner's shop, under pretence of buying some lace, to go round a cap and handkerchief, for my sister; the milliner asked [p. 7] if I was not too young a man to be a judge of lace? I replied, being young I should hope for better usage, and left it entirely to her generosity to serve me of that which was best of the kind; at this moment I fixed my eye on a particular piece; pretending to have a bad cold, took my handkerchief out to wipe my nose, laid it down on this piece of lace, which repeating again,

I took the lace up with my handkerchief, and put it in my pocket, and then told the milliner, I would stay till I was grown older; though it is clear I was too old for her now. I took my leave, and marched gravely off, without the least suspicion; and went directly to the Crown, the grand inn in Reading, hired a horse for Maidenhead, but pushed on for London, sold the horse in Smithfield for five pounds ten shillings, and lace to a milliner at Charing-cross, at a very decent price; at the same time cheapening[6] some of her lace, made bold to steal one piece.

Thus I found a method to deal among the milliners, without much danger of detection, women being less on their guard than men, and always delighted with any one who will hear them prate and chatter. Very few milliners escaped my dexterity, for my youth, simplicity of manners, and engaging behaviour, caused me always to pass without suspicion; nay, on many occasions, I have been treated with extraordinary marks of civility and politeness, and with the best the house afforded, even after I had robbed them, which sometimes has squeezed my heart a little, but I was too far gone in the road of perdition to think of returning back.

I now thought of amusing myself in the country; accordingly set out for Bath, Bristol, &c. in the first of these cities I took a room for myself [p. 8] in a widow-gentlewoman's house, who kept a shop in the drapery way; she had a daughter, a neat, pretty, genteel girl, whom I courted more for the sake of being free with her, than any real love; then the mother began to trust me, and place great confidence in me, upon her daughter's account, which continued to the mutual satisfaction of us all, till I found an opportunity to make off with between twenty-five and thirty pounds-worth of goods, taken out of the shop, and retired to Bristol, where I dealt a little among the milliners: returned for London, but being taken ill on my journey thither, I stopt two or three days at the Castle at Marlborough, where I observed a great quantity of plate, and other things of value lie very carelessly about, I only borrowed a silver tankard, and six table spoons, to assist in defraying my expences on the road: at Brentford I sold the tankard and spoons for five pounds ten shillings, and stole two pair of silver paste buckles, proceeding directly for London. I committed about fifty other robberies in the small way, which, as being trifles, are not worthy of farther mention.

I have sometimes, for the sake of variety, gone to dyers and scourers shops, in the character of a gentleman; on seeing none but a woman there, I asked for my servant, who came there for my cloaths; being told there had been none, then on asking if my cloaths were done, (they not knowing but that I had some there) shewed me several suits, clean, and not clean, but I never took a cleaned suit, always pretending they should be wore once more before cleaned, desiring my servant might be sent home as soon as ever he came; so tying them up in a handkerchief, left the poor dyers and scourers to lament their folly and precipitation. I used to serve the hatters in the same manner, both in [p. 9] gold and silver laced hats, without being in the least suspected.

I waited on a mercer on Ludgate-hill to cheapen some silks for waistcoats, with sattins, and some for gowns; I requested of the mercer to make a bill of parcels, put them up, and send his servant with me to my lodgings in Pall-mall; which being done and come there, on opening the bundle, told the servant there wanted a piece of sattin, and sent him immediately home for it: The bill amounted to forty-three pounds, and the parcel heavy, yet I easily (in the interval of the servant's departure and return) found means to walk off with all. I left an answer on the bill of parcels which was left upon the table, that my judgment was not sufficient for such a large sum, without advice whether I should pay him at his return, or never. I went directly to Mr. Howard's, in Long-lane, Smithfield, and sold the whole parcel for eighteen pounds; telling me, any quantity brought to him he would buy. This gave me great encouragement to continue in the mercers business: I served several other mercers in the same manner.

Not long after this I went to a gentleman in Long-acre, hired a chariot and pair of horses, to go to Windsor, intending to stay a fortnight; accordingly I set off, and stayed pretty near the time agreed on; I sent my servant to Eton, with a view of defrauding my landlord, and for this purpose asked him for twenty guineas, with which he very readily complied; the pretext was to purchase a pair of horses: having thus succeeded, I slipped on one side, and set off for London, leaving the man, chariot and horses to come at their leisure. The next day I sent for a sword-cutler, to bring me half a dozen swords to my own lodgings in the Hay-market, that I might take my choice in [p. 10] variety, but brought never a cut and thrust, I sent him back for some; and when he was gone, I took a walk out with the half dozen swords, with an intention never more to return.

I then took lodgings in Duke's court, St. Martin's lane, where I had not been long, but I sent the servant of the house to a jeweller, to bring me a variety of rings, the jeweller immediately sent one of his servants with some of all sorts; no sooner were they under my eye but I fixed on two, set with diamonds; I told the man, as I was no judge of their value, he would give me leave to shew them to a friend at next door, he readily assented, and so left the honest servant for his own amusement in my new lodgings: for I used to take a lodging one day, and serve a tradesman in this manner, and leave it the next.

Soon after, I put on the dress of a gentleman's servant, went to a very great milliner's in Pall-mall, as from a lady in Grosvenor-square, lately come from abroad, who wanted some assortments of her best lace, and desired one of her people with me; according to my application it had the desired effect: I brought the servant to a house under some repair, that I had the knowledge of; I took the box of laces, went up stairs to shew my pretended lady, leaving the servant in the hall, to whom immediately returning, I told her my lady was in bed, and she must come again in an hour, but must leave the laces, with a bill of the rates or prices of each sort; she went away very contentedly, and I had the generosity to follow with the whole box, and made clear off. I thought it now high time to leave off dealing with milliners. The garb of a gentleman's servant in livery, I always found the best to deceive with at this time, and made use of it on divers occasions, [p. 11] with my two companions before mentioned, Abraham Crabb, and Campbell Hamilton, and being apprehended for a small theft, made myself an

191

evidence against them both; Crabb was tried at the Old-Bailey, in February 1749–50, in the mayoralty of Sir Samuel Pennant, for stealing a peruke, value twenty shillings, and John Beaumont for receiving, knowing it to be stolen. The evidence (as an accomplice) I gave was, that I was about fifteen years of age, and deposed that I had followed the business of thieving two years; the prisoners, however, were acquitted, there being no evidence to the fact but my own.[7] Crabb was again indicted with Campbell Hamilton, for stealing on the 10th of December 1749, a silver watch, value four pounds, the property of Mr. Jonathan Scriven, in his dwelling house; and Catherine Hall, widow, for receiving it, knowing it to be stolen: my evidence was here also unsupported by any other;[8] though what I swore upon this and the former trial was nothing but the truth, with respect to all the prisoners; the silver watch belonged to the grocer in Drury-lane, already mentioned. I resolved never to have companions in any of my exploits, judging that I might one day or another be detected by my associates, as I had done by them.

Many surprizing pranks have I used with all trades in London; but at last pursued by my evil genius, I went into the shop of Mr. Honychurch, under St. Dunstan's church in Fleet-street, on the 5th of November 1750, and stole a silver watch, with which I got off, imprudently keeping it till the next day, I offered it pawn to Mr. Price on Snow-hill; it being advertised, he stopped me, sent for mr. Honychurch, and carried me out of the city to justice Fielding, who committed me to New-prison, Clerkenwell,[9] thence removed to Newgate, [p. 12] took my trial on the 10th of December 1750, in the mayoralty of Francis Cokayne, Esq; was capitally convicted, and received sentence of death with fifteen others, among whom were Mr. Baker, the sugar-baker; and Mr. Joshua West, a clerk of the Bank.[10]

In the course of my trial, which is all fact as sworn against me, it proceeds thus: Mr. Honychurch deposed that the watch was taken with the prisoner on the 6th of November, was lost on the 5th, had his name and number on it, never had been sold, and by advertising it, by that means it was stopped. William Batersby, Mr. Honychurch's servant, gave his testimony, that he was alone in the shop, the prisoner came in with a watch to have it cleaned, he then appeared in another complexion than now, he had on a laced hat, a waistcoat with either gold or silver button-holes; he desired his watch to be taken to pieces, while that was doing, he said that some of the work was dropt; adding, he was sure some of them were lost! I looked upon the ground, there were none down, but all right before me; then he was for taking it to show some other watch-maker, I said I must not take it to pieces and put it together again for nothing, he said, I will take and shew it to another man, and if he says there is nothing lost, I will bring it again; he took it not put together, also two new wheels, a third and contrite wheel away with him, which lay before me; when he stayed longer than I expected, I began to suspect him, and looking about saw a hook was empty, where a new watch hung just before he came in. I went to the watch-maker where I supposed he would go to, and asked for him; he told me no such person had been there. Then I told my master the affair, who told me by his book it was a watch he had made for a gentle[p. 13]man in Devonshire. When

Mr. Price sent for my master, I went with him, and knew the prisoner. On being asked by the court, if there been any person in the shop betwixt the time he last saw the watch, and the prisoner's coming in; replied, not one person from opening the shop, till the watch was lost, but him.

James Bruin, servant to Mr. Price, declared, that between six and seven o'clock on the 6th of November in the evening, as he was sitting in the parlour, sombody came in and asked for Mr. Price; on going into the shop saw the prisoner, who was dressed in a silver laced hat, a green waistcoat with gold button holes, who said he wanted to see the master, if he was not engaged; on being told that he could do as well, he took a watch out of his pocket, and I saw it was the watch advertised that day, I went and told my master of it, who came down stairs, and told the prisoner he had stole it, which he denied. My master sent directly for Mr. Honychurch; his man came, and said the prisoner was the person that was at his shop yesterday morning. While our man was gone, the prisoner owned to my master and I, that he had stole it; we went before justice Fielding the next day, and the prisoner was committed. So far the trial, in which the fact was but too plainly fixed on me: however, in my defence I urged that all said of me was false; I did not deny but I carried the watch to be pawned; I was coming down Snow-hill, and a well dressed man asked me if I had mind to earn a shilling; I said yes, so carried it to pawn; then the young gentleman said, there was a watch stolen, so stopped me; but neither judge nor jury paid any regard to such a pitiful come off. I put myself in a wretched habit, thinking that joined to my youth, might excite the pity of all parties.[11]

[p. 14]At this time I had many friends to make application for me in mitigation of my sentence, and had the happiness to be sent abroad in the summer of 1751, there to continue for fourteen years; I sailed from Gravesend in the ship Trial, captain Johnson, for Patomack river, in Virginia;[12] there went on board this ship with me Mr. Joshua West, before mentioned, to be transported as well as myself. As soon as the ship arrived, intelligence thereof was sent to colonel Lee's, that the convict servants were come from London; we dropped anchor on a Saturday, and the Wednesday following was sale-day, and the planters came on board to buy; there was one John Burgess, a native of the country, came to me, asking very civilly what I could do; I told him I could work, but not hard; I then asked him if there were any milliners, watchmakers, or such trades as I worked at in London, he turned his head and laughed; I told him I did not care, as my father had paid my passage, but the captain replied he had not, and I having no friends was forced to submit, and be sold as others were. My master took me on shore to an ordinary, and told me if I would be a good boy and work, I should want for nothing: I then asked him, if he and I were to go halves? he replied, in what? and I said in thieving: but on telling me I was come into a wrong country for that, and practising theft would soon bring him to ruin; I urged that would certainly be his portion if he did not let me go. He rejoiced much at his bargain, and I at his folly. We then set out for home on horse-back, I behind him, and had fifteen miles to ride; at length got home, and seeing my master's palace, I took it for a pidgeon-house: being tired and hungry, they brought me some victuals called humeny and milk, which I thought [p. 15] very sweet and good. Next morning my master roused me by-times to grind my hoe, I looked very hard at him, and told him I was not used to that kind of work; he however took me to a field to shew me how to till-up some corn; I told him the trade I was sent from London for, was much easier than this. In short, I could think of nothing but my old trade, and soon found means to break into a neighbour's house, with an intent to rob them of what I could catch, with a fixed resolution to ruin myself and my master, for work did never agree with me; however, I got two gold rings, and some wearing apparel, which I brought to my mistress, knowing her to conceal other things for us, but she would have nothing to do with my prize: this caused me to run away, and make my case known to a justice of the peace, who had me apprehended, and sent for my master, upon my own discovery; I was sent to goal, but my master bailed me out till sessions, when I received sentence to be whipped and pilloried, which was rigourously executed: my master was obliged to make a four-fold gratification for the injury I had done the party robbed.

My servitude being very intollerable to me, I determined to make a trial of another escape, and for that purpose took one of my master's horses, a suit of his cloaths, and other necessaries for my journey; but not considering the expence, the danger in crossing the rivers, and having no pass from a magistrate, I was soon taken up, and brought back to my master, who gave me a terrible whipping, he fleed me from neck to rump, so that I was obliged to lie on my belly for several days and nights; aad [and] when I was well enough to walk, he sold me into the back settlements of Virginia, I believe four hundred miles within land where I was, when general [p. 16] Braddock came with his troops from Alexandria in Virginia, on his way to the Ohio, in the year 1755, where he was defeated with great slaughter by the French; my master and his family removed for fear of the French and the scalping parties of Indians, which were scouring the country all round, and committing the most shocking and inhuman murders. I got acquainted with serjeant Campbell, of colonel Dunbar's regiment, and begged of him to let me go to the battle; he granted my request, and I got clear of my master. After our defeat, on the 9th of July, we had a very long and tiresome march back from the field of battle, near Fort du Quesne, to Philadelphia, in Pensylvania; when there being bare of cloathing, and in want of money, being withal very hungry, I took up my London trade, and soon stole a whole piece of handkerchiefs, a dozen in number; I tarried in Philadelphia till I had got good stock of cloaths and money, meeting with continual success in defrauding the public, by my old and wicked proceedings.

I travelled with all possible diligence to New York, where I found a great many milliners; I thought of immediately touching them with my London mode; into one shop I went to practise in my usual way, but going to sell the lace, I was apprehended by one of the aldermen, upon suspicion of stealing it, and the owner hearing of the affair, came and claimed the lace, brought me to trial, and I was sentenced to be whipped behind a cart, at the corner of every street in the city, which was executed upon me, brought back again to the goal, and in a few days ordered out of the city, never more to return, on pain of having my sentence again repeated. I was passed twenty miles by constables, and then left to myself to proceed wherever my fancy led me: in walking about two [p. 17] miles farther, I fell into company with one Browne, a namesake and farmer; he asked me if I could work, I told him but a little, though very willing to learn. He took me home, used me very well; however, I had not been with him long, before he sold a plantation, and observing where he put the money and the key of the chest, took my opportunity to seize all his money in dollars and paper, amounting to one hundred and ten pounds, with a horse, saddle and bridle, made off directly for New York, where altering my dress, and proceeded direct for Philadelphia, there putting up at the sign of the Indian King, I was obliged to sell my horse and buy another, intending to get a little farther out of the way of enquiry, at least for the present.

For this purpose I continued my route to Winchester, in the back settlements of Virginia; when finding myself near my old master, made enquiry for him, found him out, and made him a present of a silver watch, besides some money which contented the old man very well. He then gave me up my conviction, and went with me to Winchester, where he procured a pass as a free man for me to go wherever I had a mind without molestation. From this place I went to Port-Tobacco, to see my first master, to let him know I had mended my fortune with other peoples gains; he wished me joy on the occasion, and in a few days took me leave of him, and steered my course for Charles Town, in South Carolina, bought a gun to amuse me on the road, and had near nine or ten horses, I swapped, changed, and defrauded people off, under pretence of going with an express to Charles Town; where at length arriving, I met with my brother, that I had not seen for twelve years and upwards; he looked very cold [p. 18] and indifferent upon me, thinking I should bring him to disgrace and shame, as I had done in England. I got acquainted with one Joseph Warren, and hired myself to him, as an overseer of his Negroes. I had not been in this station long, before he sold me a horse at my own price, which I immediately sold in town, and went on board the Three Brothers, captain Holliday, bound for Antigua; the greatest reason for my retiring thus hastily from Charles Town, was, I had got acquainted with one Mrs. Broughton, a married woman; her husband swore he would cut my ears off, or take away my life, if I dared to continue any intercourse with his wife, he was extremely jealous of me, and indeed not without sufficient cause.

We proceeded on our voyage, and had got within two days sail of Antigua, when we fell in with four French privateers, after a stout resistance of sailing and plying our wooden guns, of which we had mounted twenty two, we were taken and carried into Martinico, there remained three weeks, till a cartel ship came and carried us to Antigua: in this island I assumed the character of a master painter, and got a job to paint the Duke of Cumberland privateer, belonging to George Walker, which having finished, I was paid. I now went to St. Christopher's, in the packet, where I had not been long before I entered on board the Fox privateer, captain Woolford, for a six months cruize, but had no success, we returned to the same port: as I had been thus unfortunate at sea, was willing to try my luck by land, I went into the country to a gentleman, told him I was courting a young lady of fortune, and begg'd him to lend me a suit of his cloaths, he very willingly did; I took him into a house, where we had some [p. 19] punch, which having drank, I went out and left him to amuse himself with his own folly. I sold the cloaths, without the least probability of discovery; I secreted myself a few days, and went on board a vessel then ready to sail for Philadelphia.

After my arrival, I got acquainted with a recruiting officer, beating up for volunteers against the French fort on the Ohio. I enlisted with him for four years, and to be paid half the money down, I bought a horse to go with him to Carlisle, in the back settlements of Pensylvania. There I saw my captain, who was vastly pleased with me; our company was reviewed by the major of the light horse, he having the superiour command. I was pitched on for a light horse man, under the command of captain Thompson, our general Forbes being very ill, was obliged to be carried in a horse litter, between two horses; it wanted painting, I was ordered to Carlisle to buy some paint, for that service; I was ordered by one of the officers to bring his girl from Carlisle with me, which I did, and by the way, had the pleasure of giving her the compliment of a road relish; my commiting such a rash action, made me imagine the whole camp might be set on fire by her; I thought nothing was so expedient for me as desertion, for fear of bad consequences, and went off the same night, being the 10th of July 1758, with my horse, regimentals, and accoutrements, and travelled for the back settlements of Virginia; in short, I went through many dangerous places, and almost insurmontable difficulties before I reached Williamsburg; where as soon as I arrived, sold my horse and regimentals, and put on the dress of a farmer, in order to buy corn; but nothwithstanding this scheme succeeded so well as I expected, I thought of speedily shifting my quarters. For [p. 20] which purpose, I once more thought of paying a visit to Charles Town, where I entered into a regiment of Buffs, raised by the colony of South Carolina, to go against the Cherokee nation; I was made a serjeant, and being sent one day to change a ten pound bill for my captain, I had changed it at a Jew's, who afterwards charged me with a bad bill of twenty pounds, of which I was entirely innocent; however, I was sent to Goal, and confined for two months, in as deplorable a condition, as ever poor man was. When released from prison, I was sent to the barracks, where I continued in a very bad state of health for some time. After my recovery, I became acquainted with a gentleman, he and I took to coining of bad money; which we carried on for some time with considerable success; but at length we parted good friends in the Country, and threw away our utensils. I took my course for New Bern, in North Carolina, in my way I married, and my wife's father thinking me two great a rake, to be trusted with her portion, look'd very lightly on me; but I found means to bring him greatly in debt, and made off directly, leaving the old man, daughter and all, to please themselves in the folly of their Wisdom. I made free with one of my father's horses, and made for a place called Brunswick, in the same province of North Carolina. Then I agreed with captain Wright, for my passage to Jamaica, we were weather-bound for three week. I then verily thought my wickedness was the cause of our delay, through the just vengeance of Almighty God. At last we had a fair wind, made sail, and had a very favourable passage to Port Royal; the next tide after our arrival here, we weighed anchor and made Kingston harbour.

[p. 21]On my going on shore here, being very poor and distressed, I began to think of something for my appearance in so fine a place; for this purpose I got acquainted with a taylor, and told him, I was come there to settle at my trade of a limner; by this expedient I got a very good suit of cloaths, and thought myself in a good situation. The next acquaintance I had, was one Mrs. Pembruge, who had several negroes, her own property, I thought this a fine fortune, and it was certainly so to me, though I soon found her to be a married woman, but parted according to law from her husband; she had a great many gallants, I found myself her principal favourite, and must confess, I got acquainted with one of her sparks; he told me, he had a much greater regard for her, than she had for him: and said, he had a chest at his master's accompting-house, which he believed was full of dollars: I directly acquainted Mrs. Pembruge with this, who requested me to get it from him, if possible; I then made use of every means to get the prize into my possession; he came and gave me directions how and when to send for it; I procured a negroe, and sent him agreeable to my orders; every thing succeeded, and the chest was brought to me: I went to a certain private house, examined the contents, which proved to be cambricks and lawns, which I went directly and sold for fifteen pounds sterling, leaving out two pieces for a suit of linnen for Mrs. Pembruge, but gave the gallant nothing for his pains, telling him it was of no value.

After this, I became acquainted with Mr. Torries, a Jew, who told me he had an hundred pound bill at my service whenever I pleased, and for whatever use I had a mind to apply it: I went the next morning to a store, purchased goods to the amount of one hundred and twenty pounds, desiring the [p. 22] store-keeper to send them to my lodgings; he came with the goods himself; I then shewed him the hundred pound note, told him I had borrowed it, and was to give five pistoles to the lender for two months; on this he told me, I looked like a very honest gentleman, and would give me credit for the whole for three months; I was to have gone to him the next morning, but declined that. I run in debt with many other people upon the island, to a considerable amount: I sold all the goods to the Jew, who lent me the note for fifty pounds. Mrs. Pembruge and I made off for Spanish-town, in order to settle with her husband, and get her own slaves from him. At this time, the person who let me have the chest full of cambricks and lawns, followed us; she told him how great a fool he was to follow one who he knew full well had not the least regard for him, though he had lavished away all his own honest gains, and robbed others to support her; though she was kind to me, yet I think there never was a woman of a harder heart, or of a more cruel and ungrateful disposition in the world; those who shewed a more than ordinary regard for her, were sure of the worse treatment; now living in plenty, she forgot all former want and misery; and I do verily believe, she would have cut the throat of any man who should rescue her from want, or save her life.

She was a good looking woman, and to those who knew her not, appeared an angel, but in truth a devil. The old gallant being stung to the quick at Mrs. Pembruge's base behaviour, went back to Kingston, and informed against us both, and we were taken into custody, and committed to Spanish-town goal, for the fraud of the linnen; in this prison we lay three months; at length the evidence was brought to the same goal, and the re[p. 23]gard he had for this woman being still as great as ever, he wrote a letter to her, full of the most tender professions of esteem and love; begged her pardon for being the cause of her confinement; that he was sensible the charge against her and Charles Speckman was not just; nay, that he knew us both to be innocent, and that he would so swear upon the trial; and never could rest or have quiet of mind for taking this ungenerous step, to abuse and defame the character of the best woman in the world, and that of the worthy gentleman her companion. We were removed to Kingston, to take our trials at the assizes; in the interim the evidence broke goal, and made his escape, we were for want of prosecution discharged the second court-day.

Thinking it would not be so well to continue in Kingston, I left Mrs. Pembruge, and went towards Black-river, and Savannah la Mar, where I hired a horse, and proceeded to Montague-bay: there I met with a sister, who I had not seen before for twelve years. I soon got acquaintance in the neighbourhood, and especially with a daughter of colonel Savory's; I was determined to settle here, and live in an honest way; all her family greatly caressed and loved me, and I found that I had no small interest with her friends; I found myself absolute master of the young lady's heart, my happiness was compleat. In a short time we were married; four days before, she made me a present of one hundred pounds in cash, to get necessaries: the day we were married, all the negroes came to wish me joy, and hoped I would make them a good master; the sight of them in a state of slavery, affected me very much; I wished to have made presents to them all, and wished myself on an immediate voyage for London, I had not enjoyed [p. 24] the married-state long, till my wife was taken very ill, and soon after died; she was a very worthy woman, and her departure a great loss to me. It immediately unhinged the tranquillity of my mind, so that I determined to sell all off, and return to Kingston, and to my old practices again.

Where being arrived, I enquired for and soon found out Mrs. Pembruge, and entirely forgot my deceased wife: we lived together as usual, but money falling short, I fell into the immediate exercise of my old pranks. I bought up a great quantity of flour, getting as long credit as I could, but sold it all again directly for ready money. In like manner I got linnen and other things from different stores, and sold them as I had done the flour. One man I run pretty deeply in debt with, and promised him a good horse in part payment; to accomplish this, I next morning hired a wherry to carry me to Passage Fort, where I hired a horse for Spanish-town, but instead of going there, returned to Kingston, and sold the horse to my merchant, and received some money in pocket. I confined myself during the remainder of my stay to my lodgings, being afraid to go out, my safety prompted me so to do, fearing the being detected, Kingston being but a small city, and not very populous; before I left the island I buried Mrs. Pembruge, and then bid adieu to Jamaica for ever.

I went privately on board the brigantine Betsey, captain Goodwin, bound for New-York; at this time I pretended to be a doctor, and having two other ships in company, whose hands were very sickly, I was put on board one of them to bleed several of the men, which I performed though with much fear; and one of them that I gave a draught to, gave me four dollars for the service; soon after our own people were taken ill; them I served in [p. 25] the same manner; at length I was taken ill myself, and at our arrival at Sandy-hook, was carried on shore, put to bed, and grew so much worse during three weeks, that I was obliged to have the clergy by me, thinking my end at hand: happy had it been so, but God for worthy purposes, and for the good of the world, reserved me for an ignominious death. I had extra-ordinary good usage of every kind from the gentlemen of this city: indeed, throughout all America their generosity and hospitality are almost bound-less, especially to English people. Though I was by these worthy citizens used in so kind a manner, I made them most ungrateful returns. As soon as well, I enlisted as a serjeant in captain Thompson's company of rangers, for whom I enlisted several men, but cheated them of their advance money; and went to several stores*, took up linnen, and other effects, in the captain's name, to the amount of twenty pounds. Then I hired a horse, and set off for Boston in New England; I had been no more than two days on my journey, till I was obliged to hire a chaise and harness, &c. to enable me to go through my long journey; this I did of an old gentlewoman in Connecticut, and took chaise and horse to the end of my journey, had the chaise new painted, and sold it to the best bidder; I also sold the horse and harness. My stay was but short at Boston, I went to Salem, about twenty miles from Boston, where I took lodgings, courted a widow-gentlewoman's daughter, then took a shop, set up the business of painting, and got several considerable jobs, but all the while run very much in debt with every body. I got acquainted with a gamester in this town; he wanted improvement; we contrived to [p. 26] touch all we could, and then make off. We had great success, several horses, watches, and other things in trust, were the effect of our industry. The people of Salem, are not only the most unsuspicious, but the best dispositioned, humane and friendly, and the most agreeable in all respects, in the whole world. I hired a chaise at Salem, and a single horse, to carry me out for two days pleasure; I went directly to Newport in Rhode-island, sold the chaise, bought another horse, and with my companion, went as fast as we could for Philadelphia; when arrived, we directly went on the gambling scheme, and had very great luck; but not agreeing in sharing our booty, we parted. He wanted to aspire at my art of dealing; this I chose not to trust with any one, for reasons already mentioned. The gamester took his passage for the West-Indies; I resolved to continue in Philadelphia, and had thoughts of matrimony again, that I might the better be enabled to carry on my designs, get into debt, and in due time run away. I met with a young woman, she passed for a very good fortune, we were soon married, but fortune she had none; tho' many rich and powerful relations, whose interest

---

* Warehouses or shops for the sale of European goods, are so called in America.

was for my wife, and of great service to me, I had credit every where; but being disatisfied with my wife, I told her that I had urgent business at New York, to see a commander I expected from the West Indies; as my business lay all there, I desired her to put up in a large trunk, a pair of sheets, a pillow, and other necessaries that I thought would answer my purpose: I must confess, she was a compleat housewife, and very industrious. My inclination, however, led me for England, the first opportunity: accordingly I set out on my journey towards South Carolina, hired a servant, and on the road, took all my effects out of the trunk, filled [p. 27] it with combustibles of a great weight, raised money on it, and left it in the care of my unsuspecting landlord; hired two horses, and went to Anapolis in Maryland; here I found out my wife's real character, and that she had a child at nurse, which finding out, I bought some cloaths, and presented to her, in remembrance of her mother. The next morning I set out for Edenton, North Carolina, where on my arrival, I met with some jovial company, that pleased me extremely well: I stayed three weeks with them, constantly gaming: I won more than one hundred and fifty pounds; with part of this money I bought a race horse, intending to run him as opportunity offered, on our journey to the south, which I did several times, and always won. My servant and I agreed very well, he was a trusty fellow, a good servant, kept my secrets inviolable, and without any fear. Before we reached Charles Town, we had got six or seven horses, and sold them about thirty miles from the places they were taken from. I used often to make a halt for necessaries for myself, and to the prejudice of the public.

We at length reached Charles Town, where I discharged my trusty servant; enquired after my old acquaintance Mrs. Broughton, found her, and let her know my intentions were for England; she smiled, and told me, she could not believe it, and set forth the danger and difficulty of such an enterprize from the enemy, together with the hazard of the seas. I enquired for her husband, but being told he was gone a voyage to the West Indies, this removed my fears; we drank some bottles of wine together, repeated our old scenes of action, though she had received many a hearty drubbing for what we had done before, which the husband was determined never to forgive; he was a very jealous [p. 28] man, but with great reason he was so; I knew that very well, and therefore was the more conscious of my own and her crimes.

My mind continued still to run upon England; I took a walk to the bay, and met with captain Sclater, bound for England, made a bargain for my passage, told him I had an estate fallen to me, and was going home to take possession of it; got all necessaries for the voyage, took leave of all my acquaintances, and in 1761, went on board; my servant, who still continued in town, begged to accompany me wherever I should go, but being at this time very sick, I was obliged to leave him behind me, tho' very unwilling. After being on board about three weeks, I began to write; at the same time telling the captain, I had sent the most valuable of my papers home in the West India fleet. We had a long passage of nine weeks, and the day before we made Falmouth, a most terrible hurricane came on, the oldest person on board had never before seen the like: we resigned our selves to the mercy of God, and the mountains of waves; however, we at length put into Falmouth, in a shattered condition. Captain Sclater and I went directly on shore, I then told him my intention of going up to London by land. I had a negroe of his to sell, but could not get my price for him; the gentleman I applied to, knowing my friend, desired me to be perfectly easy, as I might have ten or twenty pounds to carry me to town; I took only ten guineas, and gave him my note for it. I also settled with the captain, and gave him a note for thirty-five pounds, for the payment of my passage, and other matters betwixt us.

I set out for London along with part of the guard that came with the money, brought over in the Lisbon packet; my friend at Falmouth lent [p. 29] me one of his horses; when we came to Exeter I took a post-chaise, but not before I had borrowed twenty guineas of the landlord, who really thought I was a sharer in this fine prize, and master of the packet. The whole sum was imagined to be seventy thousand pounds. I made a bold attempt, and got some of this money, and should have got much more, but for the want of a partner. I put this and the rest of my money into the seat of the chaise, suffered a man to ride behind to the next post town, where I quitted the chaise, put the money in a box, and had it sent to town by the next waggon, and which came very safely to my hands. I was vain enough to think with proper assistance, I could have got hold of the greatest part of this cargo of money. I set out post for town on horse-back; my behaviour all the way was such as gave every body satisfaction, from the genteel treatment they all had from me on the road; they gave me the greatest character, which I turned to the best advantage, and made several little sums by the way. On searching my pockets in London, I found myself possessed of more than one hundred pounds; but thought of having another push at the treasure, which was expected in town every hour; I went to the inn in Friday-street, told the book-keeper all the circumstances relating to the money, and where I had left them on the road, with other descriptions that gave him satisfaction; and that my concern in the cash was considerable; he told me, I should be heartily welcome to all the money he had, accordingly he brought me eight guineas; after expressing my concern for giving him so much trouble, I walked away from him.

I did not think of visiting him any more; but went to Mr. Lane's in Drury-lane, where I hired a [p. 30] chariot, with a coachman and footman, in order to pay a visit to my father, whom I had not seen for fourteen years; my good father was glad to see me, I promised him to go again shortly, but never did more. The misfortunes I have undergone, had been, I am certain, intirely owing to the continual state of rebellion, that I lived in with my dear parents; and God for such unnatural practices, has been pleased to bring me to this most just and deserved punishment, I am now shortly to suffer. Oh! that from my sad fate, children would learn obedience to their parents, which will be attended with every desirable advantage on earth; be a blessing to themselves, and an honour to the human race; the enjoyment of peace and felicity in this world, and the sure and certain hope of enjoying the life which is to come. Were it known to the world, who my parents are, it could give them no satisfaction; I have been a disgrace to them, and would wish disobedient children to be warned from perpetrating those infamous actions, which may in the end work their own ruin; and such deeds, that their unfortunate parents, could neither foresee nor prevent. If children did but properly consider, the very fear of bringing their innocent parents to disgrace and shame, would prevent them from pursuing those wicked practices which end in being publickly exposed to a censorious world, and suffering an ignominious death.

I sought out all places of gaming and horse-races, till my money was all exausted. I hired a post-chaise, with an intention of going to Dublin, and went in this manner to Birmingham, where I defrauded a great many tradesmen; and at my departure, hired a horse for Park-Gate, waiting some time for a fair wind, my money running [p. 31] very short; but at length a fair wind springing up, I went on board, and there passed for Maddocks the wire dancer's brother, who had but lately been cast away in his passage from this port to Ireland. The passengers were much afraid least the same fate should attend us, as did him and his unfortunate companions; one of whom was Theophilus Cibber, the famous comedian.[13] But God's holy name be prais'd, we had a very fine passage, and arrived very safely in the port of Dublin.

I went on shore, and took me a lodging, and went the next night to the Play-House, in Crow-Street, where I made application to Mr. Barry,[14] as the brother of Mr. Maddocks, and that I wanted to perform in my deceased brother's way, though my real intention was only to borrow money of him. Mr. Barry told me he must see some of my performances first: well knowing my own inability in performances of that kind, without broken bones, I desisted from Mr. Barry and thought of making my market of Mr. Mossop;[15] but he told me it was too late in the season to engage any performers. Meeting with these two rebuffs, I went to a Goldsmith, to cheapen some buckles; he sent his boy to my lodgings with two pair of Bristol-stone buckles, set in silver: I sent the boy back for two small rings; In his absence, I marched off with the buckles, and sold them at a Bagnio for my own price. The next day the buckles were advertised, and in a few days after I was taken at the same house by the master of the Bagnio; for they were fools enough to tell of their prize to several neighbours, that they had bought two fine pair of buckles very cheap, and found themselves now in danger of much trouble for their simplicity: but the good nature of the [p. 32] master, got me off from any other punishment than that of making them a recompence for their loss. I bought me a regimental suit of cloaths, and visited the milliners as an officer; at one shop I desired them to put up a box of the best sorts of their lace to shew a lady, and send the servant with me, with which the milliner most readily complied; we went directly to my lodgings, where I directly ordered her to go and fetch me some handkerchiefs; in the interval I pushed off with the laces, and sold them all the next morning. I was immediately advertised, and taken by a thief catcher, but at the earnest intercession of his wife, he let me go; I went for the country, and at Thomolin, I was again taken by the description in the same advertisement, and brought back to Dublin; but I made the people robbed, so easy with my flattering behaviour, they did not care much what came of me, so that I meditated, and accomplished my escape, after a good supper, and drinking plenty of wine.

Money was now low with me, so that I was obliged to step into a linnen-draper's shop, and steal some handkerchiefs, made sale of them directly, and with the money paid for my passage to Park-Gate, where I found a ship bound to the Isle of Man, on which going directly on board, landed at Douglas, but I found nothing could be done here, the people being all as great thieves as myself. So in a little vessel bound for Scotland, I got on board, who landed me at Dumfries; where the moment I got on shore, I paid a visit to the merchants (the meanest shopkeeper is so here) the milliners and others, and picked up enough in defrauding them to support me tolerable. But the town being small, business promised but a short continuance. I made the best of my way [p. 33] to Edinburgh, the horse I brought with me, I sold to a drover for three pounds; and put up at one Browne's, of whom I borrowed a clean shirt to go to the play, enquired for the manager of the house, which proved to be Mr. Digges;[16] I wanted him to engage me on the same terms as I had made application to Messieurs Barry and Mossop, he said I should perform the next week, but that was too late for me. I then went to the Parliament-Close, to a silver-smith's, cheapened some of his buckles, and according to my usual method, desired him to put up two pair and two rings, let his servant go with me to my lodgings; when I sent back for something more, then went out and sold them to Mrs. Japp, at a Bagnio, where I refreshed myself for two days: but by some accident, was taken and committed to the Talbooth-Goal,[17] where I lay for three weeks, brought to my trial, and acquitted, but ordered to depart the city in three days. I must say I had very great favour shewn me, as any person could have, which was more than I either expected or deserved. On my being discharged, I hired a horse, and stole some handkerchiefs, and rode away for Berwick, where the horse was sold. I had no opportunity nor time to deal with the good people of Berwick, so went on board a ship bound for London, to which place we had a long and tedious passage: on our arrival, I thought proper to take with me, the bundle of one of the passengers, what suited me I kept, and the rest was sold.

I made but a short stay in London, hired a horse for Bristol, sold him there, and bought a stallion, with which I went to Cowbridge in Glamorganshire, there sold him, and stole a silver watch, besides some small parcels of laces. I did not like this of all the places I had ever been at; [p. 34] and set off directly for London, where I sojourned but a few days, went down to Portsmouth, took lodgings at a very creditable house, told my landlady I was a dealer in lace, desiring she would recommend me, which she did to several shops, where I got several pieces, went over to Gosport among the silver-smiths, and got some small booty there. I hired a horse in Portsmouth for London: within four miles of Kingston, I came up with two seamen, stopp'd, and demanded their money and watches, they gave me four guineas, and a silver watch; I left them, wishing them safety to London. Between Wandsworth and Vaux-Hall, I stopped a gentleman and lady in a post-chaise, robbed them of thirteen guineas, the post-boy got off his horse and ran away; but after I had secured the money, I rode after him, brought him back, and gave him a hearty flogging: the gentleman then returned me thanks in a very kind and hearty manner, and I wished him and his lady a good night. I went that night to Vaux-Hall, and between the hours of eleven and twelve, I stopped the Portsmouth machine,[18] for which I was apprehended, and carried before the sitting justices in the Borough, where they searched me, but found nothing, yet my pistols were in my breeches pockets; I was discharged as they had no proof of any thing I had done amiss: I called for my horse, and mounted, crying out to them, if any one could ride that horse better than I, they might follow me; I went directly into London, and was taken very bad, so that I was obliged to go through a salivation for one month.[19] I then began to be short of money, and was obliged to go a thieving again; accordingly I took a hackney coach, being still very weak, and not able to walk, I went to a miliner's, or lace [p. 35] shop, near the Royal Exchange in Cornhill, and stole twelve yards of point lace, to the value of thirty-six pounds, which I sold. I began to get strength daily, so one day took a walk to the Park, and so to Chelsea, where I hired a horse to ride about a little while, being tired with walking; I put my horse up at the Horse and Groom, in order to regale myself over a pint of mull'd wine: and seeing there a fine grey mare, with new bridle and saddle, I made enquiry of the owner's name in the house, and found it was Simpson; in a short time, desired the ostler to put the bridle and saddle on the mare, as I thought Mr. Simpson stayed longer than he promised; the man without the least suspicion brought the mare out, I mounted and rode into London, and at the end of Fleet-Market, was stopped by the owner, he asked if I had not that mare at Chelsea; I very frankly assured him I had, and was going on a very hasty message from the master of the Horse and Groom, into Bishop's-gate-Street, and was to return with all speed; he said it was very well, and left me to proceed where I would. I went into the Borough, and left the mare in pawn for six guineas. I went the next morning to Hyde-Park-Corner, and hired a Spanish Mare to go to Hounslow, went round the country to Epping, robbed two milliners of some lace, came back to town, and left the mare in pawn for four guineas with the landlord of the Catherine-Wheel Inn, in Bishopsgate-Street. I went out again in a few days, and at the upper end of Tyburn-Road, I hired another horse to take an airing, but went only round to Whitechapel, and left him in pawn at the Chaise and Horses there, for four pounds. A great number more horses I hired in like manner, my method was always to get the names of the stable-keepers, [p. 36] and of all the gentlemen's horses that stood with them, that I possibly could. I always called them familiarly by their names, thought I might have the knowledge of them, and their mentioning some gentleman that the acquaintance might arise from, I immediately joined with them, in affirming that it was so. I do think I have been advertised near a hundred times, for horses hired in this manner. As I had hitherto escaped, I thought it now high time to leave off dealing with the stable-keepers, and turn my hand to other branches, in which I had not been less successful.

I went into Leicester-fields to take lodgings, and the gentlewoman of the house dealt very largely in lace, which I did not know of before; I told her I was just come from the West Indies; she took me for a gentleman of distinction, as I had a servant in livery along with me. I told her, I should be glad to see some of her lace to make me ruffles; she shewed me some point, at four pounds ten shillings: I stole one piece, containing twelve yards; I sold six yards, and sent the other six to pawn: the person I sent it to, stopped it, although she had taken in pawn many pieces that she knew to be stolen by me before.[20] This event grieved me very much, as I was under the necessity of turning out again. I went to a watch-maker's in the Strand, and finding the master out, I asked his wife, if my watch was done? she not knowing but I had bespoke one, shewed me a great many; I stole a fine gold watch in this time, and went away: I met, just there, with one Smith, a bailiff's follower, to whom I sold the watch. I went into another watch-maker's, being short of money, finding only a woman in the house, she shewed me three watches, one of which I took by force, ran out of the shop with it, and got clear off. This was in the [p. 37] morning. I went to a pawnbroker's and pledged it for two guineas.

I soon heard of a particular milliner's shop at Charing-cross, Mrs. Moore, where business might be done; agreeable to this information, I hired a woman servant, sent her to Mrs. Moore's, and desired she would tell the milliner, I was lately come from abroad, and wanted some shirts, neckcloths, and other things, to the amount of eighty pounds, all of which were brought to me; but there were no black neckcloths, I requested Mrs. Moore to go back for some, and soon after sent the maid to desire her to bring two dozen; in this interval, I made off into the country, and sold all, pretending to be a dealer in lace myself. I came back to London in a few days, and paid a visit to Mr. Snow, on Ludgate-hill, as one just come from Portsmouth, where I had landed from the West Indies; I desired him to shew me some handsome rings, to shew to a young lady; as I told him he put up two that I had chosen, at six and seven guineas price; he sent his boy with me to a tavern at Temple-bar, where on our arrival, I sent the boy back for two rings, that his master had forgot; he went very readily his way, and I also with my booty. I pawned these rings to a certain man, F – Pr –, near Covent-garden, for three guineas and a half. I have pawned a great many things with this man, that I am very certain he knew to be stolen; he always received everything from me without any hesitation, reluctance, or denial, although he is a pretended honest man.

I then took my horse that I had standing by Covent-garden, and rid to the George at Hounslow; where sitting over a pint of wine, I resolved within myself that I would rob the first man I met. Going over the heath, I met with one Mr. [p. 38] Simpson, a dealer in lace, as he told me; him I robbed of fifteen pounds in money, and his silver watch; then I pushed off for Henley on Thames; and meeting with the master of the Crown inn in that town, I robbed him of a gold watch, and thirty-five shillings; afterwards went to Henley, had a pint of wine, and then returned to London. The very next night I went out again, and near the turnpike by Battle-bridge wells, I robbed two post-chaises, one of thirteen pounds, and the other of somewhat less; I came into town, put up my horse as usual by Covent-garden, and refreshed myself. I then fell ill, I believe from a fall from my horse; I made application to a doctor, and soon got well. I paid a visit to Vauxhall: going over Westminster-bridge, I robbed two gentlemen of their watches, and thirty shillings in silver, which was all they had, having left the remainder of their money with Mr. Tyre, at Vauxhall. I made directly for Covent-garden, put up my horse, and lay at a bagnio that night: I got up the next morning early, and set out for the last Ascot-heath races, where I lost a great deal of money; in short the chances run against me. In returning home, I was obliged to leave my horse in pawn at Hounslow, being short of money.

I turned out on Tuesday the 27th of September last, I took coach and paid a visit to Mrs. Dixon, a milliner, in Broad-street, Carnaby-market; the last and fatal place for me, and for which fact I am most deservedly to die. I asked her for a pair of minionet ruffles, but at this time she not having any thing to suit me (though she seemed vastly desirous to serve me) for ruffles, which I pretended to want, she very politely begged I would come again the next day; which in full expectation of bettering myself, I determined not to rob her now, [p. 39] which with ease I could have done, as she was entirely unsuspecting, and treated me with vast gentility and politeness; declaring, that if I would come the next day, she would shew me some very fine patterns of lace and ruffles. Mrs. Dixon undoubtedly took me for a gentleman; and in this she was no farther deceived than hundreds of people have been before her. Mrs. Dixon described what passed betwixt us very exactly upon my trial; that I tossed the pieces of lace about, pretending they were not fine enough, as indeed, for my purpose, they were not: according to my old custom, I clapped my hand to my head, as if not well, and had I found any lace I approved, to have taken my handkerchief out to cover it as usual. Mrs. Dixon asked me, if I was not well, and I answered her in the affirmitive; and as I had been telling her before of my buying ruffles in Jamaica, she said very smartly, sir, perhaps the air of England does not agree with you, and you may not intend to return again; to which I replied, that I certainly should, having not only a ship, but other property of great consequence there; then I took my leave of her, promising to come on the morrow, and bring a lady along with me: I accordingly went, and all things were ready for my reception; many pieces of lace were shewn me, all of them very fine indeed; I fixed my eye on a genteel and well fancied piece, began to examine my handkerchief, according to art; but two pair of eyes being too many for me, under pretence of my wanting some lace for a cravat, Mrs. Dixon sent her maid out for them; I instantly grasped my prize, slid it into my pocket, and went away, without buying any thing. Undoubtedly Mrs. Dixon was heartily vexed, to see herself so dexterously slung; but however, her prudence now began to rouze itself, for she made use of the most [p. 40] probable means either to regain the lace, discover the thief, or both. Upon some occasions, it is certainly not amiss *to set a thief to catch a thief*; but be that as it may, I am pretty certain, had not Mrs. Dixon taken the expedient of having her lace advertised at a pawnbroker's, she would never have seen thief or lace more. A pawnbroker is a most villainous employment: they not only exist by griping and grinding the faces of the poor, but are places of refuge for things stolen, few of them ever make enquiry how the party came by what they offer in pledge, and the less sum of money is demanded, the less is their desire to have it redeemed, or take notice of any advertisement; on seeing any such, they can directly make away with the matters in dispute, or send it amongst the Jews stolen cargoes to Holland.[21]

On my marching off with Mrs. Dixon's lace, I took a chair, and went to Strand-Lane, not with any intention to dispose of what I had got, but falling into conversation with Mrs. Davis and Mrs. Rogers, asked them if I might dine there, and was answered in the affirmative, discharged the chair, and dined with them on Pig; they both to me were utterly unknown before. After dinner I pulled out the lace, shewed it to them, then pretended to be short of Money, and but just come from Jamaica; I prevailed on Mrs. Rogers to go and pledge part of it, but not to take notice to Davis, what she was gone about. As soon as she was gone, I sent Davis with the other pieces I cut of, with the same injunction, not to tell the other. Though the whole of my trial is in the main, true, yet with regard to the time, Davis who pledged, and Brooks the pawnbroker, are both wrong; for it was past one o'clock when I stole it, two when I got to Strand-Lane, and at least three, when [p. 41] Mrs. Rogers went out with the first, as she justly swore. I mention not this by way of reflection, but that witnesses should consider when upon oath, they are to speak the whole truth, and in the instance it is certainly a falshood. I made a most pitiful and shuffling defence; as indeed who could do otherwise under the vast load of guilt, I had to sustain, being under a stupid infatuation, and certain that my race was run. I could very easily have escaped or eluded the most diligent search made after me, for I saw the advertisement, had information of Davis's being in custody for pledging the lace, and warned if any thing was amiss, that I would immediately fly, for fear of the bad consequences which might ensue; but all this I slighted; indeed I saw destruction before me, yet determined to make use of no means to shun it; by the persuation of a certain person who has been exceeding kind and serviceable to me under my troubles, I went to Goodman's-fields, stayed all night, returned the next day which was Tuesday the 4th of October; on our return, I heard of the enquiry made after me at this house, by very suspicious persons; however, having bought the Beggar's Opera, I was determined to go, and did, to see that play this evening: after the play was done, I returned to my lodging, and was told, two ill-looking fellows had been to see for me, and that they were at an alehouse just by; on this intelligence, I stood some time like one confounded or in a trance, and at length went into my room; where I had been scarce a quarter of an hour, till the constable and my old friend Mr. Fuller, the thief-catcher,[22] burst the door open, accosted me with, *Oh, Captain, is it you!* then took me with my friend to Covent-garden round-house, and the next day before Sir John Fielding,[23] who committed me to New-prison, as [p. 42] before mentioned: I saw several of my old acquaintances about Sir John's, and some who have deserved what I have met with; but they say they are now turned honest, though I greatly fear it is all a sham: but I was to them all unknown, at least with regard to my old pranks; they did think I dealt on the highway, and also in horses; but my old friend Mr. Fuller knew something of me with regard to horses, not much to his benefit: how can it possibly be so to people who have any concern with those of my unhappy profession?

During my long course of wickedness, I never was addicted to common
or profane swearing, to excess in eating, drunkenness, and but little to
women; to none of these I can charge the errors of my life, my faults are
all my own seeking and doing, without the advice, privity, or solicitation of
any person whatever: I never was fond of even conversing with thieves and
robbers, though at accidental meetings I have met with several, who guessing
I was of their profession, would set forth the advantage of associates, or
appearing in company to rob and plunder the honest and unwary part of
mankind. Pallister and Duplex, lately executed at Coventry, who called
themselves family men, and the heads of a great gang,[24] pressed me violently
to go on the highway with them and their companions, but all they could
say was in vain. I never would make use of, or indeed knew the flash or
cant language, in which these two men were very expert. Of all my
acquaintance, men or women, Benjamin Campbell Hamilton, and Mrs.
Pembruge* were by far the worst; of the latter I have [p. 43] already given
a particular relation; but of the former I neglected to mention, that after his
being acquitted at the Old Bailey, (my evidence not being sufficient against
him, or his mother Catherine Hall in Newtoner's-lane) he soon went into
foot-pad and street robberies, with other idle boys, committing a vast
number in the fields and streets; he was with his companions taken, tried,

---

* The Editor has been looking over some papers, shortly to be published, in which
an account is given of a woman, that in all respects far out-strips Mrs. Pembruge.
This creature, it seems, whose preceding life has been far from good, was met with
in the fields by a person who was vastly taken with the plausableness of her
demeanour, an intimacy began; she being in the utmost distress, was furnished
with money, wearing apparel, and lodging; was supported in a plentiful manner
for five years, and with a house the three last years, for which she received all the
rent, amounting to thirty pounds a year, besides an allowance of seven shillings
per week in money; but the ingratitude, baseness and corruption of manners of
the wretch, can never be parallelled: sloath, sluttishness, whoredom, drunkenness,
and gluttony, marked all her days; one of the most merciful and compassionate
of men, and the kindest benefactor to her, was treated with every mark of
ingratitude, and loaded with every kind of reproach; deprived of his peace,
happiness, content, property, reputation, and even an attempt made to take away
his life. What will be the end of this woman, cannot be ascertained; though it is
far from being improbable her days will be either finished on a dunghill, or at the
gallows.
  If there is any thing in the marks on human bodies, as the books of Astrology
and Divination would feign, this person is assuredly
  'Mark'd on the back, like Cain, by God's own hand,
  'Wander, like him, accurst thro' all the land.'
Bad as this mirror of her sex was, she had an ancient grey headed life guardian,
for her privy-councellor, confident, and servant, yet far worse than she: with this
old fellow she had lived in adultery previous to the acquaintance above-mentioned,
which continued, as opportunity offered, to the time the pious old soldier assisted
the woman to rob her benefactor of all his property, with which they retired, as
to a place of refuge, among the foot-guards and black-guards, in Peter street,
Westminster. This man makes vast pretentions to religion, and a good name; yet
it is plain, as the account saith, he has no just pretentions to either.

and executed at Tyburn on the 16th of May, 1750, with Lewis, May, and Giddis, his associates, and behaved under sen[p. 44]tence, on the way, and at the place of execution, with the utmost hardiness and unconcern, not at all forced or constrained, but talked to the mob, and his fellow sufferers in the cart, with as much disengaged ease, as if he had been going to a ball or merry-making, and continued so to within a few minutes of his death; for at the place of execution, his behaviour was most intolerably indecent, talking and laughing aloud as the executioner was tying them up; making use of most scandalous and blasphemous expressions, at the instant of his launching into eternity; and yet astonishing as it may seem, this active, wild and extravagant youth, had only lived seventeen years.

And now, O Lord God Almighty, who by thy powerful hand, and out-stretched arm, hast for the salvation of my soul, and the benefit of thy creatures, (to whom I can make no other reparation, than to make known to the public the injuries I have done) been pleased through a series of unexampled acts of injustice, brought me down to this most deserved sentence and doom; for my benefit, and that of thy most extensive mercy and goodness. Oh! that I could make recompence to the multitudes I have injured; but no means have I but this, by laying all my crimes, as red as crimson, before the world. To thee, O most merciful God, I most humbly prostrate myself: grant me in this world, knowledge of thy truth, and in the world to come, life everlasting. Amen.   C.S.

[p. 45]

Maxims, Hints, and Remarks, by way
of Caution to the Public, to prevent
or detect the Designs of Thieves and
Sharpers from being carried into
Execution.

I. NEVER place many different articles on the counter at one time; nor turn your back on the pretended customer, but let some other person put the different articles up, whilst you are intent upon the business before you.

II. It is in general to be suspected if a person pulls out a handkerchief, lays it down, and takes it up often, some ill is intended; this was my constant practice with milliners and others, in what lay in a small compass. It never failed of success.

III. The shopkeeper on seeing such methods as this made use of, should remove the handkerchief from off their goods; which will give the sharper reason to suspect his design is seen through.

IV. It is very common at haberdashers and other shops, which deal in small articles, for every one that is wanted to be paid for, the tradesman applies to his till for change; his eyes being fixed thereon, then is the time something the nearest at hand on the counter is moved off.

V. It is very easy to discover a thief or sharper from an honest person; for the sharper asks for fifty things, none of which will do, tosses them backwards and forwards, shuffles what can conveniently be done aside, and moves off with the prize, promising to come again.

[p. 46]

VI. Watch-makers and silver-smiths are imposed on principally thus; in a morning or evening the sharper, well dressed, as a sea-officer, will go to their shops, look at watches, buckles, rings, &c. when a variety of these are laid on the counter, if opportunity offers, the handkerchief is made use of with great advantage: should that fail, then the goods are ordered to a tavern, coffee-house, or private house, as best suits for ellegance or honesty; then the person is instantly sent back for something omitted, whilst the prize is secured, and the sharper moved off another way. Though this is an old and stale trick, it is amazing how successful the practitioners in it still are.

VII. Watch-makers should be extremely careful of strangers in their shops; as many watches are always lying on the work-board, and others hanging up, they should never have their eyes off the person: the handkerchief is here made use of to great advantage; if the watch is hung up, it damps any sound or tattling that might be made, and screens it intirely from the sight of the owner.

VIII. There is something in the very aspect of a cheat and sharper, which may be easily seen through: I know from experience, he continually has his eyes fixed on the shopkeeper, or person he has to deal with; has his body always in motion, whether standing or sitting. The eye of a thief continually follows the person he intends to deal upon.

IX. Dyers, scourers, and other persons, who have the property of many in their possession, should not let the appearance of a sharper, be it as genteel as it will, ever be parted with, but first by enquiring the name, and looking in their books for it; and should they by chance hit on a name, be sure to send the things in question home [p. 47] to the owner's house yourself, or send them with necessary cautions, not to part with them on any account, but to the right owner. Women and servants should never act on these occasions, in the absence of the master; or be against sending for him from a neighbouring tavern, coffee-house, &c.

X. Pickpockets are the most easily guarded against, of any kind of thieves; it is people's carelessness makes so many of this kind of rogues; nor is there more of any kind detected than of these. Whether through pride or negligence, I cannot say, but if people will go with their coats loose, a good handkerchief hanging half way out of their pocket, or the pocket flap thrust within, so that the contents, as pocket-books, &c. may easily be seen, and as easily taken away. The fob made so wide, and the chain and seals hanging down so long, that the watch will draw out as easy as water run through a pipe. People who go into crowds, or frequent the publick offices, should have their pockets open on the inside of the coat, which can easily be done; or else, as is customary with many, to have them on each side the coat, breast high; and to have a small strong strap, to button over the watch-chain, on the waistband of the breeches, will effectually and for ever prevent picking of pockets, and the loss of things of so much value. The smaller way in cutting women's pockets, &c. is but little practiced now; so that warning all people to take care, and be on their guard in churches and publick assemblies, and they will scarce have cause to complain.

XI. Footpads and street-robbers are neither to be guarded against, or prevented, in my opinion, but by the vigilance and continual care of the magistrates, in putting down bad houses, seizing su[p. 48]spected robbers, and clearing the streets of whores. None of this kind of thieves can expect to continue in their trade above a month or six weeks, and the greatest part of them not half so long.

XII. Highwaymen are also very easily detected, by the method made use of by Justice Fielding, for stable-keepers to send an account to him of the suspected robber's horse, and a necessary description of his person, especially if it answers that of the described robber.[25] But the method of thief-taking rather increase than diminish the number of robbers. And large rewards for taking highwaymen, &c. is certainly wrong, as old robbers are left unpunished, or taken, and young raw thieves hanged in their stead. The former are thief-makers, and who furnish business for the thief-takers.[26]

C.S.

The preceding narrative, with the hints and remarks, are the work of the unhappy sufferer himself. The Editor has been very faithful in adhering to the letter of the narration; and cannot help looking on it as the most extraordinary history of the kind, and of the greatest service to the public of any thing similar to it in the whole world. Unhappy for me, I knew nothing of the prisoner's intentions till Tuesday morning the 22d of November, the day before he suffered, by one of Mr. Ackerman's[27] servants; with some difficulty I got a sight of the manuscript, the reading of which filled me with amazement; and instantly determined as it would be for the public benefit for it to be printed, and resolved to see the prisoner, and agree with him directly; the time was short, the copy to be read over betwixt us, and many questions to be asked. I went into the Press-yard to him, where I found a man of genteel appearance, a likely person, thin narrow face, somewhat cloudy brow'd, [p. 49] about five feet nine inches high, of a spare slender make, his demeanour courteous and affable, and his countenance, though pale, carried the vestigia not only of serenity but innocence. On apprizing him of my business, he said, "Sir, I know you not; but trust and hope you are an honest man: my intentions in the publication, is much against the inclination of my relations; I do it to make all the satisfaction in my power, for the numberless injuries I have done to mankind, and to pay my funeral expenses, the executioner, the servants,[28] and others, to whom I am indebted. It is worth a good deal of money, but I will leave it to your generosity what I am to have for it: the Ordinary has hitherto refused me the Sacrament, under pretence of not being prepared, but in reality, to get from me an account of my life and transactions, for which he would not have given me one farthing, or his charity extended so far towards me, as to furnish me with a little food to keep soul and body together till the time of my death. That is no part of his business. I have been supported by a gentlewoman through my imprisonment in Newgate, in a most kind and christian manner; for which I trust God will bless and reward her a thousand-fold. What is farther wanted concerning me, the undertaker will inform you of himself, or let you know where the gentlewoman is to be found; who has got some other papers concerning me, and will deliver them to you."

We had just finished our business, when Mr. Cruden, famous for being the author of a Concordance of the Sacred Scriptures, the best ever yet seen in the Christian world, and well known in the republic of letters,[29] came into the prison, to pray with and comfort the five unfortunate men; who [p. 50] very cordially, and with great fervency, joined with him in prayer: Mr. Cruden adapted his whole prayer, which was delivered extempore, to their present deplorable condition, with great propriety and simplicity, to move them to a sense of their guilt, to a firm trust and affiance in God's mercy, and the certain hope and expectation, on their sincere repentance, of enjoying a state of eternal bliss in the world to come, through the blood, merits, and intercession of Jesus Christ, the redeemer of all mankind: that their state of probation here, was intended to qualify them, for a much more high and happy state; and would be their own fault if they did not attain it. To die, was natural to all men; but the time when, or place where, not worthy a wise man or a Christian's notice. Then most heartily recommending them to God, and the word of his grace, admonishing them to be chearful and resigned, he left them.

He had not been departed long, till Mr. Ordinary himself appeared; but alas! what a falling off was here! Instead of his presence being agreeable to them, as a Christian pastor should be, they looked upon him as come for nothing but his own advantage; and rather to disturb them with insignificant and impertinent questions, than to take care of their poor souls; besides being honoured with execrations from some of the bye-standers, for none but the Protestant prisoners were suffered to be in Mr. Ordinary's room: Mr. Cruden, on the contrary, desired all present to join with him, and left the door open all the time of prayer. Speckman and Broughton had the better of master Ordinary, who was obliged to leave them without accomplishing the only end he visited them for; who on coming out of the room, and perhaps smelling a rat, came up to the Editor of this narrative, with an [p. 51] assurance and countenance, that carried the *true Shannon dip*,[30] asked what he came there for; and whether he wanted any thing with *them there men*; in which being answered in the negative, he vouchsafed to stalk away, blown up with his own sufficiency and consequence.

Mr. Akerman, the keeper, to his eternal honour be it said, all this time was busily employed in procuring food, at his own expence, for the poor naked and starving prisoners, who many of them were at the point of death with the gaol distemper;[31] but the Christian reader will not be frightened at this, when he is told this distemper was only hunger. On parting with Mr. Speckman, he solemnly declared, as he trusted in God's mercies, that every part of his copy was strictly true; and now being satisfied of its publication, he should die without fear, and with perfect resignation. The Editor, on recollecting his person, and having seen him under sentence of death in the beginning of the year 1751, made enquiry of the authenticity of many robberies, &c. here related, and has found them all true in every respect.

The prisoner requested some person might come to him from me in the morning. I requested a worthy friend to do so; who went into the Press-Yard, and the prisoner speedily came down; who, on putting his leg up to have his fetters taken off,[32] lifted his hands and eyes up towards the heaven, and said in a kind of extasy, *This is the finest Morn, that ever I have seen.* As soon as this was performed, he was taken on one side to be haltered and pinioned, which he suffered to be done with patience and resignation; praying with uncommon fervency all the time. And then going with this friend to the upper end of the Press-Yard, they read and prayed together for some time, and was [p. 52] then asked if he had any thing farther to say concerning his life; replied, It is all truth, but if Mr. S. finds anything therein, which may be thought not for the public good, that may be left out if he pleases. At the conclusion of this he addressed himself to the people, requesting their prayers, for his happy entrance into eternity; declaring that he deserved to die, but had great consolation in his last moments; that he never had beat, ill treated, or murdered any one, save in one instance of the post-boy.

The friend was then desired to take some money out of his left breeches pocket, which proved to be eight-pennyworth of half-pence, and to give them to one of the servants who attended on him, desiring his acceptance of that and his wig, which he had ordered to be sent to him: Then wishing farewell to his friend, Mr. Melville a prisoner, and the persons about him; was led by the officer to the cart: which for the first time was hung in mourning, this added much to the solemnity of the occasion. On the way to, and at the place of execution, he was perfectly resigned to his irrevocable doom; and to the last carried himself with the greatest decency and devotion, in full expectation and hope of enjoying the life to come, in the blessed regions of eternal day.

His body was taken care of by his friends, put into a coach and carried to an Undertaker's in Moorfields, where on searching his pockets, there was found a prayer copied by him from a printed one, two farthings, half a walnut-shell, into which was thrust a long narrow slip of paper, on which he had wrote, "*I beg of you to let your trust be in God, for there is your trust, and in no man living;*" intending it for the young woman before mentioned. His body was decently interred on [p. 53] Sunday evening the 27th of November, in Tindall's Burying-ground, Bunhill-fields; aged 29 years: and the service of the church of England, at his own request when living, was there performed.

Since writing the above, I have seen the Ordinary's Account of Speckman and the other criminals, and that he hath given what he calls the Life of Speckman; which if the reader will give himself the trouble of perusing, he will find nothing but absurdity and contradiction; and that the unhappy man, at the instant of his being turned off, told him was nothing but deceit, asked Master Ordinary forgiveness, whose truly Christian disposition was on this imminent occasion pleased to comply, and pray for the sufferer. This undoubtedly is a laudable act, though the Ordinary did no more than his duty, which I hope he'll not think too much for him, to make his only rule and guide for the time to come: as a pastor of such a flock he hath much to do, and his constant presence and residence as near the scene of action as the keeper; the necessity and obligation of taking care of the souls of the prisoners, should go hand in hand with the care of their bodies.

Such a wretched paper as the public is drenched with every execution, it is hoped they will be no more bothered with, but if that should be the case, it is confounded hard to pay six-pence for two sheets of whited brown paper rubbed over in a very slovenly manner, but the writing itself is truly inimitable, none but himself can be his parallel; finally, should it ever fall in Mr. Ordinary's way, to find any of his brother pastors neglecting their duty, he will recommend to them the following spirited admonition of a famous poet on occasion of the corrupted state of our ra[p. 54]tional clergy, and under the similitude of a shepherd; which cannot fail of bringing them back to the original prurity and usefulness.

'Of other care they little reckoning make,
'Than how to scramble at the shearers feast,
'And shove away the worthy bidden guest;
'Blind mouths! that scarce themselves know how to hold
'A sheep-hook, or have learn'd aught else the least
'That to the faithful herdman's art belongs!
'What recks it them? what need they? they are sped;
'And when they list their lean and flashy songs,
'Grate on their scrannel pipes of wretched straw;
'The hungry sheep look up, but are not fed,
'But swol'n with wind, and the rank mist they draw,
'Rot inwardly and foul contagion spread:
'But that two handed engine at the door,
'Stands ready to smite once, and smite no more.'[33]

FINIS

NOTES

1 Speckman said that he adopted aliases 'to avoid exposing his family'. Other names he used were Woodward, Evans, Saunders, Tafrail and Dougan: Ordinary of Newgate, *Account*, 23 November 1763.
2 Speckman told the Ordinary (ibid.) he was born in Antigua, but to someone else he said he was born in Barbados. He also told the Ordinary that he had been educated in Boston and had then gone to Philadelphia, only moving to London in 1763 – this seems a little unlikely since he was on trial at the Old Bailey in 1750. The Ordinary reported that a friend of Speckman's in London had said that he was about 35 years old but according to the text he was 29 years old at his death (p. 213).
3 According to Speckman's evidence at the trials of Abraham Crabb and Campbel Hamilton in 1750, this method was used in the theft of a watch from Jonathan Scriven in 1749 with which the two were charged: OBSP, 28 February to 7 March 1750.
4 Presumably, Crabb and Hamilton.
5 The bills of mortality were the records of burials and baptisms kept by parish clerks in the central area of London based on the town as it was in the seventeenth century. The term was also used – as here – to describe the area itself.

6 To cheapen is to bargain for an item.

7 The offence took place on 18 November. According to the report in OBSP, 28 February to 7 March 1750, 'Abraham Cribb' was charged with stealing a peruke and John Beaumont with receiving, but the only evidence was provided by Speckman, a self-confessed accomplice aged about 15 years, and 'not being back'd by evidence of credit, the prisoners were acquitted' (editor's note). This requirement of corroboration for those who impeached their criminal comrades led to bitter criticisms from Henry Fielding, the Bow Street magistrate, who argued that it made the task of breaking gangs very difficult: H. Fielding, *An Enquiry into the Late Increase of Robbers, &c.*, London, 1751.

8 Speckman said at the trial that he, Cribb and Benjamin Hamilton lodged with Hall, Hamilton's mother, in Drury Lane: OBSP, 28 February to 7 March 1750; *Whitehall Evening Post*, 10–12 May 1750.

9 *Whitehall Evening Post*, 6–8 November 1750; *Penny London Post*, 7–9 November 1750.

10 *Whitehall Evening Post*, 8–11 December 1750.

11 OBSP, 5–11 December 1750.

12 This is the Potomac river. See also P.W. Coldham, *The Complete Book of Emigrants in Bondage, 1614–1775*, Baltimore, 1988, p. 104.

13 Theophilus Cibber (1703–58), son of actor-playwright Colley Cibber, was drowned in October 1758 when on his way in the *Dublin Trader* out of Park Gate to the Theatre Royal, Dublin. He had been engaged to play there by Sheridan as part of a strategy to oppose the newly opened theatre in Crow Street: *Dictionary of National Biography*; *Gentleman's Magazine*, 1758, vol. 28, p. 555.

14 Spranger Barry (1719–77), a silversmith-turned-actor, built the theatre in 1758: *Dictionary of National Biography*.

15 Henry Mossop (c. 1729 to c. 1774) acted with Barry at Crow Street, but then opened the rival Smock Alley Theatre: ibid.

16 West Digges (1720–86).

17 Tolbooth Gaol.

18 Portsmouth coach.

19 A medical treatment involving the use of mercury.

20 Pawnbrokers were under constant attack for their alleged role as receivers of stolen goods. Sir John Fielding (died 1780), the Bow Street magistrate and half-brother of Henry Fielding, devised a plan by which the theft of goods would be reported to Bow Street and then advertised in the *Public Advertiser* (in which Sir John had a share) to which pawnbrokers would subscribe: J. Fielding, *A Plan for preventing Robberies within Twenty Miles of London*, London, 1755; J. Styles, 'Sir John Fielding and the problem of crime investigation in eighteenth-century England', *Transactions of the Royal Historical Society*, 1983, 5th series, vol. 33, pp. 127–49. On John Fielding generally see R. Leslie-Melville, *The Life and Work of Sir John Fielding*, London, [1935].

21 The allegation that stolen goods were sent to Holland (particularly, Amsterdam) was not uncommon: *A Full, True and Impartial Account Of all the Robberies Committed in City, Town, and Country, For several Years past By William Hawkins, In Company with Wilson, Wright, Butler Fox, and others not yet Taken*, London, 1722, pp. 5–6.

22 Richard Fuller was involved in the arrest of some of the Coventry Gang (see *The Discoveries of John Poulter*), although it seems that this was as a result of his having been arrested and pressed to impeach his comrades: [J. Hewitt], *A Journal of the Proceedings of J. Hewitt*, Coventry, London, [1779], pp. 117–220 *passim*.

23 On Fielding see note 20.

24 John Duplex, alias John Phillips, and William Pallester or Palliser, alias William

Ogden or Ugden, led the Coventry Gang. They were tried in June 1763 and both hanged in the following August. At their trial the judge and counsel declared they never tried two such 'dangerous villains'. Pallister was said to have been born in Ireland and was 29 years old when he died; he was 5 feet 10 inches tall and 'of a genteel make'. Duplex was about 28 years old, 5 feet 8 inches and 'a strong well built man'. For a fascinating account of their arrest see [J. Hewitt], *A Journal of the Proceedings of J. Hewitt*, pp. 117–220 *passim*; see *The Discoveries of John Poulter* in this volume.

25 On the plan and Fielding see note 20.
26 This was a common complaint, especially after the conviction of the M'daniel Gang in 1756 for setting up young men on charges of robbery: R. Paley, 'Thief-takers in London in the age of the MacDaniel Gang, *c.* 1745–1754' in D. Hay and F. Snyder (eds.), *Policing and Prosecution in Britain 1750–1850*, Oxford, 1989, pp. 301–42.
27 Akerman was the Keeper of Newgate Prison.
28 The custom was for the hangman and his servants to claim the hanged person's clothes, so prisoners often gave money to avoid having their bodies stripped after death.
29 Alexander Cruden (1701–70).
30 Those who take the 'Shannon dip' (a reference to the Irish river) are supposedly cured of bashfulness.
31 See C. Harding, W. Hines, R. Ireland, and P. Rawlings, *Imprisonment in England and Wales: A Concise History*, London, 1985.
32 The chains were removed by the prison authorities before the prisoner was formally handed over to the sheriff's officers.
33 This is from J. Milton, 'Lycidas', lines 116–31 in B.A. Wright (ed.), *Milton's Poems*, London, 1956 (many thanks to Allen Rawlings for pointing this out).

INDEX OF NAMES

INDEX OF SUBJECTS

INDEX

Marxism 15
men 22–3
Methodism 6, 17
middling classes, middle classes 4, 17, 18, 20

North America 80, 82, 94, 96–8, 133, 168, 182, 187, 193–200
novel 9, 10, 18; relationship with biography 10, 11

Old Bailey 25, 117
Old Bailey Sessions Paper (OBSP) xi, 26, 115
Ordinary of Newgate xi, 4–6, 7, 21, 23, 44, 114–17; *Accounts* of xi, 4–6, 7, 8, 24, 26, 43, 114–17, 118, 181–2, 211–14

pardon 6, 8, 171
picaresque literature 10
pillory 81
police 25, 80, 81
popular art 18
popular literature 9, 10, 13–14, 16, 17
Portugal 80
pregnancy 134
prison: disease in 8; *see also* prisoners; prisons; ordinary of Newgate
prisons: Clerkenwell bridewell 52; New Prison 41, 47, 51, 54, 59, 63, 71, 86, 94; Newgate 5, 7, 39, 40, 41, 44, 47, 51, 52, 55–6, 57, 58, 59, 62, 63–9, 93, 94, 96, 99, 122, 133, 136, 211; Poultry compter 57, 75; St. Giles's roundhouse 47, 49, 51; Tollbooth, Edinburgh 6; Tothill-Fields bridewell 90; Westminster Gatehouse 63, 146; Wood Street compter 93, 101, 103
prisoners 5, 6, 7–8
prosecution 104

punishment as spectacle 81

readers 3–4, 7, 11
receivers of goods 125, 127, 128, 130, 133, 142, 151–4, 156–7, 161–6, 175
repentance 5, 115
rewards 80, 107, 171, 175, 176, 216
ruling class 4, 14, 15, 16; *see also* gentry

sailors 24
Scotland 187, 203
slang 116–7, 125
smugglers, smuggling 128, 149, 153, 174
societies for the reformation of manners 48, 69
soldiers 24
Spain 80, 95
Stamp Act (1711) 114
Strawberry Hill 4
surgeons: protection of corpse from 8

thieftakers 80, 143, 149, 207; *see also* Wild; Arnold; Fuller, Richard; M'daniel gang; Waller, John; Willis, Michael; Willis, Robert; Willis, Thomas
transportation 12, 26, 81, 89, 93, 94, 95, 122, 123, 133, 134, 143, 169
Transportation Act 1718 81, 96
trial 25
Tyburn, procession to 136

West Indies 80, 97, 169, 187, 195, 197
whipping 81
witness for the Crown 70, 79, 80, 107, 139–40, 143–4, 145
women 19, 22–3, 43, 48, 49, 81–3, 86, 87, 113–14; *see also* gender

youths 19